Report on the Agrarian Law (1795) and
Other Writings

ECONOMIC IDEAS THAT BUILT EUROPE

Economic Ideas That Built Europe reconstructs the development of European political economy as seen through the eyes of its principal architects and interpreters, working to overcome the ideological nature of recent historiography. The volumes in the series – contextualized through analytical introductions and enriched with explanatory footnotes, bibliographies and indices – offer a wide selection of texts inspired by very different economic visions, and stress their complex consequences and interactions in the rich but often simplified history of European economic thought.

Series Editor
Sophus A. Reinert – Harvard Business School, USA

Editorial Board
David Armitage – Harvard University, USA
Steven L. Kaplan – Cornell University, USA
Emma Rothschild – Harvard University, USA
Jacob Soll – Rutgers University, USA

Report on the Agrarian Law (1795) and Other Writings

Gaspar Melchor de Jovellanos

Edited with an Introduction by Gabriel Paquette and
Álvaro Caso Bello
Translated by Yesenia Pumarada Cruz

ANTHEM PRESS

Anthem Press
An imprint of Wimbledon Publishing Company
www.anthempress.com

This edition first published in UK and USA 2016
by ANTHEM PRESS
75–76 Blackfriars Road, London SE1 8HA, UK
or PO Box 9779, London SW19 7ZG, UK
and
244 Madison Ave #116, New York, NY 10016, USA

British Library Cataloguing-in-Publication Data

A catalogue record for this book is available from the British Library.

Library of Congress Cataloging-in-Publication Data
A catalog record for this book has been requested.

ISBN-13: 978-1-78308-629-0 (Hbk)
ISBN-10: 1-78308-629-7 (Hbk)

This title is also available as an e-book.

CONTENTS

ILLUSTRATIONS

EDITORS' BIOGRAPHIES

Gabriel Paquette is a professor of history at Johns Hopkins University. He is the author of *Enlightenment, Governance and Reform in Spain and Its Empire, 1759–1808* (2008) and numerous articles on aspects of eighteenth-century intellectual history published in *European History Quarterly*, *History of European Ideas*, *Bulletin of Spanish Studies*, *Modern Intellectual History* and *Journal of Latin American Studies*, among other academic journals.

Álvaro Caso Bello is a PhD candidate in history at Johns Hopkins University, where he also obtained his MA in history. He has published articles in academic journals in Spain and Latin America, such as *Ariadna Histórica* and *HIb-Historia Iberoamericana*, as well as book chapters in volumes such as *El Sur en Revolución* (2015) and *La Subversión del Orden por la Palabra* (2015).

NOTE ON THE TEXT

The translation of the *Report on the Agrarian Law* was made on the basis of the 1795 original, *Informe de la Sociedad Económica de esta Corte al Real y Supremo Consejo de Castilla en el Expediente de la Ley Agraria extendido por su Individuo de Número, El Sr. D. Gaspar Melchor de Jovellanos a nombre de la Junta Encargada de su Formación y Arreglo a sus Opiniones* (Madrid: En la Imprenta de Sancha, 1795).

The translations of the four additional texts were made on the basis of those published in nineteenth-century editions of Jovellanos's collected works: *Sobre la necesidad de unir al estudio de nuestra legislación el de nuestra historia y antigüedades* (1780), the *Oración sobre la necesidad de unir el estudio de la literatura al de las ciencias* (1797) and the *Elogio de Carlos III* were taken from *Obras del Excelentísimo Señor D. Gaspar Melchor de Jovellanos* (Barcelona: Imprenta de Francisco Oliva, 1839–1840), vols. 2 and 3. The *Oración Inaugural a la apertura del Real Instituto Asturiano* was taken from *Colección de varias obras en prosa y verso del Exmo: Señor D. Gaspar Melchor de Jovellanos* (Madrid: Imprenta de León Amarita, 1830), vol. 2.

Some terms without an English language equivalent have been left in the original Spanish, and several of the most important of these are accompanied by a footnote with an "Editors' Note" or "E. N." Jovellanos's footnotes in Spanish have been translated into English, but his Latin footnotes have been left in the original language. The style and format of Jovellanos's footnotes are the same as those in the original texts.

ACKNOWLEDGMENTS

The editors wish to thank Sophus Reinert and Francesca Viano for their generosity in using the grant they received from the Institute for New Economic Thinking (INET) to underwrite the translation of Jovellanos's *Report on the Agrarian Law*. Yesenia Pumarada Cruz undertook and completed the translation with impressive skill, which greatly facilitated the editors' task of revising the translation and preparing the present volume for publication. The editors would have been unable to complete their work without the unfailing support of the History Department of Johns Hopkins University.

INFORME

DE LA SOCIEDAD ECONÓMICA

DE ESTA CORTE

AL REAL Y SUPREMO CONSEJO

DE CASTILLA

EN EL EXPEDIENTE DE LEY AGRARIA,

EXTENDIDO

POR SU INDIVIDUO DE NUMERO

EL S.ʳ D. GASPAR MELCHOR DE JOVELLANOS,
á nombre de la Junta encargada de su formacion, y con
arreglo á sus opiniones.

CON SUPERIOR PERMISO.

MADRID: *EN LA IMPRENTA DE SANCHA,*
IMPRESOR DE LA REAL SOCIEDAD.

AÑO DE M.DCC.XCV.

Illustration 0.1 Title page of the original 1795 edition of the *Report on the Agrarian Law*. Reproduced with the permission of Wesleyan University Library.

INTRODUCTION: LIBERTY (*LIBERTAD*), KNOWLEDGE (*LUCES*) AND REFORM (*AUXILIOS*) IN THE ECONOMIC AND POLITICAL THOUGHT OF JOVELLANOS

Jovellanos, the Bourbon Reforms and the Spanish Enlightenment

Gaspar Melchor de Jovellanos (1744–1811) was a leading figure of the late eighteenth-century Spanish Enlightenment. His life and career coincided with what is known to historians as the period of the Bourbon Reforms, called "Bourbon" for the dynasty that ruled Spain and its Atlantic empire from the first decades of the eighteenth century. The reforms the Crown undertook, which touched all aspects of Spanish political, economic and social life, reached their apogee in the final third of the century.[1] Many historians, though not all, have understood these reforms to have been influenced by the new currents of thought often associated with the Enlightenment, and thus classify the quickening of the pace of government action to reshape society as "enlightened reform."[2] Bourbon reformers rejected the notion of Spain as an eclipsed power. They endeavored to assert the Crown's rejuvenated sovereignty over its far-flung empire against the relentless encroachments by competitor imperial states, like Britain. Bourbon reformers attempted to turn away from the stable, resilient "composite" monarchy structure and, in its place, erect a unified nation-state, subservient to the monarchy and capable of inculcating a new patriotic spirit.[3] They took practical steps—though sometimes tentatively,

---

1 Among the most important overviews, in English, of the Bourbon reform period are the following: D. A. Brading, "Bourbon Spain and Its American Empire," in Leslie Bethell, ed., *The Cambridge History of Latin America* (Cambridge: Cambridge University Press, 1984), vol. 1: 389–440; Stanley J. Stein and Barbara H. Stein, *Apogee of Empire: Spain and New Spain in the Age of Charles III, 1759–1789* (Baltimore and London: Johns Hopkins University Press, 2003); and Allan J. Kuethe and Kenneth J. Andrien, *The Spanish Atlantic World in the Eighteenth Century: War and the Bourbon Reforms, 1713–1796* (Cambridge: Cambridge University Press, 2014).

2 For a discussion of the historiography for and against linking enlightenment with political and economic reform, see Gabriel Paquette, *Enlightenment, Governance and Reform in Spain and its Empire, 1759–1808* (Basingstoke: Palgrave Macmillan, 2008), "Introduction."

3 J. H. Elliott, "A Europe of Composite Monarchies," *Past and Present* 137 (1992): 48–71; J. H. Elliott, *Empires of the Atlantic World: Britain and Spain in America 1492–1830* (New Haven and London: Yale University Press, 2006), 307–308.

erratically and with few tangible results—in both the Old World and the New to further this aim.[1]

The strenuous reform effort expended in Spain and Spanish America was formidable, even if it was seldom matched by the permanent results attained. Contemporaries witnessed fresh incursions into Amerindian-controlled lands, the spasmodic settlement of rustic peripheries from Patagonia to modern British Columbia and the military repossession of Florida, Louisiana and the Mosquito Coast. There were Crown-led attempts to overhaul the navy, improve and expand the army and colonial militias, revamp coastal fortifications and ports, modify university education, enact a less-regulated trade regime, boost mineral yields, encourage export-led agricultural production and wrest control of church property and patronage.

Whether caused by these attempts or merely coterminous with them, Spain's empire experienced remarkable urban, mercantile and demographic growth in the eighteenth century. This surge was sparked by export-led production and galvanized by the dramatic influx of African slaves, particularly explosive in Caracas, Havana, Buenos Aires and their hinterlands. The average value of exports from Spain to America was 400 percent higher in 1796 than it had been in 1778, though problems were gathering on the horizon. The techniques employed to raise revenue and consolidate centralized control sparked tax riots and broader undercurrents of resistance across Spanish America, from the Quito Revolt of 1765 to the Túpac Amaru revolt in Peru and the *Comuneros* uprising in New Granada in the 1780s. Spain's involvement in the French Revolutionary Wars in the 1790s caused further problems and decelerated reform. British blockades from 1796 and the naval debacle at St. Vincent in 1797 served as a prelude to the devastating defeat at Trafalgar in 1805, which confirmed peninsular Spain's commercial separation from its American dominions. Spain's military and commercial enervation in the first decade of the nineteenth century thus stood in stark contrast to the previous half-century's trajectory. When Napoleon's armies flooded across the Pyrenees, forcing Charles IV and Ferdinand VII to abdicate in 1808, the era of enlightened reform under the Bourbons had come to a sudden, ignominious close.

Jovellanos's career was intermeshed with the tumultuous age through which he lived: he was a jurist; an influential member of several learned societies; a Crown official who held

---

4   Though the acceleration of the pace of these initiatives may be dated to Charles III's accession in 1759, they clearly had their origins not only in the *Nueva Planta* decrees of the early decades of the century and the writings of mid-eighteenth-century political economists but also in the reformist tendencies so pronounced in Ferdinand VI's reign (1746–1759). On the timing of, and proper periodization for, the Bourbon reforms, see Manuel Lucena-Giraldo, "The Limits of Reform in Spanish America," in Gabriel Paquette, ed., *Enlightened Reform in Southern Europe and Its Atlantic Colonies, c. 1750–1830* (Farnham and Burlington: Ashgate Publishing, 2009), 307–320; on reforms before Charles III's accession, see the essays in José Miguel Delgado Barrado, *Quimeras de la Ilustración (1701–1808): Estudios en Torno a Proyectos de Hacienda y Comercio Colonial* (Castelló de la Plana: Publicacions de la Universitat Jaume I, 2009); and Adrian Pearce, *The Origin of Bourbon Reform in Spanish South America, 1700–1763* (Basingstoke: Palgrave Macmillan, 2014); on political economy in Spain before Charles III's accession, see Stanley Stein and Barbara Stein, *Silver, Trade and War: Spain and America in the Making of Early Modern Europe* (Baltimore and London: Johns Hopkins University Press, 2000).

many ministerial posts; an indefatigable reformer of many aspects of society in his native kingdom of Asturias and Spain as a whole; and a prolific writer whose oeuvre ranged from poetry to pedagogy to political economy. His full, active life befit his century: he frequented *tertulias*, where he cultivated a universalist conception of knowledge; he became embroiled in the intrigues endemic to Court life, leading to two separate periods of banishment; and he contributed to the revolutionary upheavals that transformed Spain, first as a member of the Junta Central resisting the Napoleonic occupation, and then, posthumously, as an inspiration to those who framed Spain's first written constitution, the 1812 Cádiz Constitution.[5]

The complete works of Jovellanos are now available online in Spanish, part of a resurgence of interest accompanying the commemoration of the bicentenary of his death in 2011.[6] The 14 volumes of his *Obras Completas* (Collected works), which include both his correspondence and writings, are a compilation of almost 5,000 separate texts. Thus, the five texts selected for inclusion in this book represent merely a small fraction of Jovellanos's overall output. The texts selected, however, rank among the most representative of his thought and the most influential of his works, and this volume includes the only two works on economic themes to be published in his lifetime.[7] The principal text published here, the *Informe de Ley Agraria* ("Report on the Agrarian Law," hereafter the *Informe*), first published in 1795, sparked debate and informed policy in the nineteenth and twentieth centuries. Historian Richard Herr has hailed it as "the culmination of Spain's intellectual flowering in the second half of the eighteenth century and [it] ranks among the great works of the Enlightenment in any language."[8] The *Informe*, probably more than any other work or deed, earned Jovellanos the plaudits of succeeding generations, especially of Spanish liberals who fitfully sought to enact parts of his economic program during their brief periods in power during the first half of the nineteenth century. One leading liberal politician, the Conde de Toreno, hailed Jovellanos in the following terms: "In his person was united the honorable dignity and elegance of the eighteenth century with the knowledge and exquisite taste of our own century."[9]

---

5   The best intellectual biography of Jovellanos is Vicent Llombart, *Jovellanos y el Otoño de las Luces: Educación, Economía, Política y Felicidad* (Gijón: Ediciones Trea, 2012).
6   The *Obras Completas* are available in the following website: http://www.jovellanos2011.es/web/biblio/.
7   These were the *Elogio* and the *Informe*; Vicent Llombart indicates the vastness of Jovellanos's writings on economics when he notes that he penned at least 57 works on some aspect of the Asturian economy alone. See Llombart, "El pensamiento económico de Jovellanos y sus intérpretes," in Ignacio Fernández Sarasola et al., eds., *Jovellanos, el valor de la razón (1811–2011)* (Gijón: Instituto Feijoo de Estudios del Siglo XVIII, 2011).
8   Richard Herr, *Rural Change and Royal Finances in Spain at the End of the Old Regime* (Berkeley: University of California Press, 1989), 50; for overviews of Spanish political economy, see Vicent Llombart, "El Pensamiento Económico de la Ilustración en España (1730–1812)," in Enrique Fuentes Quintana, ed., *Economía y Economistas Españoles. Vol. III: La Ilustración* (Barcelona: Galaxia Gutemberg-Círculo de Lectores, 1999); and Jorge Cañizares-Esguerra, "Eighteenth-century Spanish Political Economy," in his *Nature, Empire, and Nation: Explorations of the History of Science in the Iberian World* (Stanford: Stanford University Press, 2006), 96–111.
9   Conde de Toreno, *Historia del Levantamiento, Guerra y Revolución de España* (Madrid: Imprenta de Don Tomas Jordan, 1835), vol. 2.

Scholarly assessments of Jovellanos as an economic thinker tended until recently to coalesce into two broad camps. On the one hand, there are scholars who consider Jovellanos a proponent and Spanish interpreter of economic liberalism often associated, misleadingly or not, with Adam Smith and the French physiocrats.[10] On the other hand, a second cohort of scholars maintain that Jovellanos was a less-than-original, late-mercantilist author whose writings merely offered a systematic classification and elegant elucidation of other Spanish economists from the seventeenth and eighteenth centuries.[11] Part of this debate turns on the *Spanish-ness* of Jovellanos's ideas. Were his economic ideas largely derivative of non-Spanish authors or was he an *original* thinker, steeped in Spanish economic thought, responding to specific and sui generis aspects of the Spanish political and economic experience?

The most recent scholarship emphasizes the eclecticism of Jovellanos's political economy. Specialists such as Vicent Llombart have argued that the very diverse texts that Jovellanos read, cited and (arguably) was influenced by were not perceived by him as "contradictory" or "mutually exclusive."[12] This new scholarship is less concerned with the influences that might have informed Jovellanos's thought, and more interested in the ways in which Jovellanos read, adapted and integrated diverse authors and influences

---

10 Among these are Miguel Artola, Pedro Schwartz Girón, Robert Sidney Smith, John H. R. Polt or Joseph A. Schumpeter. Artola is considered by some of the best historiographers on Jovellanos as the figure who reintroduced the idea of Jovellanos as a follower of Smith's principles (V. Llombart, "Una Aproximación Histórica y Analítica al Pensamiento Económico de Jovellanos," *Asociación Española de Historia Económica-Documentos de Trabajo*, 1012 [2010], 8). Miguel Artola, "Vida y Pensamiento de D. Gaspar Melchor de Jovelanos," introductory study to *Obras Publicadas e Inéditas de D. G. M. de Jovellanos* (Madrid: BAE, 1956); J. H. Polt, "Jovellanos and His English Sources: Economic, Philosophical, and Political Writings," *Transactions of the American Philosophical Society*, New Series 54, Nº 7 (1964): 1–74; Schumpeter's characterization of Jovellanos in the 1954 *History of Economic Analysis* was that of an "applied economist" who expounded the principles of "economic liberalism, but judiciously tempered by practical considerations"; see Schumpeter, *History of Economic Analysis* (New York and London: Routledge, 2006), 168; Pedro Schwartz Girón, "La recepción inicial de 'La Riqueza de las Naciones' en España," *Facultad de Ciencias Económicas y Empresariales-Universidad Complutense de Madrid-Documento de Trabajo*, 9034 (1990); Robert Sydney Smith, "The Wealth of the Nations in Spain and Hispanic America, 1780–1830," *Journal of Political Economy* 65:2 (1957): 104–125.

11 Llombart mentions, among others, mid-century historian Jesús Prados Arrate who classified Jovellanos as a "post-mercantilist author, detached from physiocracy and Smithian liberalism." Another mid-century author mentioned by Llombart is Valentín Andrés Álvarez who "reedited the *Informe* in 1955 in the Instituto de Estudios Políticos, indicating that it was among the jewels of Castilian prose, and coinciding with the view of Manuel Colmeneiro (1863) regarding the lack of originality of its doctrines." Vicent Llombart, "Una Nueva Mirada al *Informe de Ley Agraria* de Jovellanos Doscientos Años Después," *Revista de Historia Económica* 13:3 (1995), 557–558. Jesús Prados Arrarte, "Jovellanos, economista," in his, *Jovellanos: su vida y su obra* (Buenos Aires: Centro de Estudios Asturianos, 1945); Valentín Andrés Álvarez, "Prólogo" to the *Informe sobre la Ley Agraria* (Madrid: Instituto de Estudios Políticos, 1955).

12 Llombart, "Una Nueva Mirada," 570. After noting the difficulties inherent in characterizing Jovellanos's thought, Ignacio Fernández Sarasola argues that the author should be referred to as an "enlightened" political writer, *El Pensamiento Político de Jovellanos: Seis Estudios* (Oviedo: In Itire-Servicio de Publicaciones de la Universidad de Oviedo, 2011), 63–70.

in his own work. Indeed, references to classical authors, such as Columella or Pliny, are interspersed with citations of contemporary political writers, whether Britons like Edward Gibbon and Smith or Spaniards like Campomanes and Uztáriz.[13]

The position taken by the editors of the present edition of Jovellanos's texts is close to that reached by recent scholarship: Jovellanos drew on the many political vocabularies of late eighteenth-century Europe, combining them in ways specific to the particular problems he was addressing. Such a pragmatically oriented eclecticism is on full display in the *Informe* especially. This mode led him to take inspiration from Smith, for example, but to reject aspects of his doctrine that he believed were inapplicable to Spanish circumstances, including his analysis of the grain trade. In fact, the *Informe* explicitly attacked Spaniards' "mania for imitation" of foreigners.[14] By contrast, Jovellanos repurposed debates, discourses and vocabularies from other parts of Europe and adjusted them to Spanish circumstances. So, the justification of the pursuit of individual interest as consistent with natural law possibly required recasting self-interest as virtuous, located within a framework of communal well-being. The epitome of Jovellanos's conceptual reconfiguration is the patriot farmer who, by means of his diligent labor, both supports his household and increases the nation's wealth.

The dispute about the originality or derivativeness of Jovellanos's thought forms part of a broader debate on the nature of the Enlightenment in Spain.[15] With the exception of certain distinguished luminaries who, by dint of their genius, have merited periodic, even if perfunctory, inclusion in the canon of "great thinkers" or "important writers" of the eighteenth century, figures such as Feijoo, Mayans and Jovellanos, the older historiography, both within and outside of Spain, held that Spain's Enlightenment was feeble, limited and brief. This unfavorable conclusion may be attributable to at least two causes. First, there was a tendency to look for evidence of the Enlightenment in the "public sphere" or in "civil society," realms supposedly beyond the state's regulation. As these realms were smaller in Spain as compared to other European states, it was assumed that the extent of the Enlightenment was smaller as well. Second, there has been a tendency among historians to privilege printed books and pamphlets over other types of sources. This meant that the vibrant oral culture, epitomized in the *tertulias*, as well as unpublished manuscript sources, which percolated widely in Spain, were largely neglected by historians.

These tendencies nurtured older assumptions (now increasingly discarded) about the geography of the Enlightenment. The chief assumption was that the Enlightenment (singular) was a Paris-based phenomenon, one characterized by a set of anticlerical prejudices, hostility to institutions bequeathed by tradition and a cosmopolitan outlook. As historian Carla Hesse has noted, "the geography of the advance of the Enlightenment

---

13 For a useful table of his citations in the *Informe* as well as a discussion of additional, uncited influences, see Llombart, *Jovellanos*, 103–106.

14 *Informe*, section 326 (all sections numbers cited in this introduction correspond to their 1795 original edition; their numeration was also respected in the translation).

15 The new directions in the historiography are well represented in Jesús Astigarraga, ed., *The Spanish Enlightenment Revisited* (Oxford: Voltaire Foundation, 2015).

thus mirrored that of modernity itself, producing a natural landscape with advanced and backward areas of Europe, with leader nations and follower nations […] the story of diffusion from a Western European core to the peripheries of the continent and beyond."[16]

The absence of revolution in Spain until 1808 reinforced the prejudice that Spain was tradition-bound society, inert to outside influences. This notion came about because the Enlightenment was considered a phenomenon whose central tenets underpinned or inflamed (if not caused) revolutionary upheaval. It was therefore necessarily subversive of the established order. In this way, a purported, yet faulty, link between Enlightenment and revolution (that is, where there is Enlightenment, there will be revolution) led many historians to conclude, erroneously, that the absence of a revolution was evidence for the absence of Enlightenment in that country. Spain's seeming immunity to revolutionary upheaval until 1808—and then sparked only by the external stimulus of the Napoleonic invasion—and the revanchist restoration of the Bourbon dynasty in 1814 prompted many historians to assume that it was a reactionary country, wedded to tradition and impervious (indeed hostile) to Enlightenment currents.

For scholars interested in the prevalence of Enlightenment in Spain, this now-antiquated conception gave rise to several distortions. First, it resulted in a misleading tendency to equate the paucity of works sharing the convictions of the *philosophes* with the absence (or weakness) of the Enlightenment in Spain. Second, it encouraged some historians to view the dissemination (or lack thereof) of French ideas as the chief measure of the Enlightenment's impact in Spain. Hence the flurry of books and articles on the dissemination of Rousseau's or Voltaire's writings in Spain, which historians took to be indicative of (or a proxy for) the Enlightenment's impact.[17]

Two subsidiary observations to this second point deserve mention. First, the monolithic nature of "the Enlightenment", a purportedly singular phenomenon with little national variation, was assumed by most scholars working on Spain. Enlightenment was necessarily universalist and cosmopolitan; it was therefore reducible to a fixed number of immutable features identifiable across Europe. Second, almost by definition, Enlightenment was considered to be French, specifically Parisian, a view that gave rise to the notion that "the Spanish Enlightenment" resulted exclusively from the diffusion of ideas and texts from abroad, that it was necessarily derivative, a phenomenon drawing on borrowed ideas.[18] The notion of a peculiarly "Spanish Enlightenment", distinct from that of France in terms of both form and content, was seldom considered a real possibility.

16 Carla Hesse, "Towards a New Topography of Enlightenment," *European Review of History* 13:3 (2006): 500.

17 See, for example, J. R. Spell, *Rousseau in the Spanish World before 1833: A Study in Franco-Spanish Literary Relations* (Austin: University of Texas Press, 1938).

18 Even two great early works share this assumption: Jean Sarrailh, *La España Ilustrada de la Segunda Mitad del Siglo XVIII* (Mexico City: Fondo de Cultura Económica, 1957); and Richard Herr, *The Eighteenth-century Revolution in Spain* (Princeton and Oxford: Princeton University Press, 1958); for a useful correction of this view, with citations to pertinent scholarship, see Jesús Astigarraga, "Introduction: *Admirer, rougir, imiter.* Spain and the European Enlightenment," in Astigarraga, *Spanish Enlightenment*, 1–27.

The third distortion afflicting the older historiography was that the association of the Enlightenment with implacable hostility toward existing institutions and traditions meant that the sphere where it could be found was extremely limited. Enlightenment could be found neither in the bureaucratic apparatus, in the church nor in the universities. The ubiquitous *tertulias* held at aristocratic homes, though venues for the polite exchange of ideas, were also deemed ineligible. So, too, were the royal patriotic or economic societies, operating under the approving gaze of the Crown, and so important to the genesis of Jovellanos's *Informe*. Any activity, then, that fortified the "Old Regime" to which the *philosophes* were supposedly implacably opposed was out of bounds. Interestingly, the court, now considered a chief site for the diffusion, discussion and debate of Enlightenment texts and ideas, was previously dismissed out of hand as impervious to the *luces*.[19]

Historians of Spain were left, then, with a very narrow range of possible subjects, sites and texts for the study of the Enlightenment. "Enlightened" Spaniards were necessarily radical (or, in the old parlance, "heterodox") thinkers, hounded by the Inquisition and/ or forced into exile abroad. The paradigmatic trajectory of Jovellanos's early mentor, Peruvian-born Pablo de Olavide—from arch reformer and cosmopolitan man of letters to disgraced exile—thus attracted great historiographical interest, pointed to as both an example of the thwarted "radical" Enlightenment in Spain, the Francophilia of Spain's few *philosophes*, and also as a symbol of the limits of Enlightenment in Spain.[20] There is little doubt that the church did limit the spread and impact of purportedly heterodox doctrines, but it was far from impermeable and, in fact, sheltered many enlightened thinkers.[21] Its relationship to the Enlightenment was ambivalent and somewhat, to modern scholars, ambiguous.

Jovellanos's trajectory provides some insight into the ambiguity and ambivalence characterizing relations between church and Enlightenment in Spain. Jovellanos, who early in his career seriously considered pursuing an ecclesiastical vocation, received in 1771 a license to read "forbidden books," something impossible for the vast majority of Spaniards. He partly owed his meteoric rise (and special dispensation to read illicit books) to the patronage of the powerful minister Pedro Rodríguez de Campomanes (1723–1803), later Count of Campomanes, who himself had run afoul of the ecclesiastical establishment in the mid-1760s for his brazen assertion of regalist principles.[22] Campomanes had argued that

---

19 On the importance of the court, see Charles C. Noel, "In the House of Reform: The Bourbon Court of Eighteenth-century Spain," in Paquette, *Enlightened Reform in Southern Europe*, 145–166.

20 Luís Perdices, *Pablo de Olavide (1725–1803): El Ilustrado* (Madrid: Editorial Complutense, 1993).

21 See, for example, the essays contained in Ulrich Lerner and Michael Printy, eds., *A Companion to the Catholic Enlightenment* (Leiden and Boston: Brill, 2010).

22 As Noel has explained, regalism "aimed to enhance royal authority over the church and the clergy in Spain; to reduce that of the Pope and Roman Curia; and to employ royal authority to force certain clerical reforms." See Charles C. Noel, "Charles III of Spain," in H. M. Scott, ed., *Enlightened Absolutism: Reform and Reformers in Later Eighteenth-century Europe* (Ann Arbor: University of Michigan Press, 1989), 132; on Campomanes's political, economic and juridical thought, see Antonio Álvarez de Morales, *El Pensamiento Politico y Juridico de Campomanes* (Madrid: Instituto Nacional de Administración Publica, 1989); and Vicent Llombart, *Campomanes, Economista y Político de Carlos III* (Madrid: Alianza Editorial, 1992).

the Crown should seize economically unproductive church property (*desamortización*), and his unrepentant attack on the Jesuits culminated in their expulsion from Spanish territory in the Old World and the New in 1767.[23] The impact of Campomanes's regalism may be detected strongly in several parts of the *Informe*. Jovellanos's embrace of such principles provoked the ire of the church and laid bare the doctrinal constraints under which he operated. In 1800, an *Anonymous Denunciation* spuriously claimed that Jovellanos's writings were infused with the doctrine of the "*Novatores*, of whom, unfortunately, and perhaps for our common punishment, our Spain, which before was an empire of Catholicism, now abounds."[24] The smear campaign precipitated charges against Jovellanos and, ultimately, a trial resulting in his imprisonment on Majorca (1801–1808).

In Jovellanos's writings, however, there are few criticisms of Catholicism as a doctrine but many concerning the church's role in various aspects of society. In the *Informe*, for example, he called for a return to the "pure and ancient discipline of the church."[25] In his address to the Instituto Asturiano on the need for uniting the study of the sciences and literature, Jovellanos called for the study of ethics "perfected and sanctified by the Gospel," which was "the peak and the foundation of our august religion." In the *Eulogy in Praise of Charles III*, he also criticized "ecclesiastical studies" and "scholasticism," which "hoarded the attention that was owed to morality and dogma." Jovellanos claimed that Carlos III's reign, the apex of enlightened reformism in Spain, had emancipated the country from the "barbaric voices" of "Thomism, Scotism, and Suarezian scholasticism." What was important was thus to "free" religion from "the Aristotelian yoke" and to make it return to "its purest sources, the Holy Scripture, the Councils, the Church Fathers, the history and discipline of the church."[26]

The recent historiographical recognition of the existence of "national" Enlightenments (note the plural) and even the introduction of the concept of "Moderate Enlightenment,"[27] in which church, state, and Enlightenment are compatible, instead of antithetical, has propelled the reconsideration of eighteenth-century Spanish texts as worthy of inclusion as part of the broader European Enlightenment. Viewed in light of the old historiography, this new tendency is undeniably salutary. But this approach does not mean that it is without shortcomings. The problem with a focus on variations across linguistic, national

23 Paquette, *Enlightenment, Governance and Reform*, ch. 2; estimates vary, but it is safe to estimate that the church in Castile possessed roughly one-seventh of the region's agricultural and pastoral lands.

24 *Anonymous Denunciation* against Jovellanos, cited by: José Miguel Caso González, *Jovellanos: Biografía/Biography* (Oviedo: Fundación Cristina Masaveu Peterson, 2011), 248. It should be noted that political economy itself was not inherently irreligious. As John Robertson explains, "In focusing on bettering the human condition in this world, it set aside the next […] it did not challenge theology as such." See Robertson, "Enlightenment, Public Sphere and Political Economy," in Jesús Astigarraga and Javier Usoz, eds., *L'économie politique et la sphère publique dans le débat des Lumières* (Madrid: Casa de Velázquez, 2013), 30.

25 *Informe*, section 181.

26 *Inaugural Address* and *Eulogy in Praise*.

27 Jonathan Israel, *A Revolution of the Mind. Radical Enlightenment and the Intellectual Origins of Modern Democracy* (Princeton and Oxford: Princeton University Press, 2010).

and territorial boundaries and the embrace of the plurality of "Enlightenments" is that it might distract attention from the ways that the Enlightenment was unitary, with shared intellectual preoccupations and characteristics, a movement that trespassed, and often transcended, borders and boundaries of all types—intellectual, doctrinal and geographical. So, even as the study of the Enlightenment drifts away from the stultifying emphasis on a canon populated by too few "great" books of rather limited provenance and linguistic range, it is crucial to retain an awareness of certain shared themes, problems and epistemological preferences, as historian John Robertson has proposed.[28] Such awareness underpins the case for the inclusion of Spain as part of a broader movement of the Enlightenment in Europe (and beyond).

The Life and Career of Jovellanos

Born to a respected family in the port city of Gijón, Asturias, in the north of Spain, Jovellanos prepared for a career in the church from an early age.[29] As was customary, the eldest son inherited the entirety of the family's estate as a result of *mayorazgo*, which is equivalent to primogeniture in English. The remaining children were left to pursue careers in the military, the church, law or government service. Jovellanos, the tenth child overall and the fourth male child, thus commenced his ecclesiastical studies in his native Gijón. In 1757, at age 13, he relocated to nearby Oviedo, the capital of Asturias, to begin his philosophical studies.

From Asturias, Jovellanos moved to Castile, where he was supposed to continue his ecclesiastical training and, in turn, pursued studies in canon and civil law in Ávila, Osma and, finally, in Alcalá de Henares. In Ávila, he probably gained proficiency in the Latin classics, particularly Horace, Virgil, Cicero, Sallust and Pliny, among others. In Osma, he received a degree in canon law, which was later validated by the more prestigious University of Ávila, which granted him a *licenciatura* in canon law.[30] Most biographers coincide that apart from studying canon law during this period, he also trained extensively in civil law.[31] In Alcalá, he received a fellowship to study at the prestigious Colegio de San Ildefonso, which opened crucial doors to elite circles in Spanish society.[32]

---

28 John Robertson, *The Case for the Enlightenment: Scotland and Naples, 1680–1760* (Cambridge: Cambridge University Press, 2005).

29 Many important biographical treatments of Jovellanos's life are available, beginning with the biography written by painter, fellow Gijón native and friend Juan Agustín Ceán Bermúdez, *Memorias para la vida del Excmo. Señor D. Gaspar Melchor de Jovellanos y Noticias Analíticas de sus Obras* (Madrid: En la Imprenta que fue de Fuentenebro, 1814). Among the more recent biographies, see Javier Varela, *Jovellanos* (Madrid: Alianza Editorial, 1988); John H. R. Polt, *Gaspar Melchor de Jovellanos* (New York: Twayne Publishers, 1971); the above-cited Caso González, *Jovellanos*; and Llombart, *Jovellanos*.

30 Caso González, *Jovellanos*, 71.

31 Some scholars affirm that the University of Osma granted him degrees in both canon and civil law whereas others insist that he solely received degrees in canon law. The first position is that of his original biographer (Céan Bermúdez, *Memorias*, 6). Alternatively, Caso González posits that Jovellanos was the recipient of canon law degrees (*Jovellanos*, 71).

32 Caso González, *Jovellanos*, 71–72.

Upon graduation, Jovellanos still contemplated an ecclesiastical career, but he was persuaded instead to pursue law and, in 1768, was appointed as a criminal judge (*alcalde de crimen*) in Seville. The experience was transformative. In Seville, he attended the *tertulias* of Pablo de Olavide, then the intendant of Seville. It was under Olavide's influence that Jovellanos applied for and received the aforementioned license to obtain and read prohibited books. He read these and other books voraciously in these years. At Olavide's *tertulias*, Jovellanos mixed with influential Spanish intellectuals.[33] In 1774, his career reached another milestone when Charles III named him judge (*oidor*) of the High Court (*Audiencia*) of Seville. During his decade in Andalusia, Jovellanos was a founding member of Seville's *Sociedad Económica de Amigos del País*, which had its statutes approved in 1777. Approximately 80 such economic societies (sometimes called patriotic societies) were created across Spain and Spanish-America between 1770 and 1820. Based on the model of the European agricultural improvement association—such as those established in Dublin (1731), Zurich (1747), Florence (1754) and Bern (1758)—, they were designed to diffuse "useful knowledge" and promote "improvement" of the cities or regions in which they were located. They pursued this objective through regular meetings, publications, prizes, public events, schools and classes of instruction and the formation of specialized libraries containing works of agronomy and political economy.[31]

In 1778, Jovellanos was transferred to Madrid. First, he served as *Alcalde de Casa y Corte*, and doubled as a criminal judge.[35] In 1780, he was appointed to a new post as a member of the Council of Military Orders. He caught the attention of Campomanes, a fellow Asturian, who would rise to the presidency of the Council of Castile, the very apex of Spain's government. Under Campomanes's patronage (and tutelage), Jovellanos was soon inducted into numerous academies and learned societies, the most important of which were the Real Academia de la Historia (Royal Academy of History) (inducted 1779) and the Royal Economic Society of Madrid—commonly known as *La Matritense*—(1778), the latter of which he would serve briefly as director (1784–1786).[36] Three of the five works published in the present volume were given originally as speeches or else published under the auspices of these two cultural bodies. Jovellanos

---

33 The 1778 catalogue of his library indicates the presence of the following modern authors (among many others): Bacon, Hume, Milton, Dryden, Pope, Addison, Fontenelle, La Fontaine, Montesquieu, Voltaire, Rousseau, Beccaria, Muratori. Ibid., 80.

34 R. J. Shafer, *The Economic Societies of the Spanish World (1763–1821)* (Syracuse: Syracuse University Press, 1958); Maria Consolación Calderón España, ed., *Las Reales Sociedades Económicas de Amigos del País y el Espíritu Ilustrado: Análisis de sus Realizaciones* (Seville: La Real Sociedad Económica de Amigos del Pais, 2001); and, most recently, Koen Stapelbroek and Jani Marjanen, eds., *The Rise of Economic Societies in the Eighteenth Century: Patriotic Reform in Europe and North America* (Basingstoke: Palgrave Macmillan, 2012); on the contemporary Spanish-American Societies, see Paquette, *Enlightenment, Governance and Reform*, ch. 4; on "improvement" as a pan-European ideology in the long eighteenth century, see Richard Drayton, *Nature's Government: Science, Imperial Britain and the "Improvement" of the World* (New Haven and London: Yale University Press, 2000).

35 Caso González, *Jovellanos*, 85.

36 Varela, *Jovellanos*, 47; *La Matritense* was the largest of the Economic Societies, boasting 450 members in 1795, the year it published Jovellanos's *Informe*. See Shafer, *Economic Societies*, 73.

was a polymath, and his varied interests and expertise led to membership in other prestigious bodies, including the Real Academia de Bellas Artes de San Fernando (1780),
the Real Academia de la Lengua (1781), and the Academia de Cánones, Liturgia,
Historia y Disciplina Eclesiástica (1781).

Mixing in circles bearing scant resemblance to those of his provincial upbringing in
Gijón, he forged friendships with famous artists, such as Goya, who painted his portrait
twice, and others influential members of the Spanish elite, including the financier and
economist Francisco Cabarrús. In fact, it would be Jovellanos's defense of Cabarrús,
in 1790, accused of fraud in relation to the recently founded Bank of San Carlos, that
caused the Asturian's estrangement from court. The scandal involved María Luisa, wife
of Carlos IV and Queen Consort of Spain. Jovellanos's defense of Cabarrús paved the
way for his banishment—probably aided by the fact that María Luisa allegedly harbored
"a nearly irrational hatred" toward him—and prompted an exile to his native Gijón that
lasted for the first half of the 1790s.[37]

During his *destierro*, Jovellanos embarked on a series of productive ventures. He
penned several reports on mines and manufactures in northern Spain. He founded the
Real Instituto Asturiano de Náutica y Mineralogía, another learned society as well as
school created to foster the "useful" sciences and the "advancement" of the province.[38]
It was positioned as a counterpoint to the tradition-bound University of Oviedo, with
its scholasticism-infused curriculum. The antipathy was mutual: the University tried
to prevent the opening of the Institute.[39] Nevertheless, the Institute, bearing the royal
imprimatur, opened its doors to commoners and nobles alike, in January 1794. The Latin
motto of the Institute was "Quid Vero, Quid Utile," often translated as "Truth and Public
Utility," and, unsurprisingly, the curriculum was weighted in favor of mathematics and
the physical sciences, and applied "sciences" such as political economy, though literary
studies were not neglected, as one of Jovellanos's orations to the Institute, reproduced in
this volume, makes clear. Jovellanos favored the Institute with vigorous and lavish patronage. Unfortunately, within a decade of its founding, the Institute had fallen on hard times,
largely connected to the vicissitudes of Jovellanos's own career, described in the following
paragraphs.[40]

---

37 Caso González, *Jovellanos*, 206.
38 On the Asturian economy in the Age of Jovellanos, see Gonzalo Anes, *Economía y Sociedad en la
    Asturias del Antiguo Régimen* (Barcelona: Editorial Ariel, 1988).
39 The creation of the Institute must be situated in the context of the general opening of second-
    ary education following the 1767 expulsion of the Jesuits, who at their peak in 1749 admin-
    istered 117 colleges (*colegios*). While universities had generally fallen under the purview of the
    Franciscans, Dominicans and other orders, the Institute, a hybrid *colegio*-university, represented
    a secular threat to previous ecclesiastical hegemony. See William J. Callahan, "The Spanish
    Church," in Callahan and David Higgs, eds., *Church and Society in Catholic Europe of the Eighteenth
    Century* (Cambridge: Cambridge University Press, 1979).
40 One of the final acts of Jovellanos's life (1811) was to pledge half of his salary to the revival
    of the Institute, remarking that "the nation needs not only brave defenders, but also well-
    educated ones"; on this bequest, see Llombart, *Jovellanos*, 173.

It was during his 1790s Asturian exile that Jovellanos completed his *Informe de la Ley Agraria*, perhaps the most important work of eighteenth-century Spanish political economy, as the subsequent sections of this introduction should make clear. But first it is crucial to describe the final phases of Jovellanos's career. In 1797, he was rehabilitated thanks to the recently ascendant prime minister and royal favorite Manuel de Godoy, who named him as minister of justice. The seemingly triumphant return to Madrid proved ephemeral; it lasted a mere 18 months. Jovellanos was again dismissed from office in 1798 and returned, in disgrace, to Gijón. In 1801, as previously mentioned, he was arrested as a political prisoner and exiled to the island of Majorca, in the Mediterranean, where he remained in Bellver Castle for almost seven years (1802–1808).

With the abdication of Charles IV, and then Ferdinand VII, in the face of the French occupation of the Iberian Peninsula in 1808, Jovellanos was released from his Balearic confinement, returning to the Peninsula.[11] He was soon elected as an Asturian delegate to the Junta Central, the principal body resisting Joseph I (José I), Napoleon's elder brother, who had been installed by the French as the new king of Spain. The Junta Central assumed for itself the power to act on behalf of the imprisoned Ferdinand VII for the purpose of maintaining Spanish sovereignty and contesting French ascendancy. A flurry of activity marked Jovellanos's association with the Junta Central: he wrote an extensive plan for the reform of education in Spain as well as a defense of the Junta's activity, including its controversial convocation of a Cortes, an extraordinary parliament convened in Cádiz and empowered to draft a written constitution for Spain and its empire. Jovellanos died in 1811, at age 67, after the Cortes had begun its deliberations yet before its famous 1812 Constitution was promulgated.[12]

The Contexts and Reception of Jovellanos's *Informe*

Though the lion's share of the *Informe* was written during Jovellanos's exile in Gijón, the seminal work published in 1795 was not the work of an isolated genius. On the contrary, it has a long, tangled and fascinating history involving many individuals, and institutions, intersecting with an array of social and economic problems. The *Informe* may of course be situated in the pan-European literature related to agrarian reform, whether the debate over restrictions on the grain trade or of the connection (and contested primacy) between the agrarian, commercial and industrial sectors of a nation's

---

41 There is no shortage of high-quality descriptions of these episodes in English. See, for example, Charles Esdaile, *Spain in the Liberal Age: From Constitution to Civil War, 1808–1939* (Oxford: Blackwell, 2000); and Raymond Carr, *Spain, 1808–1975* (Oxford: Clarendon Press, 1982). For an overview of the historiography of Latin American Independence, see Gabriel Paquette, "Dissolution of the Spanish Atlantic Monarchy," *Historical Journal* 52:1 (2009), 175–212.

42 There are many good accounts of the Cortes and Constitution of Cádiz, but see, most recently, Natalia Sobrevilla Perea and Scott Eastman, eds., *The Rise of Constitutional Government in the Iberian Atlantic World: The Impact of the Cádiz Constitution of 1812* (Tuscaloosa: University of Alabama Press, 2015).

economy.[13] The *Informe* bears the traces of Jovellanos's extensive reading in European political economy, in particular his engagement with Scottish Enlightenment giants Adam Ferguson and Smith, though his embrace of these figures was partial, and his thought was notable for its eclecticism, as previously has been established.[14]

The *Informe* also has a more specific Spanish context.[15] The middle of the eighteenth century witnessed a growing awareness of the difficulties facing Spanish agriculture. Agricultural prices rose in the early 1750s and, by the early 1760s, the discrepancy between the food requirements of Spain's growing cities and the plenitude of its harvests became evident, and the specter of famine stalked the country, as it did elsewhere in Mediterranean Europe, including Southern Italy. In 1765, grain price controls were eliminated and the freedom to ship grain throughout Spain was confirmed. Greater demand for basic staples not only led to higher prices but also produced spillover effects in the rural economy, where the price of lands and rents rose, often with disruptive consequences.[16]

Abolishing restrictions on the grain trade was merely a first step to remedy the plight of Spanish agriculture. Numerous other obstacles remained and were subject to assault by Spanish writers.[17] Jovellanos's *Informe* would describe and criticize many of these obstacles, connecting what appeared to be disparate phenomena with a singular brilliance and cogency. Among the panoply of problems identified by Spanish writers was the use, or misuse, of land. The church's land ownership came under special criticism. The church must be understood here as the aggregate of cathedral chapters, religious orders, pious charities and related, sundry institutions and bodies. Not only did the church's possessions include highly desirable, fertile territory, which reformers complained was grossly underutilized, but also church-owned land could not be sold. Effectively taken off the market, it was reduced to *manos muertas*, or mortmain. The church's income derived from rents on this land held in mortmain.

---

43 The debate over physiocracy in Spain, though beyond the scope of the present introduction, deserves mention. See Ernest Lluch and Lluís Argemí, "Physiocracy in Spain," *History of Political Economy* 26:4 (1994), 613–627. On physiocracy more generally, see Elizabeth Fox-Genovese, *The Origins of Physiocracy: Economic Revolution and Social Order in Eighteenth-century France* (Ithaca and London: Cornell University Press, 1976).

44 On Jovellanos's engagement with Smith and Ferguson, see Smith, "The Wealth of Nations in Spain and Hispanic America"; Polt, "Jovellanos and his English Sources"; and María del Carmen Lara Nieto, *Ilustración Española y Pensamiento Inglés: Jovellanos* (Granada: Editorial Universidad de Granada, 2008). Polt rightly notes that Jovellanos did not "fall victim to a foolish and superficial anglomania," 68; on the ambivalence (and perhaps rejection) of Jovellanos toward Smith, see Ernest Lluch, *Las Españas Vencidas del Siglo XVIII: Claroscuros de la Ilustración* (Barcelona: Crítica, 1998), 202–208; on the changing reception (and perceptions) of Smith in the eighteenth and nineteenth centuries, see Emma Rothschild, *Economic Sentiments: Adam Smith, Condorcet and the Enlightenment* (Cambridge, MA: Harvard University Press, 2001).

45 The reconstruction of the Spanish context of the *Informe* relies on the following works: Polt, *Jovellanos*, 94–98; Gonzalo Anes, *La Ley Agraria* (Madrid: Alianza Editorial, 1995), 152–61; Varela, *Jovellanos*, 110–120; and Herr, *Rural Change*, 42–50,

46 Herr, *Rural Change*, 10, 15, 19, 34.

47 The following paragraphs are indebted to, and follow closely, Herr, *Rural Change*, 19–27.

A second form of land practice that aggravated reformers was that of primogeniture entail, or *Mayorazgos* (and sometimes called *vínculos legos*), in Spanish. Here families established inalienable and indivisible units of land that passed from generation to generation by primogeniture.[48] The concentration of land in a few hands was criticized by some contemporaries as pernicious because many landowners with vast estates were bankrupt or impoverished, yet *mayorazgo* prevented them from selling off even a fraction of their property to those possessing capital. Thus, in the eyes of critics, lands would lie fallow, underutilized or worked with rudimentary methods, instead of new, capital-intensive techniques.

A third type of land use tendency against which reformers directed their pens was the phenomenon of the *tierras baldías*, or *baldíos*. Such lands were neither owned privately nor ceded for the exclusive use of a municipality. Instead, *baldíos* encompassed a wide array of uncultivated "waste" lands, including woods, rough hills of scrub growth, mountains and the like. *Baldíos* would increasingly be targeted by Spanish reformers as an underexploited resource over which the Crown had authority and should encourage its use. The most famous example of the Crown's efforts to utilize the neglected, much maligned *baldíos* was that undertaken by Jovellanos's first patron and mentor, Olavide, the colonization project in the Sierra Morena, Andalusia, in the 1760s, known as the Nuevas Poblaciones. As Olavide noted, "today these [lands] are despised as useless, but they will flourish with an infusion of manure and sweat."[49] Olavide believed that excessively large plots were less productive than smaller ones. In Andalusia's *baldíos*, he distributed small plots to the colonists, while holding valleys and mountainsides in common for livestock.[50] The partial success of the Sierra Morena scheme—with nine towns founded and 13,000 homesteaders settled in previously unpopulated, barren territory—undoubtedly shaped Jovellanos's ideas toward the *baldíos* in the *Informe*, particularly the ideal of the small, independent property owner able to pursue his interest unencumbered by rights and privileges of groups like the *Mesta*.

The fourth and final land practice that came under increasing criticism from the mid-eighteenth century onward was the *Mesta*. Established in the thirteenth century, the *Mesta* was a guild composed of powerful owners of vagrant merino sheep. These sheep pastured in the central and northern mountains in the summer months, before being driven south prior to the onset of winter. This annual migration of transhumant sheep was incredibly disruptive: thousands of sheep followed the *cañadas*, long-established migratory paths. At its inception, this practice received the full support of the Spanish Crown,

---

48 As Herr rightly points out, *mayorazgo* encompassed not just real estate but also extended to all forms of property, including royal bonds (*juros*), ownership of local public offices, seigneurial jurisdiction and other privileges. See Herr, *Rural Change*, 21–22; written in the wake of the publication of Jovellanos's *Informe*, the following eighteenth-century account of the history of the *mayorazgo* by one of Spain's leading political economists still merits rereading: Juan Sempere y Guarinos, *Historia de los Vínculos y Mayorazgos* [1797] (Alicante: Instituto de Cultura Juan Gil-Alber, 1990).

49 Olavide, quoted in Herr, *Rural Change*, 67.

50 Anes, *Ley Agraria*, 20–21, 125–133.

which profited handsomely from the trade in merino wool, for which there was demand in Northern Europe in particular. An appreciative Crown had granted the members of the *Mesta* something called the right of *posesión*. Essentially, these owners of sheep could use any pasture they had ever (since the thirteenth century) utilized without an increase in the level of rent. As Herr notes, "the right of *posesión* was a disguised form of entail, which restricted land to its present use."[51] The impact of the annual migration of sheep was deleterious, too, in the view of reformers, as it disincentivized bringing communal lands into cultivation and made precarious private holdings bordering the *cañadas*.

The vacillating, fickle fortunes of Spanish agriculture sparked a tremendous outpouring of writing on these institutions and practices, much of it written by members of the flourishing economic societies or reform-minded Crown officials. Over the course of the eighteenth century, thousands of complaints, analyses and suggested remedies concerning Spanish agriculture had been submitted to the Council of Castile, the most important decision-making body in the Peninsula. The Spanish state was far from unresponsive. The effort to reform the *baldíos* of the Sierra Morena in the 1760s has been mentioned already, part of a surge of Crown activity to address perceived agricultural problems. Following the expulsion of the Jesuits in 1767, Jesuit property was disentailed and sold, whereas the Mesta's right of *posesión* was curtailed in 1786.

But while treatises, pleas and reports proliferated, and some, albeit halting, government action was taken, there was scant convergence regarding the causes of, or solutions to, these purported ills preventing Spanish agriculture's efflorescence. Jovellanos's *Informe* may be seen as an attempt to sift through, make sense of and (if possible) harmonize these reform proposals, laments and analyses. The specific origins of the *Informe* itself may be located in a 1777 request by Campomanes to Madrid's Economic Society. Campomanes was in that year both a member of the Council of Castile and director of the Economic Society.[52] He entrusted the Society with the manuscripts pertaining to agriculture that the Council had accumulated, requesting that the Society attempt to make sense of them, with a view toward proposing the lines along which a comprehensive agrarian law, a panacea to remedy the myriad ills diagnosed as afflicting Spain with a single blow, might be framed. These documents were quite heterogeneous, ranging from reports written by various intendants (including a 1768 *Informe* written by Jovellanos's early mentor and patron, Olavide, while intendant of Seville) to a hodgepodge of narrower, local complaints submitted by smallholders to the judgments of myriad legal cases pertaining to sundry aspects of agrarian affairs.

Faced with this avalanche of heterogeneous and largely anecdotal data, very little headway was made by the Society. In the early 1780s, it requested that the Council of Castile, of which Campomanes recently had become president, condense the unwieldy morass of

---

51 Herr, *Rural Change*, 24.
52 Campomanes would be interim president or president of the Council of Castile from 1783–1791; Campomanes had some reservations about Madrid's Economic Society, complaining that its classes hardly met, a sign of the apathy and indolence of its members. Jovellanos, who became director in 1784, came to harbor a similar complaint, believing the infrequency of its meetings was an indication of pernicious decrepitude. See Schafer, *Economic Societies*, 55–56.

documents related to agriculture into something more manageable before it executed the commission it had accepted. The Council complied and, in 1784, furnished the Society with an *expediente* (dossier), an extensive abstract of the various writings. This *expediente*, which was published in 1785, was turned over to a 12-member junta (subcommittee) of the Society devoted to agricultural matters. The junta, of which Jovellanos was a member (he also served as director of the *Matritense* in 1784–1786), was meant to write an *informe*, or report, that could serve as a guide or set of prescriptions for comprehensive agrarian legislation. It made scant progress. In 1787, following a speech to the junta that was praised for its lucid exposition of the problems facing Spanish agriculture and the principles that should inform any solutions proposed, Jovellanos was asked to write up, in extended form, the arguments and evidence that he had conveyed orally. He agreed, only after the junta aided his efforts by submitting its views on the various issues identified in the *expediente*.

It is worth mentioning the junta's areas of agreement in order to understand the constraints under and parameters within which Jovellanos labored to compose the *Informe*, an undertaking that lasted almost eight years. The junta's members unanimously held that the level of taxation was excessive and the form of collection flawed; the privileges of the *Mesta* required modification; population was poorly distributed in Spanish territory, with vast underpopulated zones; Spain lacked an adequate number of canals and roads for the grain trade to flourish (which led to price distortions); the absence of liberty with regard to the use and disposal of property was a problem; and entail needed to be addressed.[53]

Jovellanos received his commission in 1787 yet did not submit his draft to the Society until 1794. Besides the enormity of the task, the slow pace may be attributable by changes in Spanish politics. As noted previously, he was exiled to Gijón from 1790–1796, placing him far from the center of political life. More broadly, Spanish and European politics was transformed between the year of his commission (1787) and the year he submitted the draft of the *Informe* (1794) for the Madrid Economic Society's approval (which was received with enthusiasm in October 1794). With regard to Spanish high politics, Jovellanos's chief patron was Campomanes, who, as president of the Council of Castile, tentatively undertook some of the reforms the Society meditated, protecting local farmers, for example, from the powerful *Mesta*. In 1791, the new King Charles IV (r. 1788–1808) relieved Campomanes of his duties, a prelude to the *Mesta*'s reassertion of its privileges and disruptive practices.[54] With regard to European politics, the advent of the French Revolution in 1789 and, especially, the radical turn of the Revolution after 1792, produced a chilling effect on reformers in Spain, particularly those whose ideas threatened entrenched and powerful landed interests. Jovellanos, then, bereft of his chief protector at court and viewing the political cataclysm unfolding across the Pyrenees, may have judged it prudent to proceed with caution.

These circumstances notwithstanding, the *Informe* was published by the Society in 1795, with the support of Godoy, who likely hoped it would provide him with a rationale

---

53 These areas of agreement are described well in Anes, *Ley Agraria*, 152.
54 Herr, *Rural Change*, 42; the *Mesta* was the target of legislation at the Cortes of Cádiz in the 1810s, but would not be abolished definitively until 1836.

for imposing new taxes on church-owned lands.[55] The Inquisition, less enamored of the *Informe* than Godoy, also took an interest. Its censors initiated an investigation, but this process was suspended in 1797, coinciding with Jovellanos's elevation to the ministry.[56] The longevity of the *Informe*'s impact is suggested by the fact that it was placed on the Vatican *Index of Prohibited Books* in 1825, where it remained for 52 years. Before then, the Cortes of Cádiz recommended the *Informe*'s diffusion and implementation. It became a cherished text for Spanish liberals throughout the nineteenth century, who reprinted it and also published new editions, including the 1820 edition published by exiles in Bourdeaux, France, the cover of which is reproduced in this introduction (see Illustration 0.2). Historians estimate that there were over 30 editions of the *Informe* between 1795 and 1995.

Before it could be banned, however, it was diffused widely, both in Spain and abroad. A French translation of the *Informe* was published in 1806 in St. Petersburg, Russia, and a more widely disseminated French translation undertaken by Napoleonic diplomat (and prolific travel writer) Alexandre de Laborde (1773–1842) appeared in 1808, which served as the basis for the translation of the *Informe* in English, published in 1809. The title page of this 1809 English translation of Laborde's book and the first page of the translation of the *Informe* embedded in it are reproduced, respectively, in this introduction (see Illustrations 0.3 and 0.4). There was an extensive review of the St. Petersburg French translation of the *Informe* in the *Edinburgh Review* in 1809, which some historians attribute to James Mill. There also were Italian and German translations in 1815 and 1816, respectively.[57]

Between Practical Politics and Philosophical History: An Outline and Analysis of Jovellanos's *Informe* as a Work of Political Economy

Putting aside the acclaim and posthumous fame he gained, Jovellanos's reputation as author of the *Informe* remains somewhat curious. He evidently viewed himself merely as the mouthpiece of his *Matritense* colleagues, synthesizing their views, and believed himself

---

55 Godoy's new taxes on church property foreshadowed Charles IV's decision in 1798 to commence a general disentailment of properties under ecclesiastical control. See Herr, *Rural Change*, 45.

56 Polt, *Jovellanos*, 99.

57 Llombart, "El Pensamiento Económico de Jovellanos y sus Intérpretes," 93–94; and, more extensively, Vicent Llombart, "Jovellanos, Economista de la Ilustracíon Tardía," in Gaspar Melchor de Jovellanos, *Escritos Económicos*. Ed. Vicent Llombart (Madrid: Real Academia de Ciencias Morales y Politicas, 2000), 138–46; further details concerning the first English translation deserve mention: it was a translation of a French translation, published by Alexandre de Laborde in 1808. It had been included in Volume 4 of his *Itinéraire descriptif de l'Espagne et tableau élémentaire des différentes branches de l'administration e de l'industrie de ce royaume* (Paris, 1808). The complete translation of the *Informe* was published as "Memoir on the Advancement of Agriculture and on Agrarian Laws," appearing in the English translation of Laborde's *A View of Spain; Comprising a Descriptive Itinerary of Each Province, and a General Statistical Account of the Country*, vol. 4 (London: Longman, Hurst, Rees, and Orme 1809); the translation of the *Informe* may be found on pp. 111–315 of the English edition. The present edition, as far as it can be determined, is the first direct translation of the Spanish original.

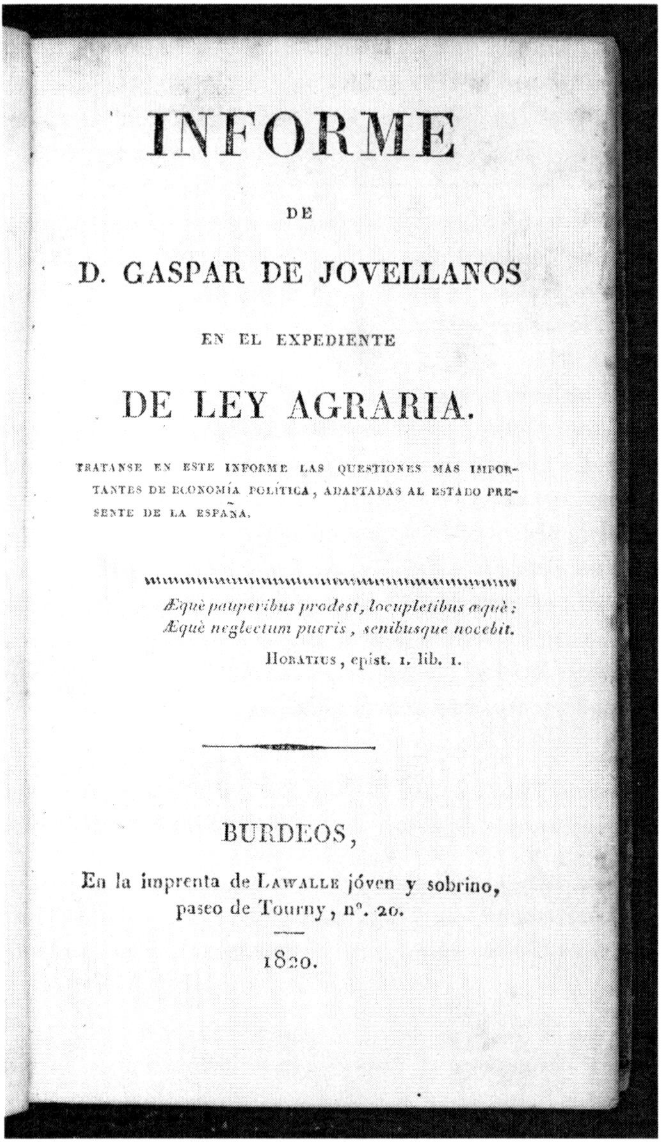

INFORME

DE

D. GASPAR DE JOVELLANOS

EN EL EXPEDIENTE

DE LEY AGRARIA.

TRÁTANSE EN ESTE INFORME LAS QUESTIONES MÁS IMPOR-
TANTES DE ECONOMÍA POLÍTICA, ADAPTADAS AL ESTADO PRE-
SENTE DE LA ESPAÑA.

Æquè pauperibus prodest, locupletibus æquè;
Æquè neglectum pueris, senibusque nocebit.

HORATIUS, epist. 1. lib. 1.

BURDEOS,

En la imprenta de LAWALLE jóven y sobrino,
paseo de Tourny, n°. 20.

1820.

Illustration 0.2 Title page of *Informe de D. Gaspar de Jovellanos en el Expediente de la Ley Agraria* (Bordeaux: Lawalle, 1820). Reproduced with the kind permission of the George Peabody Library, The Sheridan Libraries, Johns Hopkins University.

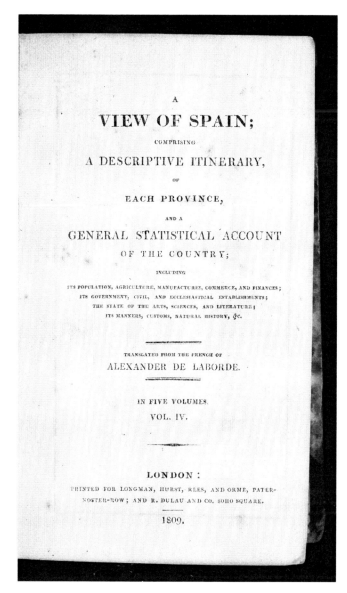

Illustration 0.3 Title page of Alexandre de Laborde, *A View of Spain; Comprising a Descriptive Itinerary of Each Province, and a General Statistical Account of the Country*, vol. 4 (London: Longman, Hurst, Rees, and Orme 1809). Reproduced with the kind permission of the George Peabody Library, The Sheridan Libraries, Johns Hopkins University.

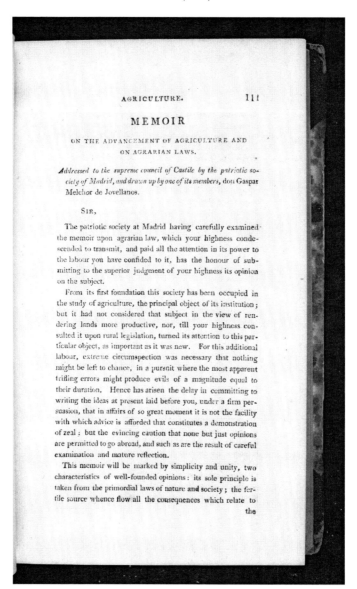

Illustration 0.4 First page of [Jovellanos,] "Memoir on the Advancement of Agriculture and on Agrarian Laws," published in Laborde, *A View of Spain*, vol. 4. Reproduced with the kind permission of the George Peabody Library, The Sheridan Libraries, Johns Hopkins University.

to have moderated his own views in order to concoct a compromise, pragmatic document that could be endorsed by the entire economic society, with its notable range of opinions, as well one that might be palatable to the Council of Castile. In his diary, for example, Jovellanos indicated that he intended to explain his conciliatory pragmatism to his friends: "I did not propose the absolute abolition of every kind of entail and amortization, which I consider necessary; why I blocked free grain exports, which I consider just; and other matters in keeping with the demands of these times."[58]

Sections of the *Informe* recall the philosophical history so common to Jovellanos's century, evocative of masterworks such as Abbé Raynal's *Histoire des Deux Indes* (1770–1780), William Robertson's *History of America* (1777), Ferguson's *Essay on the History of Civil Society* (1767), Marquis de Condorcet's, *Esquisse d'un Tableau Historique des Progrès de l'Esprit Humain* (1794–1795), and Gibbon's *Decline and Fall of the Roman Empire* (1776). Indeed, Jovellanos had long wished to remedy what he considered to be the defects of Spanish history writing by infusing it with the spirit and philosophical preoccupations of his age. In a 1779 letter, for example, he lamented that historians had heretofore "troubled themselves little to provide us with information regarding the civil aspects of our history, as if the only thing worth bequeathing to future generations was material relative to warfare, of battles and domestic political disputes, the only things of which they write."[59] The *Informe*, often considered as the centerpiece of Jovellanos's thought and certainly at the core of this volume, was chiefly a work of philosophical history, even if its specific target was an analysis of the obstacles that hindered agricultural progress in Spain—and, more generally, it could be argued, economic improvement—and the means to overcome such impediments.

For Jovellanos, the branches of learning that in an age of specialization have come to be understood as distinct, were inextricable, necessarily cross-pollinating one another. Two of the orations reproduced in the present volume, from 1780 and 1797, respectively, make clear how the study of law and history, and literature and science, had to be bounded together. Not only was each subject enriched by the study of the other but also, Jovellanos strongly argues, each was incoherent without the other. Political economy was no different: its study demanded thorough immersion in and awareness of the intersections among, law, politics, history, moral science, natural science and many other branches of knowledge. In the *Informe*, Jovellanos grouped the obstacles into three categories: political obstacles (those imposed by legislation), moral obstacles (those imposed by opinion or custom) and physical obstacles (those imposed by Nature). It is the political obstacles that merit the reader's closest attention here, but it should be noted how these three types of obstacles are entwined and interpenetrating for Jovellanos. This provides some context for the inclusion of the four shorter texts in this volume, which collectively make the case that scientific, historical, literary, mathematical and legal education were the proper and indispensable foundation of the study of political economy.

---

58 Quoted in Polt, *Jovellanos*, 104.
59 Jovellanos to José Gil Araújo, January 1779, quoted in Varela, *Jovellanos*, 63.

Jovellanos's *Informe* is best known for its scathing critique of the institutions and customary practices that purportedly impeded Spanish agriculture's efflorescence. Jovellanos's vehemence was directed at what he maligned as antiquated institutions, the *baldíos* and the *Mesta* especially. He famously called for the removal of obstacles that thwarted the interest of individual agents and an overhaul of existing legislation in order to make the laws affecting economic life coincide with self-interest.[60] In Jovellanos's *Informe*, the familiar eighteenth-century language of "private vices and public benefits" is undoubtedly present. Yet in Jovellanos's work, the pursuit of self-interest is valorized as a public virtue, to be encouraged and rewarded amply. The protoliberal dimension of the *Informe* has often been stressed, with some reason. As Jovellanos stated toward the end of the *Informe*, addressing Charles IV, "all that our country needs to achieve prosperity is a single wave of your Highness's powerful hand to remove the obstacles that block our way."[61] Jovellanos made extensive use of the languages of liberty and interest in his economic writings, which is starkly apparent in the *Informe*.

As the *Informe*'s purpose was to restore Spain's prosperity, Jovellanos emphasized the need to remove the many obstacles that restricted liberty in agriculture, which he saw as the basis of the economy. The *Informe*, according to Jovellanos, was not aimed at curtailing manufacturing and commerce but at establishing and demonstrating that both were dependent upon agriculture.[62] The *Informe* thus focused on the ways to revive Spanish agriculture from its state of stagnation. The language of liberty was invoked to characterize the types of policy Spanish agriculture required. The protection dispensed over the centuries by the Crown to certain groups and institutions—nobles, clergymen, shepherds and so forth—brought about pernicious consequences to agriculture, and thus to the Spanish economy as a whole. Spanish agriculture's plight in the late eighteenth century was characterized by Jovellanos with language antonymic to the idiom of liberty. Land was "enslaved" by legislation that protected primogeniture entails (*mayorazgos*) and made the Catholic Church the largest landowner of thousands of square kilometers of arable land, most of it either unused or underutilized. Property was also "enslaved" by entails, taxes, and legal restrictions that prevented the alienation of land.[63] The market for basic staples was also "enslaved" because prefixed prices deterred the circulation of agricultural produce.[64] Semantically adjacent to these words used to describe limitations to liberty were the terms describing the concession of monopolies on certain goods (*estancos*).

In the case of the *baldíos*, Jovellanos predicted that breaking them up into a great number of smaller properties would prove an inducement to economic activity, providing the substrate upon which stifled self-interest would operate. As for the *Mesta*, Jovellanos sought to give the owners of land the right to enclose their property and thus avoid the disruptive (and often harmful) effects of transhumance. Other long-standing institutions,

---

60 *Informe*, sections 19, 29.
61 Ibid., section 433.
62 Ibid., section 328.
63 Ibid., sections 205, 222.
64 Ibid., section 230.

mortmain and entailment in particular, are subjected to a similar scrutiny. They are found to be either anachronistic or flagrantly hostile to the dictates of Reason.

The liberation, and thus improvement (*fomento*), of Spanish agriculture was a matter of creating incentives to induce specific actions. Jovellanos attributed Spain's late eighteenth-century situation to the absence of positive stimuli to excite the "naturally active interest" of agriculture's "agents."[65] For Jovellanos, the unencumbered operation of interests on a standing of "equal protection" was a precondition of economic prosperity.[66] One of the main problems that Spain faced was the differentiated protection given to certain interests relative to others. The plan outlined in the *Informe* consisted in the repeal of the privileges enshrined in legislation and enjoyed by the nobility, the clergy, the members of the *Mesta*, those belonging to guilds and the holders of monopolistic supply contracts, among many others groups. A rather nakedly visible hand would be needed to intervene temporarily to promote agriculture to compensate for, or counterbalance, centuries of neglect. Once restored to its natural place, the interests would be able to operate and intermingle freely, and prosperity would ensue.

Due to Jovellanos's emphasis on the benefits of deregulation, legal reform (that is, making legal codes more rational and uniform by extirpating the byzantine exemptions, exceptions and allowances that had accumulated over the centuries), the pursuit of individual self-interest and the inviolability of property—as the examples of the *baldíos* and the *Mesta* demonstrate—many scholars have drawn attention to the influence of Smith and Ferguson, among others, on Jovellanos, with good reason, as these were authors whom Jovellanos read during the gestation and writing of the *Informe*. Yet the *Informe*, as has been argued in the preceding paragraphs, was far from a paean to an atomistic vision of rent-seeking automatons requiring the dead hand of the state, custom and anachronistic institutions either to wither or else be swept away. Though Jovellanos's views were sometimes indistinguishable from those of his predecessor Smith, understandings of Jovellanos's reading of Smith is based on a limited interpretation of Smith as merely steeped in the language of natural law.[67]

But if the civic humanist dimension of Smith's thought is appreciated adequately, then Jovellanos's own embrace of civic humanist themes might reflect a more nuanced engagement with Smith than has often been recognized.[68] He advocated the eradication of a decrepit legal and institutional past in order to resurrect a long-defunct agrarian society, and accompanying moral order, suitably updated for his eighteenth-century present. He imagined a well-populated rural society, filled with "simple and virtuous" subjects, enjoying "the peace that comes from being ruled by conjugal, paternal, filial, and fraternal love, as well as concord, charity and hospitality."[69] Elsewhere in the *Informe*, he

---

65 Ibid., section 24.
66 Ibid., section 110.
67 Ibid., section 19.
68 Nicholas Phillipson, "Adam Smith as a Civic Moralist," in Istvan Hont and Michael Ignatieff, eds., *Wealth and Virtue, the Shaping of Political Economy in the Scottish Enlightenment* (Cambridge and New York: Cambridge University Press, 1985), 188–189. See also Donald Winch's essay in the same volume.
69 *Informe*, section 89.

described agriculture as "the mother of innocence and of honest labor [...] the primary support of nations' strength and splendor."[70] Understood in this way, self-interest could be (or become) "virtuous": far from being tied to vanity or self-glorification, it could be made consonant with "simplicity," "frugality," "abundance," "peace" and "laborious-ness." Self-interest of this sort, when unleashed on the countryside, would (somewhat paradoxically) bring about a return to rustic virtue and a primeval simplicity of manners and mores. For Jovellanos, then, agriculture was the proper object of study because of the outsized moral and societal consequences of agriculture's fortunes as well as the eco-nomic viability (and advisability) of rural life.

In the *Informe*, agriculture was lauded as the "wellspring of prosperity" and presented as a precondition of both commerce and industry.[71] But European states had not acted with this understanding in mind, Jovellanos lamented. The neglect of agriculture, which contrasted sharply with the favor lavished on commerce and industry, he argued, was repeated across Europe, not just in Spain. "How much protection and solicitude," he asked, "have they not swindled from voiceless and defenseless agriculture?"[72] Jovellanos did not disparage commerce and industry, but rather held that agriculture was the foun-dation of the other two, without which they were doomed. To fail to recognize this order of priority, the necessity of this sequence, these stages of economic development and to foment industry and commerce while agriculture languished, was simply wrongheaded and, in the long run, insecure. As he put the matter, it would be comparable to "tak-ing the road backward."[73] Jovellanos favored agricultural over commercial society for another reason, too, one specific to Spain. A large and ecologically diverse territory, like Spain, did not require international trade to meet its basic needs, thus making it quite distinct from smaller polities, such as Holland and the Italian Republics. Instead, if appropriate policies were implemented, Jovellanos contended, Spain was the ideal place—as he believed it had been under Roman rule—in which to foster small and medium landholdings and diverse agricultural production that would secure alimentary self-sufficiency and also provide for an exportable surplus. Toward the conclusion of the *Informe*, Jovellanos went so far as to describe as "shameful" the contrast between Spain's opulent, burgeoning cities and the "barren-ness and desolation of the countryside."[74] He speculated that the resurgence of agriculture would trigger a reverse migration, from the city to the countryside, and he foresaw the economic, moral and political benefits of this shift.

Jovellanos's ideal Spain, however, differed from the Jeffersonian vision of yeoman farmers, of sturdy freeholders, who were secure in their property, self-regulating/gov-erning and unencumbered in pursuit of their individual interest. Jovellanos may have delighted in such a vision, but he went far beyond it. The preferred economic future for Spain was predicated on a concatenation of flourishing smaller cities, towns, villages and

---

70 Ibid., section 321.
71 Idem.
72 Ibid., section 324.
73 Ibid., section 328.
74 Ibid., section 415.

hamlets, all enlivened and supported by the abundance generated by the agricultural sector's recovery. Interestingly, he predicted that wealth would be widely distributed and more equally divided in such a society. Thus, for Jovellanos, pernicious social ills would be alleviated through a combination of government action (to remove obstacles to economic activity), a recognition of the proper source of the wealth of nations (land and agriculture) and the resettlement, due to the aggregate workings of self-interest, of much of the population in the countryside from the cities.

Several caveats, however, must be mentioned with regard to Jovellanos's advocacy of freeing self-interest from the shackles of outdated legislation and oppressive tradition. Far from a protolibertarian thinker, Jovellanos's *Informe* consistently argued for the indispensability of the protection offered by the central authority, the monarchy, to bring about and sustain the agrarian society he envisaged. Such protection would take the form of forceful interventions to diminish the disproportionate economic and political clout wielded by certain privileged groups. These interventions would be required for his ideal political community to flourish.

Jovellanos's denunciation of the Mesta Council is indicative of his view. He derided it as "an association that is interested only in concentrating in a certain class of owners [...] the protection that the law grants to all."[75] Though he paid lip service to the social value and continuing utility of the nobility, as well as the clergy, there is little doubt that civil and ecclesiastical mortmain as well as civil entailment were the targets of his ire: "the enslavement of property hinders the liberty of cultivation."[76] A similar lamentation may be found in his criticism of the clergy's exemption from certain provincial contributions: "Can such a privilege really be granted to one class of persons without overburdening the other; and without destroying that fair equality without which taxation loses all possibility of being equitable and fair?"[77] The theme of monarchical intervention to ensure justice emerges again in his discussion of how agriculture had suffered due to exceptions/exemptions given to other sectors (industry and commerce): everyone, he claimed, had been granted "exemptions" that had proven deleterious to agriculture. If only agriculture were the object of policy and care, he claimed, "the mercantile profession would need nothing more than equal protection."[78]

The monarchy in Jovellanos's *Informe*, then, is recast in novel ways: specifically, it furnishes protection for the weak against powerful agents, and it propels (and directs) economic activity by removing harmful legislation and extirpating detrimental special interests. The monarchy serves as the arbiter among antagonistic social groups, preventing one from dominating the rest. It thus keeps open avenues for subjects to pursue their own self-interest, which in turn produces additional, if unintended, benefits for the commonwealth. That is, the resulting material bounty would further fortify its legitimacy and provide coveted resources to enable it to compete with other states. In its role as harmonizer and protector, Jovellanos offered a solution—through growth—to

---

75 Ibid., sections 135–138.
76 Ibid., section 222.
77 Ibid., section 315.
78 Ibid., sections 328–329.

the old fiscal-military conundrum as well as a curiously regalist interpretation of the relationship between the Crown and corporations and intermediate bodies. The *Informe* is thus a rich document, valuable as a source for understanding how political economy was conceptualized in late eighteenth-century Spain as it endeavored to reinvigorate domestic production and markets in order to compete globally with rival states. It also offers a philosophical history of Spain's political and economic development, a meditation on Spain's historical evolution that takes into account not just legislative changes and shifts in mores and manners, but also the interaction of these with the limitations imposed by the environment and technological knowledge. Taken together with the other four shorter texts included in this volume, it is hoped that the publication of this translation of the *Informe* will establish Jovellanos for contemporary Anglophone scholars and students as an Enlightenment writer of the first rank, thus drawing attention to the intellectual ferment and vivacity south of the Pyrenees in the eighteenth century that is all too often neglected.

Bibliography

Álvarez de Morales, Antonio. 1989. *El Pensamiento Político y Jurídico de Campomanes*. Madrid: Instituto Nacional de Administración Publica.

Andrés Álvarez, Valentín. 1955. "Prólogo" to the *Informe sobre la Ley Agraria*. Madrid: Instituto de Estudios Políticos.

Anes, Gonzalo. 1988. *Economía y Sociedad en la Asturias del Antiguo Régimen*. Barcelona: Editorial Ariel.

———— 1999. *Cultivos, Cosechas y Pastoreo en la España Moderna*. Madrid: Real Academia de la Historia.

Artola, Miguel. 1956. "Vida y Pensamiento de D. Gaspar Melchor de Jovelanos." In *Obras Publicadas e Inéditas de D. G. M. de Jovellanos*, 1–87. Madrid: Biblioteca de Autores Españoles.

Astigarraga, Jesús. 2015. "Introduction: *Admirer, rougir, imiter*. Spain and the European Enlightenment." In *The Spanish Enlightenment Revisited*, edited by Jesús Astigarraga, 1–27. Oxford: Voltaire Foundation.

Brading, David A. 1984. "Bourbon Spain and Its American Empire." In *The Cambridge History of Latin America*, edited by Leslie Bethell, volume 1, 389–440. Cambridge and New York: Cambridge University Press.

Calderón España, María Consolación, ed. 2011. *Las Reales Sociedades Económicas de Amigos del País y el Espíritu Ilustrado: Análisis de sus Realizaciones*. Seville: La Real Sociedad Económica de Amigos del Pais.

Callahan, William J., and David Higgs, eds. 1979. *Church and Society in Catholic Europe of the Eighteenth Century*. Cambridge and New York: Cambridge University Press.

Cañizares-Esguerra, Jorge. 2006. *Nature, Empire, and Nation: Explorations of the History of Science in the Iberian World*. Stanford: Stanford University Press.

Carr, Raymond. 1982. *Spain, 1808–1975*. Oxford: Clarendon Press.

Caso González, José Miguel, and Caso Machicado, María Teresa. 2011. *Jovellanos: Biografía/Biography*. Oviedo: Fundación Cristina Masaveu Peterson.

Caso Machicado, María Teresa. 2011. "Gaspar Melchor de Jovellanos: Diez Momentos." *e-Legal History Review* 11: 1–11.

Ceán Bermúdez, Juan Agustín. 1814. *Memorias para la vida del Excmo: Señor D. Gaspar Melchor de Jovellanos y Noticias Analíticas de sus Obras*. Madrid: En la Imprenta que fue de Fuentenebro.

Corredera, E. J. 2015. "Labouring Horizons: Passions and Interests in Jovellanos' *Ley Agraria*." *Dieciocho* 38(2): 267–290.

Delgado Barrado, José Miguel. 2009. *Quimeras de la Ilustración (1701–1808): Estudios en Torno a Proyectos de Hacienda y Comercio Colonial*. Castelló de la Plana: Publicacions de la Universitat Jaume I.

Drayton, Richard. 2000. *Nature's Government: Science, Imperial Britain and the "Improvement" of the World*. New Haven and London: Yale University Press.

Elliott, J. H. 1992. "A Europe of Composite Monarchies," *Past and Present* 137: 48–71.

――― 2006. *Empires of the Atlantic World: Britain and Spain in America 1492–1830*. New Haven and London: Yale University Press, 2006.

Esdaile, Charles. 2000. *Spain in the Liberal Age: From Constitution to Civil War, 1808–1939*. Oxford: Blackwell.

Fernández Sarasola, Ignacio. 2011. *El Pensamiento Político de Jovellanos: Seis Estudios*. Oviedo: In Itire-Servicio de Publicaciones de la Universidad de Oviedo.

Fox-Genovese, Elizabeth. 1976. *The Origins of Physiocracy: Economic Revolution and Social Order in Eighteenth-century France*. Ithaca and London: Cornell University Press.

Herr, Richard. 1958. *The Eighteenth-century Revolution in Spain*. Princeton and Oxford: Princeton University Press.

――― 1989. *Rural Change and Royal Finances in Spain at the End of the Old Regime*. Berkeley: University of California Press.

Hesse, Carla. 2006. "Towards a New Topography of Enlightenment." *European Review of History* 13(3): 499–508.

Israel, Jonathan. 2010. *A Revolution of the Mind: Radical Enlightenment and the Intellectual Origins of Modern Democracy*. Princeton and Oxford: Princeton University Press, 2010.

Kuethe Allan J., and Andrien, Kenneth J. 2014. *The Spanish Atlantic World in the Eighteenth Century: War and the Bourbon Reforms, 1713–1796*. Cambridge and New York: Cambridge University Press, 2014.

Lara Nieto, María del Carmen. 2008. *Ilustración Española y Pensamiento Inglés: Jovellanos*. Granada: Editorial Universidad de Granada, 2008.

Lerner, Ulrich, and Printy, Michael, eds. 2010. *A Companion to the Catholic Enlightenment*. Leiden and Boston: Brill.

Llombart, Vicent. 1992. *Campomanes, Economista y Político de Carlos III*. Madrid: Alianza Editorial.

――― 1995. "Una Nueva Mirada al Informe de Ley Agraria de Jovellanos Doscientos Años Después." *Revista de Historia Económica* 13(3): 553–580.

――― 1999. "El Pensamiento Económico de la Ilustración en España (1730–1812)." In *Economía y Economistas Españoles. Vol. III: La Ilustración*, edited by Enrique Fuentes Quintana. Barcelona: Galaxia Gutemberg-Círculo de Lectores.

――― 2000. "Jovellanos, Economista de la Ilustracion Tardía." In *Gaspar Melchor de Jovellanos, Escritos Económicos*, edited by Vicent Llombart, 138–146. Madrid: Real Academia de Ciencias Morales y Politicas.

――― 2010. "Una Aproximación Histórica y Analítica al Pensamiento Económico de Jovellanos." *Asociación Española de Historia Económica-Documentos de Trabajo*, N°1012.

――― 2011. "El pensamiento económico de Jovellanos y sus intérpretes." In *Jovellanos, el valor de la razón (1811–2011)*, edited by Ignacio Fernández Sarasola, Elena de Lorenzo Álvarez, Joaquín Ocampo Suárez-Valdés, Álvaro Ruiz de la Peña Solar, eds., 59–88. Gijón: Instituto Feijoo de Estudios del Siglo XVIII, 2011.

――― 2012. *Jovellanos y el Otoño de las Luces: Educación, Economía, Política y Felicidad*. Gijón: Ediciones Trea.

Llombart, Vicent, and Ocampo Suárez-Valdés, Joaquín. 2012. "Para leer el *Informe de Ley Agraria de Jovellanos*." *Revista Asturiana de Economía* 45: 119–143.

Lluch, Ernest, and Argemí, Lluis. 1994. "Physiocracy in Spain." *History of Political Economy* 26(4): 613–627.

Lluch, Ernest. 1998. *Las Españas Vencidas del Siglo XVIII: Claroscuros de la Ilustración*. Barcelona: Crítica.

Lucena-Giraldo, Manuel. 2009. "The Limits of Reform in Spanish America." In *Enlightened Reform in Southern Europe and Its Atlantic Colonies, c. 1750–1830*, edited by Gabriel B. Paquette, 307–320. Farnham and Burlington: Ashgate Publishing.

Noel, Charles C. 1989. "Charles III of Spain." In *Enlightened Absolutism: Reform and Reformers in Later Eighteenth-century Europe*, edited H. M. Scott, 119–144. Ann Arbor: University of Michigan Press.

——— 2009. "In the House of Reform: The Bourbon Court of Eighteenth-century Spain." In *Enlightened Reform in Southern Europe and Its Atlantic Colonies, c. 1750–1830*, edited by Gabriel B. Paquette, 145–166. Farnham and Burlington: Ashgate Publishing.

Ocampo Suárez-Valdés, Joaquín. 2014. "Jovellanos: la reconstrucción de un clásico." *Estudios de Economía Aplicada*, 32(1): 83–110.

Paquette, Gabriel B. 2008. *Enlightenment, Governance and Reform in Spain and its Empire, 1759–1808*. Basingstoke: Palgrave Macmillan, 2008.

——— 2009. "Dissolution of the Spanish Atlantic Monarchy." *Historical Journal* 52(1): 175–212.

Pearce, Adrian J. 2014. *The Origins of Bourbon Reform in Spanish South America, 1700–1763*. Basingstoke: Palgrave Macmillan.

Perdices, Luís. 1993. *Pablo de Olavide (1725–1803): El Ilustrado*. Madrid: Editorial Complutense, 1993.

Phillipson, Nicholas. 1985. "Adam Smith as a Civic Moralist." In *Wealth and Virtue, the Shaping of Political Economy in the Scottish Enlightenment*, edited by Istvan Hont and Michael Ignatieff, 179–202. Cambridge and New York: Cambridge University Press.

Polt, John H. R. 1964. "Jovellanos and His English Sources: Economic, Philosophical, and Political Writings." *Transactions of the American Philosophical Society*, New Series 54, 7: 1–74.

——— 1971. *Gaspar Melchor de Jovellanos*. New York: Twayne Publishers.

Prados Arrarte, Jesús. 1945. *Jovellanos: su vida y su obra*. Buenos Aires: Centro de Estudios Asturianos.

Queipo de Llano, Jose María (Conde de Toreno). 1835. *Historia del Levantamiento, Guerra y Revolución de España*. Madrid: Imprenta de Don Tomas Jordan.

Robertson, John. 2005. *The Case for the Enlightenment: Scotland and Naples, 1680–1760*. Cambridge and New York: Cambridge University Press.

——— 2013. "Enlightenment, Public Sphere and Political Economy." In *L'économie politique et la sphère publique dans le débat des Lumières*, edited by Jesús Astigarraga and Javier Usoz, 10–32. Madrid: Casa de Velázquez.

Rothschild, Emma. 2001. *Economic Sentiments: Adam Smith, Condorcet and the Enlightenment*. Cambridge, MA: Harvard University Press.

Sarrailh, Jean. 1957. *La España Ilustrada de la Segunda Mitad del Siglo XVIII*. Mexico City: Fondo de Cultura Económica.

Schumpeter, Joseph. 2006. [1954]. *History of Economic Analysis*. New York and London: Routledge.

Schwartz Girón, Pedro. 1990. "La recepción inicial de 'La Riqueza de las Naciones' en España." *Facultad de Ciencias Económicas y Empresariales-Universidad Complutense de Madrid-Documento de Trabajo*, Nº 9034.

Sempere y Guarinos, Juan. 1990. [1797]. *Historia de los Vínculos y Mayorazgos*. Alicante: Instituto de Cultura Juan Gil-Alber.

Shafer, R. J. 1958. *The Economic Societies of the Spanish World (1763–1821)*. Syracuse: Syracuse University Press.

Smith, Robert Sydney. 1957. "The Wealth of the Nations in Spain and Hispanic America, 1780–1830." *Journal of Political Economy* 65(2): 104–125.

Sobrevilla Perea, Natalia, and Eastman, Scott, eds. 2015. *The Rise of Constitutional Government in the Iberian Atlantic World: The Impact of the Cádiz Constitution of 1812*. Tuscaloosa: University of Alabama Press.

Spell, J. R. 1938. *Rousseau in the Spanish World before 1833: A Study in Franco-Spanish Literary Relations*. Austin: University of Texas Press.

Stapelbroek, Koen, and Marjanen, Jani, eds. 2012. *The Rise of Economic Societies in the Eighteenth Century: Patriotic Reform in Europe and North America*. Basingstoke: Palgrave Macmillan.

Stein, Stanley J. Stein, and Stein, Barbara H. 2000. *Silver, Trade and War: Spain and America in the Making of Early Modern Europe*. Baltimore and London: Johns Hopkins University Press.

———— 2003. *Apogee of Empire: Spain and New Spain in the Age of Charles III, 1759–1789*. Baltimore and London: Johns Hopkins University Press, 2003.

Varela, Javier. 1988. *Jovellanos*. Madrid: Alianza Editorial.

Winch, Donald. 1985. "Adam Smith's 'enduring particular result': a political and cosmopolitan perspective." In *Wealth and Virtue*, edited by Hont and Ignatieff, 253–270.

REPORT ON THE AGRARIAN LAW (1795)

REPORT OF THE ECONOMIC SOCIETY OF THIS COURT [MADRID] TO THE ROYAL AND SUPREME COUNCIL OF CASTILE ON THE AGRARIAN LAW DOSSIER, SUBMITTED BY ITS MEMBER, MR. DON GASPAR MELCHOR DE JOVELLANOS, ON BEHALF OF THE JUNTA COMMISSIONED TO CONSIDER THE SAID DOSSIER, AND IN ACCORDANCE WITH ITS OPINIONS*

"Æque pauperibus prodest, locuplentibus æque:
Æque neglectum pueris, sensibus nocebit."
Horatius epist. 1. Lib. 1.

---

* *Informe de la Sociedad Económica de esta Corte al Real y Supremo Consejo de Castilla en el Expediente de la Ley Agraria extendido por su Individuo de Número, El Sr. D. Gaspar Melchor de Jovellanos a nombre de la Junta Encargada de su Formación y Arreglo a sus Opiniones* (Madrid: En la Imprenta de Sancha, 1795).

INDEX OF THE ARTICLES CONTAINED IN THE REPORT ON THE AGRARIAN LAW[1]

---

1   Numbers are those of the sections, not page numbers.

1. Sire: The Patriotic Society of Madrid, after reviewing the dossier [*expediente*] on the Agrarian Law that Your Highness deigned to send for its examination, and having dedicated a most mature and diligent meditation to the honorable task entrusted to it, has the honor of bringing its views to Your Highness's supreme attention.

2. From its founding, the Society has devoted itself to the study of agriculture, which is the first among its objectives. But considering it only as the art of cultivating the land, a long time would have passed before the Society examined agriculture's political aspect if Your Highness had not summoned its attention to such an inquiry. Engaged then with such a new and difficult examination, it proceeded with great circumspection and care, for discovering the truth in questions in which error can cause a broad and pernicious influence is no trifling matter. This was the reason behind the slowness with which the Society concluded this report, which it submits today for your supreme judgment with the certainty that, in such a grave matter, it is better to be right than to be hasty.

3. This report, Sire, presents the simplicity and unity that distinguish truth from mere opinion because it is based on a single principle derived from the primitive laws of nature and society. This principle is so fertile that it contains in itself all that is relevant to its great object; and, at the same time, it is so certain and constant that, on the one hand, it is confirmed by all of the facts consigned in the dossier on the Agrarian Law while, on the other hand, it eliminates all of the erroneous inferences that have been derived from these very facts.

4. The great many deviations from reason and assiduity that are found in the reports and recommendations gathered in the dossier on the Agrarian Law must be based either on false assumptions, which gave way to false inferences; or on misinterpreted facts. The Society could cite many examples of both these sources of error were it not as uninterested in censuring them as it is in following them; and if it did not believe that they would not remain concealed from Your Highness's penetrating gaze when you deign to examine this report.

5. One of these errors in particular caught the Society's attention because it can be identified as the source of many other errors; and it is the widely held assumption that our agriculture is in a state of great decadence. The very zeal displayed by Your Highness in your paternal concern for our agriculture's prosperity belies this notion; and even though it is a well-known fact that in the present century our agriculture has experienced a most considerable growth, many still lament and ponder its degeneration or conjure up imaginary systems.

6. The Society, Sire, knows better than anyone that Spanish agriculture is still far from enjoying the prosperity that it might indeed attain, and which is the object of Your Highness's request [to the Society]; but it is equally convinced that the notorious claim concerning our agriculture's decadence is mistaken, for if it were true, we would have witnessed a fall from a prosperous and flowering state to one of despondency and neglect. And after having examined the progression of our

agriculture in different historical periods, the Society can assure Your Highness that our agriculture has never been as extensive, or as flourishing, as it is today.

THE HISTORICAL DEVELOPMENT OF OUR AGRICULTURE

7. Its first historical period was that of the Roman Empire, which, uniting all of the peoples of Spain under a common legislation and government, and accelerating the progress of civilization, must have also greatly stimulated their agriculture. Nonetheless, the evils that afflicted it for nearly two hundred years, during which time this land was the theater of countless and bloody wars, are enough to prove that, until the peace of Augustus, agriculture in Spain enjoyed neither stability nor great development.

8. Subsequently, protected by laws and perfected by the progress of enlightenment [*el progreso de las luces*] that the nation received following the introduction of the Roman language and customs, agriculture must have developed rapidly; this, indeed, was one of its most glorious periods. But the immense accumulation of landed property and the establishment of great estates;[2] the use of slaves in its direction and cultivation;[3] and the consequent abandonment that this produced, along with the denigration and contempt[4] it brought upon the profession, could do nothing but leave agriculture oppressed by vice and despondency, which in the understanding of the ancient agronomists[5] and modern economists are inseparable from such conditions. Columella already bitterly lamented these evils, and he came soon after Augustus; and in the time of Vespasian, Pliny the Elder complained that, after ruining agriculture in Italy, large estates were doing the same in empire's subject regions: *Latifundia*, he said, *perdiere Italiam, jam vero & provincias.*[6]

---

2   Modum agri (says Pliny H. N. bk. 18, ch. 6) in primis servandum antique putavere; quipped ita censebant, satius esse minus serere, & melius arare; qua in sentential, & Virgilium fuisse video. Verumque confitentibus, *latifundia perdidere Italiam, jam vero & provincias.* Sex Domini semissem Africae possidebant, cum interfecit eos Nero Princeps: non frauddando magnitudine ac quoque sua: en Popmeyo, qui nunquam agrum mercatus est coterminum. Vide Senec Ep. 89. This evil lasted until the end of the fourth century. (Probus says Amm. Marcell. 27. II) claritudine generis & potential, & opum magnitudine cognitus *Orbi Romano, per quem universum pene patrimonia sparsa possedit.* See also the history of the decline of the empire cited below, ch. 31.

3   The weakness of cultivation directed by slaves can be seen in M. Varro (I.17) in Columella (I.7) and in Smith (*An Inquiry into the Nature and Causes of the Wealth of Nations*), bk. 3, ch. 2.

4   Nec post haec reor, says Columella (in praef.) intemperantia coeli nobis ista, sed nostro potius accidere vitio, qiu rem rusticam pessime cuique Servorum, velut carnifici noxe dedimus quam majorum nostrorum optimus quisque optime tractaverit.

5   Editors' note (hereafter E. N.): In the original Spanish the expression used was *geopónicos antiguos*, which has no equivalent in English. The 1846 Salvá Dictionary equated *geopónica* with *agricultura*. Similarly, it defined *geopónico* as "Lo que pertenece a la agricultura o trata de ella. || m.- El escritor o maestro de agricultura." Vicente Salvá, *Nuevo Diccionario de la Lengua Castellana* (Paris: Vicente Salvá, 1846), 552, 1.

6   Columella (R.R., bk. 1, ch. 3) more praepotentium, says, qui possident fines gentium, quos nec circumire equis quidem valent, sed proculcandos pecudibus, & vastaudos ac populados feris derelinqunt.

9. After that period, the state of agriculture certainly worsened, because Spain, subjected like the other provinces to the tax on wheat [*canon furmentario*], was, due to its greater fertility, even more vexed than the rest with taxes and levies and with continuous exactions of people and wheat that the praetors then used to furnish their armies and supply the capital.[7] These contributions became progressively more exorbitant under Vespasian's successors, who increased property taxes and food taxes [*sisas*], especially after Constantine. The Society could not be more persuaded that, as ill-treated as it was, Spanish agriculture then could compare favorably to what we have today.[8] Thus, the ponderings of Latin writers regarding the fertility of Spain led not to the flourishing of its agriculture, but to its continual extenuation due to the immense succor it was forced to provide to the armies and to Rome, to feed military tyranny and to support the slothful and insolent unrest of that great people.

10. Surely we could not consider the agriculture of the Visigothic period as superior to that of today; for, without taking into account the ravages of the horrendous conquest that preceded it, the plundering of the former estates and the allocation of two-thirds of all the lands to the conquerors were enough to upset and destroy the most flourishing cultivation. Moreover, these barbarians were as weak and lazy in peacetime as they were fierce and diligent in war; and not only did they abandon their crops to the hands of their slaves, but they also regarded livestock farming as superior to cultivation, for cattle were the only true source of wealth in the countries from which they hailed. These conditions necessarily must have a poor and reduced agriculture.

11. And notwithstanding the state of agriculture under the Visigoths, it perished during the Saracen invasion, and many centuries were to pass before what we can properly refer to as the rebirth of our agriculture. It is true that in the climates that were best suited to their canons, the Andalusian Moors set up a Nabataean agriculture, establishing it firmly in our Levantine and Meridional provinces; but the despotism of their government, the harshness of their exacted contributions, and the internecine discord and warfare that agitated them could not have permitted it to flourish, even if the incursions and conquests that we continually carried out on their frontiers had allowed it.[9]

12. When, due to these conquests, we had recovered a great part of the national territory, it remained difficult for us to reestablish agriculture. There was scarcely

---

7   There are abundant testimonies in our histories of the vexations produced by the Praetors and their impunity; these can be seen in Ferreras and Mariana, especially in the last bk. 2, ch. 26.

8   (I) The increasing harshness and excess of the empire's contributions can be seen in the excellent history written by the Englishman Gibbon (*The History of the Decline and Fall of the Roman Empire*, especially ch. 17: *mihi*, vol. 3, pp. 81–92).

9   E. N.: The "*Nabateos*" were those "*naturales de Nabatea*" in reference to the ancient kingdoms nucleated around the Middle Eastern cities of Petra and Palmyra. Real Academia Española, *Diccionario de la Lengua Castellana* (Madrid: Viuda de Ibarra, 1803), 577, 1.

any farming beyond the northern provinces until the reconquest of Toledo. In the lowlands of León and Castile, exposed to constant incursions by the Moors, [the population] was forced to take shelter behind the walls and in the shadow of castles and forts, and to prefer the mobile wealth of livestock, capable of surviving the accidents of warfare, to that of tillage. After the conquest from the Moors provided more stability and territorial extension, continuous agitations perturbed agricultural work on the other side of the Sierra de Guadarrama, distracting laborers from their occupation. The history of that period shows our peasants dragged by their masters to undertake the great conquests that recovered the kingdoms of Jaén, Córdoba, Murcia and Seville until the second half of the thirteenth century; History then shows us some of them turning their weapons against others like themselves in the shameful divisions incited by the system of privileges and favors known as *privanzas* and *tutorías*. What might the state of our agriculture have been under such circumstances until the end of the fifteenth century?

13. It is true that, after the reconquest of Granada, the unification of the many Crowns under a single one and the expansion of the empire with the discovery of a New World, an epoch commenced that could have been most favorable to Spanish agriculture; and it is indisputable that, in fact, agriculture expanded and was greatly improved. Yet far from removing the obstacles that blocked its prosperity, it appears that legislation and politics obstinately persisted to increase them.

14. Distant and continuous foreign wars, extraneous to the interests of the nation, exhausted its population and its wealth little by little; the religious expulsions that considerably aggravated both evils; the privileged protections given to livestock, which ruined the fields; the civil and ecclesiastical entailment or mortmain tenure that sank the greater and most profitable properties into idle hands; and, finally, the diversion of capital from the cultivation of the soil to commerce and industry, a natural effect of the stagnation and scarcity of land, determinedly opposed the progress of agriculture that, had it been favored by the law, would have increased prodigiously the wealth and glory of the nation.

15. Such were the many factors that caused the great torpor into which our agriculture fell at the beginning of this century. Yet from that point until the present day, the obstacles decreased and the stimuli increased. Even though it was harmful in some respects, the war of succession led to the preservation at home of funds and labor that in earlier periods had perished beyond [Spain's borders], and it even attracted some from foreign provinces and set them to work alongside ours. By mid-century, peace had restored agriculture with a tranquillity previously unknown and under the influence of which it began to grow and prosper. With it, industry and the population also prospered, and new resources of public wealth became available. Legislation, not only more vigilant, but also more enlightened, encouraged rural settlements in the Sierra Morena, in Extremadura, in Valencia and in other parts, favoring in all of them the tilling of uncultivated fields; it limited the privileges of livestock farming; it stabilized the price of grain; it encouraged the trade of fruit; and it produced, in short, this healthy ferment, these

demands that to many are the evidence of our agriculture's decadence, and yet in the view of this Society are the best harbinger of its future prosperity and recovery.

THE INFLUENCE OF LEGISLATION ON THE DEVELOPMENT OF AGRICULTURE

16. Such is the brief and simple history of the nation's agriculture, and such are the changes it has undergone throughout its different periods. The Society has been unable to confront the facts that constitute it without making some key observations that will serve to guide the present report. All of them lead us to conclude that agriculture has always adapted itself to the political situation in which the nation found itself, and that the latter's influence upon the former has been of such significance that neither the temperate and benign nature of the climate nor the excellence and fertility of the soil, nor its capacity for the most varied and rich production, nor the country's advantageous position in maritime commerce, nor any other gifts that nature has seen fit to grant our land have been powerful enough to overcome the obstacles that politics has placed in its path.

17. Yet, at the same time, the Society also has recognized that when the political situation was not unfavorable to cultivation, the obstacles that most immediately and predominantly hindered it were those derived from the laws that were meant to regulate it; so that cultivation prospered more or less depending on the agrarian laws that encouraged or discouraged the self-interest of its agents.

18. This last observation, even as it led the Society by the hand to discover, so to speak, the principle upon which it based its final assessment [*juicio*], also inspired it with the confidence that its hopes regarding agriculture could be fulfilled. Because recognizing, on the one hand, that our present political situation supports the flourishing of agriculture, and, on the other, that the fortune of our agriculture depends entirely upon the laws, what hopes are we not to harbor upon witnessing the great dedication that Your Highness devotes to the improvement of this most important branch of our legislation? The zealous ministers who have responded to Your Highness with ideas and plans for reform in the dossier on the Agrarian Law have also understood the influence of legislation on agriculture, but they have erred in the application of the aforementioned principle. All of them demand new laws to improve agriculture, without reflecting upon the fact that the causes for its backwardness are found mostly in the laws themselves. And it follows that such laws should not be multiplied, but, on the contrary, diminished: instead of passing new laws, old laws should be repealed.

LAWS SHOULD LIMIT THEMSELVES TO AGRICULTURE'S PROTECTION

19. However briefly one were to meditate upon this matter, one would come to understand that agriculture naturally tends to perfect itself. Therefore, only those laws that encourage this tendency are favorable to it. Also, such favor does not derive

from providing incentives but from removing those hurdles that impede or slow its progress. In a word, the only object of laws pertaining to agriculture should be to protect the self-interest of its agents, eliminating all of the obstacles that can obstruct or hinder their actions and movements.

20. This principle, which the Society endeavors to elucidate in this report, is found in the eternal laws of nature, and most particularly in the first that man's omnipotent and merciful Creator dictated for him, when, so to speak, He placed him on the Earth and made him its master, condemning him to live off the fruit of his labor. Thus, upon granting man the right to rule over nature, the Creator imposed upon him the duty of cultivating it, and inspired him with the love of life and activity that were necessary to secure his subsistence through work. To this sacred interest man owes his conservation and the earth its cultivation [*cultura*].[10] He alone has weeded and plowed the fields, cleared the forests, dried the lakes, diverted the rivers, mitigated the climates, domesticated the beasts, selected and perfected the seeds and secured in their cultivation and reproduction the portentous multiplication of the human species.

21. The same principle is found in the primitive social laws [*leyes primitivas del derecho social*], because when such multiplication forced men to join together in societies and to divide the dominion of the earth among them, it necessarily legitimated and perfected their interests, determining a sphere for every individual, so that he could devote all of his energy to it. Hence, individual interest was more vigorous the more it was employed on better-known activities, which were best suited to the strength and capabilities of each person, and most conducive to individual happiness.

22. Men, taught by this very interest to use and increase the products of nature, multiplied more and more; hence, men distinguished a different sort of property, separate from that over land: the property arising from labor. The earth, endowed as it was by the Creator with marvelous fecundity, only granted its bounties when these were solicited by cultivation, and as it rewarded the laborious with abundant and plentiful fruit, it gave the slothful only thistles and thorns. More toil always yields greater produce: it was therefore necessary to apportion labor according to the character of the crops: when assistance was necessary to carry them to fruition, those who helped were made participants of the yield; and from then on, the products of the earth were not the sole property of the owner of the land, but divisible between him and his assistants, whether laborers or tenant farmers.

23. Labor, precisely because it was a more precarious and uncertain property [than land], was exercised more vigilantly and ingeniously. Observing first the necessities, and then the desires of men, [labor] invented with the arts the means to satisfy both; it presented new objects each day for their comfort and taste, making them

---

10   E. N.: "Cultura. S.f. Las labores y beneficios que se dan a la tierra para que fructifique." Real Academia Española, *Diccionario de la lengua castellana* (Madrid: Viuda de Ibarra, 1791), 281, 3.

accustomed to these; and it created new necessities; it enslaved these necessities to its desires and, from then on, the sphere of the property of labor became more varied, more comprehensive and more independent.

THIS PROTECTION SHOULD BE LIMITED TO THE REMOVAL OF THE OBSTACLES THAT THWART THE [SELF-]INTEREST OF AGRICULTURE'S AGENTS

24. These reflections, derived from the simple observation of human nature and of its progress in the social state, reveal that the role of laws with regard to the ownership of land and labor should not be to excite or to direct, but to protect their agents' interest, which is naturally active and well suited to its object. They have also revealed that such protection cannot consist in anything but the removal of the obstacles that thwart the action and movement of this interest, for the latter's activity is intertwined with man's very nature and its direction is therefore dictated by man's needs. And, finally, it is evident that without the intervention of laws, the art of cultivating the land can reach, and, indeed, among some peoples it has reached, the highest levels of perfection, so that wherever laws protect the ownership of land and labor, such perfection certainly will be obtained, along with all the goods that depend upon it.

25. However, two very plausible reasons have steered lawmakers away from this simple principle: first, their mistrust of individuals' activity and intelligence; and, second, their fear of such activity. Seeing men so often driven away from their true interest and carried away by passions [*arrastrados por las pasiones*] in the pursuit of a good that deserves this name in appearance rather than in substance, it is easy to believe that they would be better governed by laws rather than by their own personal desire. But this supposes that nobody can dictate better laws than those who, freed from the illusion of personal interests, act only for the general public interest. With such a perspective, lawmakers did not limit themselves to protecting land and labor ownership; instead, they stimulated and directed agents' interests through laws and regulations. They were not guided by individual utility, but by the common good, and, since then, the law has often been at odds with the interests of individuals, and the actions of this interest have been less animated, less diligent and less ingenious, the more restricted its agents have been in their elections and in the execution of the means to fulfill it.

26. But in proceeding this way, lawmakers did not recognize, first, that the more men are engaged in promoting their interests the more they listen to the dictates of reason than to the dictates of passion; second, that the object of their desire is always analogous to the object of the law; third, that when a man acts against this object, he acts against his true and solid interest; and, fourth, that even when a man steers away from it, the same passions driving him are the same ones that cause him to stop by showing him, from the consequences of his misdirected effort, the punishment for his misguided illusion. And this punishment is swifter, more effective and more infallible than that which can be imposed by the law.

27. Also hidden from view was how the continuous conflicts of interests that animate men establish a natural equilibrium that can never be emulated by the law. It is not only just and honest men who respect their neighbors' interests, but unjust and greedy men, too. They certainly do not respect them out of a sense of justice; rather, they do so out of a sense of convenience and utility. The fear that one's own interests may be injured is what safeguards the interests of others. It is in this sense that it can be said that in any society [*orden social*] the individual's particular interest is better protected by common wisdom [*opinión*] than by the law.

28. The Society does not conclude from this that the excesses of private interest should not be limited by law. Indeed, it acknowledges that this will always be legislation's most salutary and sacrosanct duty, one of its primary objectives. It merely concludes that, as long as private interest remains within the confines defined by justice, the law should protect its freedom of action and confront it only when it begins to go beyond those confines. In sum, Sire, the great and general principle of the Society may be reduced to this: that the protection afforded by the law to agriculture should be limited to the removal of the obstacles that thwart the free action of its agents' interests within the sphere determined by justice.

[ON THE] CONVERGENCE OF THE OBJECT OF THE LAWS WITH THAT OF SELF-INTEREST

29. This principle, applicable to all economic legislation, is even more perspicuous in its relation to agrarian laws. Do these perchance have any other purpose than that of increasing public wealth to the highest level possible by means of cultivation? Well, the same goes for agriculture's agents, taken collectively, for while each wants to increase his individual fortune as much as possible through cultivation, it is clear that this object is identical to that of the agrarian laws, so that both have the same end and the same tendency.

30. Agrarian laws can only achieve this goal by securing three ends: the growth, perfection and utility of cultivation; and agriculture's agents are naturally driven toward these same ends by their self-interest. For which one among them, knowing his capital, his strength and his current situation, will not plant as much as he can, or as well as he can? And who would not prefer to have the most valuable as opposed to the least valuable produce? Thus, to secure the object at which it aims, agrarian legislation must favor the freedom of agriculture's agents to pursue their interests, for they naturally share the same object.

31. The Society, Sire, has gone to great lengths to firmly establish this principle, because though it is obvious and simple, it is not among those that underlay the dossier of the Agrarian Law as well as most of the texts that so far have dealt with the same issues. Convinced that many of its opinions may seem new, the Society has wanted to present the solid foundation from whence this indisputable principle is derived, hoping that Your Highness will pardon the length of the explanation devoted to demonstrating this important truth.

[ON THE NEED TO] INVESTIGATE THE OBSTACLES THAT OPPOSE SAID INTEREST

32. If laws designed to favor agriculture are limited to protecting its agents' self-inter-
     est, and if the only way to protect this interest is by removing the obstacles that
     impede their natural tendencies and movements, nothing can be more important
     than inquiring what those obstacles might be, and understanding them well.

33. The Society believes that these obstacles are of three kinds, namely political,
     moral and physical, because they can only come from legislation, opinions or
     nature. These three points will guide the division of the present report, in which
     the Society will answer the following questions: what obstacles does our cur-
     rent legislation place in the path of agriculture's progress? Which [obstacles]
     are placed by our present opinions? And, finally, which [obstacles] derive from
     the nature of our soil? In describing and demonstrating what these different
     obstacles are, the Society will also suggest the simplest and safest means of
     removing them. Let us delve into the matter at hand and examine the political
     obstacles first.

FIRST KIND

POLITICAL OBSTACLES, OR THOSE DERIVED FROM LEGISLATION

34. When the Society studied Castilian agrarian legislation, it could not help but be
     surprised at the great number of laws that crowd our codes with such a simple
     object. Would [the Society] dare to declare before Your Highness that the greater
     part of these laws have been, and still are, completely contrary, or very harmful, or,
     at the very least, of no use, to their intended goal? Well, why pass over a truth that
     Your Highness has already acknowledged when, with your characteristic zeal and
     wisdom, you decided to overhaul this precious part of our legislation?

35. Castile is certainly not alone in suffering from this ill: the agrarian codes of all
     nations are plagued with laws, ordinances and rules that, intending to improve agri-
     culture, are quite contrary to it. At least ours have the advantage of having been
     dictated by necessity, demanded by the people [*pedidas por los pueblos*] and adapted to
     the situation and circumstances that made them desirable at the time.[11] But at the
     time, lawmakers ignored that the greater evils usually came from other laws; that
     what was needed was to repeal, and not to issue, more laws; and that the new laws
     produced new obstacles and these, in turn, new evils. But what people on this earth,

---

11 E. N.: *Pueblos*, in early-modern Hispanic parlance, was both related to the more abstract notions
    of "people" that contemporaries now associate with the "nation," and, at the same time, it
    stood for the concrete, specific space of a village or town. In the mind of an eighteenth-century
    political writer like Jovellanos, it is not unlikely that these were two faces of the same coin,
    inasmuch the people who lived in a specific locale were conceived as possessing more abstract
    qualities—such as political power—while being simultaneously identifiable as the inhabitants
    of that specific place.

however learned it may be, has not fallen prey to this error, pushed by the more than pardonable concern that is respect for antiquity?

36. On the other hand, social economy [*economía social*], a science of this century, or perhaps the science of our times, has never informed the drafting of agrarian laws. Jurisprudence alone did this, and jurisprudence, unfortunately, has been reduced among us, as among the other peoples of Europe, to a fistful of maxims of private justice taken from Roman law and adapted to each and every nation. Unfortunately, the most precious part of Roman law, public law, was the most commonly ignored. Being less suited to the constitution of modern empires, it was only natural that, indeed, it would be disregarded and overlooked.

37. Therein lies the origin of all the political errors that our current agrarian laws have but sanctified, Sire. The Society, unable to review them individually, will reduce them to certain major sections, so as to concentrate on the principle that shall guide its maxims, and to avoid being bogged down by a useless and tiresome endeavor.

1st. Baldíos

38. If individual interest is the first instrument to secure agriculture's prosperity, then without a doubt, no laws would be more contrary to the principles of the Society than those that, instead of increasing, have diminished this interest, by reducing the number of individual properties and the number of proprietors. Such laws are those that by a kind of political apathy have left a precious portion of Spain's arable lands without landlords or tenants, depriving them of the labor of such individuals and thus defrauding the state of all the production that individual interest would have obtained—such are the *baldíos*.

39. The Society refers to this neglect as political apathy because the disposition that has led to the *baldíos*' survival does not deserve a more decorous name. Their origins are found in none other than the time of the Visigoths, who occupied and distributed two-thirds of the conquered lands among them and left one-third for the conquered; and eventually abandoned and left ownerless all of those lands that the population, so diminished after the war, could not settle. These lands were designated as vacant fields, and are what constitute today most of our *baldíos*.

40. The war that had at first reduced the population would later thwart its natural growth with another, stronger obstacle: the conquerors' aversion to cultivation and all such industrious activities. These barbarians knew nothing beyond fighting and sleeping, and they were incapable of embracing the toil and diligence that agriculture demanded, so they preferred animal husbandry to cultivation, and pastures to crops. It followed that the vacant fields were respected as reserves for common pastures and to increase the size of the herds, as the various testimonies that abound in our *Fuero Juzgo* regarding this rustic policy demonstrate.

41. This legislation was restored by the kings of Asturias starting with Alfonso "the Chaste," adopted by the Crown of León starting with Alfonso V, and later transferred

to Castile and obeyed until the reign of Ferdinand III [*San Fernando*]. Thus a system spread throughout the realm more suitable to the character of the Goths and to the Middle Ages, when the enemy was in the very heart of the empire [*en el corazón del imperio*] and in plain sight, and it was necessary to invest in animal husbandry, an activity that was less vulnerable to the clash of arms to secure both personal livelihoods and to increase public wealth. Even after the conquest of Toledo, frontier lands, which extended from Extremadura to La Mancha and New Castile, were marked by more livestock than crops, and their flocks pastured in open, public fields, or commons, rather than in privately owned meadows or plots, which could only be cared for alongside crops.

42. Once the Moors were expelled from our continent [*nuestro continente*], *baldíos* should have been broken down into private holdings. Politics and piety both demanded an increase in the means of support that population growth made increasingly necessary, but each took a different route. Politics, finding the fatal system of livestock legislation so deeply entrenched, continued to favor it, excessively reserving the use of *baldíos* to farming. And piety, looking upon them as the patrimony of the poor, strove to maintain them: neither one nor the other realized that the communal character of *baldíos* allowed the rich to use and enjoy them more than the poor. Therefore, it would be a better politics, and more pious, to transform them into the basis of independent livelihoods, rescuing a great number of poor families from misery, instead of allowing their free and common use to spur the greed of the wealthy cattle magnates and remain useless for the needy.

43. Those who hope to encourage the increase of livestock by means of *baldíos* fool themselves. As enclosed private farms, their soils fertilized, their potential fully exploited, would they not enjoy a greater quantity of pasture land and support considerably larger herds or flocks?

44. Some argue that, thus transformed, all would turn to cultivation and the herds would diminish considerably. This proposition is untrue because it is easily demonstrated that *baldíos* that are converted into private properties can readily support both crops and the same, if not a greater, number of livestock than they do today. But let us suppose for an instant that the proposition were true. Could we deny that nations where men and produce abound are wealthier than those that are rich in livestock?

45. Perhaps there is fear that the price of meat, a major food staple, would rise extraordinarily, but let us reflect further upon this: if the price of meat were to rise, interest would naturally be aroused, and then, would [interest] not prefer to dedicate itself to livestock instead of cultivation, without the need for any external stimulus? Equilibrium, so desirable in this matter, is reached more fully without laws than with them.

46. These reflections should be sufficient to demonstrate to Your Highness the need to undertake the distribution of all of the kingdom's *baldíos*. With such vast and rich lands converted into private properties, where individual interest could devote itself

to populating them, cultivating them, filling them with livestock and producing in them as much as labor and pasture could produce, would this measure not open up a source of great wealth?

47. It is worthy of Your Highness's attention to observe that the countries that are richest in *baldíos* are the poorest in population, and that this lack of people, and therefore, of laborers, makes operations carried out in their immense and badly cultivated fields wasteful and chaotic. The transformation of *baldíos* into private property would multiply the population with their means of subsistence, procuring the quickest, most just and easiest remedy to this evil.

48. With regard to the transfer of the *baldíos*, the Society abstains from proposing plans or systems like those that abound in the Agrarian Law dossier. Let *baldíos* become individual properties and the state will reap great benefits. If they are sold for money or credit, distributed through emphyteutic leases, or converted into large or small holdings, the utility of the operation may be larger or smaller, quicker or slower, but it will be infallible, because the interest of *baldío* purchasers eventually will lead to the establishment of the most suitable divisions and activities, according to their strength and their financial capacity, and the climate and the soil. And, certainly, if legislation were to let them operate freely, we need not fear that they would choose the least profitable options.

49. On the other hand, a general and uniform method might prove inconvenient due to the local differences among the provinces. A free distribution of small allotments would seem to favor the population most immediately, but it would place the lands in the hands of poor persons incapable of carrying out the necessary improvements or setting up the most profitable operations. Sales, in contrast, place the lands in the hands of the rich, favoring the accumulation of property, and lead to the establishment of immense estates in areas of low population, so cultivation is wasteful and unproductive. Enfeoffments undertaken by the public and for the public have the inconvenience of being difficult to set up and administer. Moreover, they are exposed to fraud and collusion, and are not conducive to cultivation's progress insofar as, by separating the dominion over land from the dominion over the surface, interest in improving property is discouraged. It is therefore necessary to adapt to the different situations of each province, and use the most suitable means in each of them.

50. In Andalusia, for instance, where depopulation is a significant concern, it would be best to begin by allowing poor and industrious households to acquire small plots that can provide for their families through a *censo reservativo*. In this way, they can use the land by paying a moderate interest for it [*rédito*]. Eventually, they would pay the full price of the property in installments in order to acquire absolute ownership over it. The interest paid on the use of the land would be higher for those who would not occupy the plots but instead commute from surrounding villages, and lower for those willing up to reside on the plots. It will be necessary to ensure, however, that the highest interest never exceeds 2 percent of capital, that the lowest never goes

below 1 percent and that they are equitably estimated, because high interest could prove too onerous for a new farm while with very low interest there would be no inducement to pay off the debt on the land in its entirety. This scheme would simultaneously encourage population growth and agriculture in a kingdom [Andalusia] whose fertility promises the greatest progress.

51. The remaining lands (because the *baldíos* in Andalusia are immense, and there will be enough for all of this) could be sold as lots of different sizes, from the smallest to the largest. After a first round of sales for ready money or payable in fixed installments along with suitable securities, the rest could be leased in perpetuity. In this way, these precious *baldíos* would be divided and occupied, for it is unlikely that with the daily accumulation of wealth produced by commerce in that realm, particularly in Málaga, Cádiz, Seville and other coastal towns, there would be a shortage of buyers.

52. In the Two Castiles, which are neither as depopulated nor as rich in *baldíos* as Andalusia, the process could start with the sale of small portions of land for cash or credit, with contracts safeguarded by suitable securities that stipulate annual payments on the purchase price, toward which end the latter could be divided into ten or twelve installments. Since these provinces lack commerce and industry, and therefore capital, outright sales of land would be unlikely. And if in the end there were still not a sufficient number of buyers, it would be convenient to distribute the remaining land in plots that are suitable for the subsistence of poor families in perpetual leases, as described above; the same goes for Extremadura and La Mancha.

53. But in the Northern provinces, which run from the foot of the Pyrenees to Portugal, where, on the one hand, there is a vast population but little money, and, on the other, *baldíos* are few and not very fertile, it would be most useful to enfeoff [*foros otorgados*] laborers after the country's custom, without payment of entry fees and with moderate rents [*pensiones*] paid to the land's owners in kind. Of its large populace, one can expect not only that the labor needed to put these lands under cultivation will be readily available, but also that the lands will soon be peopled and improved; because application and work would satisfactorily compensate for the lack of capital that characterizes those parts.

54. In sum, Sire, the Society believes that no general rule would be suitable for determining the distribution of the *baldíos*. Instead, this measure should be preceded by a careful examination, to accommodate it not only to each province, but also to each district. Moreover, the provincial juntas [*juntas provinciales*] and town councils [*ayuntamientos*] should be in charge of this measure's execution, under Your Highness's direction, in order to ensure impartiality and success. Finally, it is our belief that what is urgent is to order the distribution of the *baldíos*, and the rest will follow, so that if Your Highness deigned to decree this measure, the main step toward a great good will have been undertaken.

2nd. Municipal lands [Tierras concejiles]

55. Perhaps it would be advisable to extend the same measure to the *tierras concejiles* [municipal lands], placing them in the sphere of individual interest and putting them under useful cultivation. Though on the one hand, this property is as sacred and worthy of protection as that of individuals, and perhaps more so, because its rent is destined to the conservation of the civic state [*estado cívico*] and support of the municipal institutions [*establecimientos municipales*] in their respective jurisdictions; on the other hand, it is almost inconceivable that until now we have not tried to unite the interests of the towns themselves with the interests of the individuals who inhabit them, and turn these lands into a fruitful source of personal livelihoods and public wealth. Divided and distributed in emphyteusis or perpetual leases, they would remain the towns' patrimony and would continue to meet and indeed surpass all of the needs of municipal governance. Moreover, they could also house a great number of families, who, exercising upon them their self-interest, would make them quite productive, generating great benefits for themselves as well as their communities.

56. Your Highness demonstrated awareness of this truth when, in your decrees of 1768 and 1770, you ordered the distribution of *tierras concejiles* to the towns' poorest farmers and peasants.[12] But permit the Society to point out that these decrees would have been even more perfect if the distribution were to have been carried out everywhere, and been applied to all municipal properties; if this were done by emphyteusis or by *censos reservativos*, and not by temporary (albeit indefinite) tenancies; and if, moreover, residents were provided with the redemption of their annuities and allowed the acquisition of the absolute property of their allotments [*suertes*]. Without these conditions, the effect of such a salutary decree will remain partial and uncertain; because only a true and certain property can inspire that active interest without which lands are never entirely improved; that interest which, in embodying all of the landlord's wishes, is the first and strongest stimulus defeating his sloth and driving him to diligent and incessant work.

57. The Society would not find it inappropriate either if these lands were to be freely and permanently sold to individuals. In fact, it finds quite odd a maxim that so religiously maintains municipal properties while, at the same time, deprives communities of the most useful initiatives. The product of these sales could be destined to draining a lake, or making a river navigable, or building a port, a canal, a road or a bridge, favoring the town's cultivation and industry, facilitating the abundance of its markets and the extraction of its produce and manufactures; in sum, permanently

---

12 E. N.: The continuum of power was expressed with phrases such as this one, in which "Your Highness," and the possessive pronoun "your," while historically referred to the late King Charles III, were used in a writing addressed to the reigning King Charles IV.

securing an entire district's happiness. Would it really matter that the community sacrificed its holdings to obtain such benefits? It is true that without these properties each household would have to pay thereafter a contribution [*repartimiento*] for the maintenance of the municipal institutions but, with their wealth so multiplied, would they not prefer to have four and pay two, rather than pay nothing and have nothing?

58. Henceforth, though the Society finds more justice and greater advantages in the distribution of these lands, it would not object to the sale and alienation of some portions of them in places where their abundance and the eagerness of buyers were to make this option desirable. Proceeds from sales destined to the public coffers could be more profitable for communities, and the administration of their revenues would be easier and more secure. Moreover, were such funds used for necessary or extremely useful works, they would give the towns greater, more certain and longer-lasting advantages than those produced by the ordinary investment of the municipal rents [*rentas concejiles*] obtained today.

59. The custom of endowing town councils with common pasturelands to raise oxen and horses may elicit qualms regarding this measure. The need for such resources is dependent upon the present disorder of our agrarian policies [*policía rural*]. Your Highness should have no doubt that, were this branch of law perfected, this dependence would entirely disappear; for then, not only would these pasturelands be unnecessary but they would be damaging as well. Work animals always receive the most dedicated attention from farmers, and if there are no common pasturelands, all private holdings will have within their allotments small meadows where the climate permits it, or artificial grasslands where it does not, for the care of the herds. Is this not what one finds in the more populated and better-cultivated provinces, where there is no such thing as common pastureland?

60. The conservation of good and noble horse breeds for the army is very commendable, to say the least, but can there be any doubt that self-interest would not perfect the breeding of such horses better than municipal institutions and laws? Can we doubt that the very scarcity of good horses, which is at times perhaps even a consequence of the distribution of communal pasturelands for horses, would itself constitute the greatest stimulus for breeders, because of the rise in prices that would accompany it? Why are the best Andalusian horses bred in private pastures, and with the utmost care, if not because they fetch high prices? Is there indeed any other stimulus behind the increase in mule breeding than the utility of this activity? The latter are raised with the utmost care in the fresh pastures of Asturias and Galicia. From there, foals are taken and sold in the markets and fairs of León, from where they go to La Mancha to be fattened on its abundant [*pingües*] dried grasses before they finally are brought to the court's stables. Could anyone who reflected upon this matter harbor any doubts concerning its truth? It is therefore necessary to bolster this interest by multiplying the number of individual properties, and thus give greater inducements to agriculture.

3rd. *The openness of lands* [La apertura de las heredades]

61. But when Your Highness, seeking to favor, increase and encourage cultivation, has transformed the common lands into private properties, will you be able to tolerate the shameful right, which at certain times and occasions, turns private property into *baldíos?* A barbaric custom, born in barbaric times and worthy only of them, has introduced the barbarous and shameful prohibition of land enclosures, impinging upon private property's very essence and putting in place one of the most powerful obstacles that prevents cultivation's progress.

62. The Society, Sire, judges this custom severely because it is not only absurd and ruinous, but also unfair and irrational. Despite having studied and explored the codes and orders of our legislation, seeking to understand its legitimate origin, the Society has been unable to identify a single general law that expressly authorizes it. On the contrary, it found that such a prohibition repugnantly contradicts all of the principles of Castilian legislation, and it thinks that only the ignorance of these principles combined with the interest of the wealthy proprietors of flocks has allowed it to be introduced in the tribunals and elevated into the concept of an *unwritten right* [*derecho no escrito*], against all reason and laws.[13]

63. Under the Romans, it was not customary in Spain to break down the walls that enclosed private lands so that their produce could be enjoyed by all. Civil laws fully protected landed property, giving owners the absolute right to defend themselves from any usurpation, and severely punishing violators. Nowhere in the texts of legal scholars, in the texts of Latin agronomists, in all the works of Columella, a Spanish writer who knew the Spanish agrarian policy of that period very well and was the best of all these scholars, is there the smallest trace of such abuse. On the contrary, nothing was as recommended as highly among his precepts as the need to enclose and defend one's lands at all times. Indeed, in his exposition on the different means of making fences and hedges, Marcus Varro praises those walls with which lands were enclosed in Spain.

64. There was no such prohibition among the Visigoths either, for even though the common enjoyment of the spontaneous fruit of the lands was, according to some authors, customary among northern peoples, it is also true that in this, as in many other regards, the Visigoths in Spain adopted the Roman law. The evidence supporting this interpretation is in the laws of the third title, eighth book of the *Fuero Juzgo*, specifically in law number 7, which fines the person who broke into an enclosure where there were no crops to be harvested, and establishes a higher fine for those who trespass where there was produce ripe for harvest as well as compensation for the damage caused to the owner. This is a clear argument in favor of the protection of property and the exclusive nature of its enjoyment.[14]

---

13 Italics in the original.

14 E. N.: For clarity's sake, the original sentence in which Jovellanos mentions the specific fines is included here: "y señaladamente en la 7ª., que castiga con el cuatro tanto al que quebrantase el cercado ajeno si en la heredad no hubiere fruto pendiente, y si le hubiere con la pena de un

65. The true origin of the custom [of tearing down enclosures and opening lands] must be in those times in which our agriculture was, so to speak, uncertain and precarious; because a ferocious and nearby enemy harassed it constantly; when husbandmen, forced to seek shelter under the protection of fortresses, were contented with planting and harvesting what they could; when due to lack of security, the fields were neither enclosed nor improved nor settled in, because they were constantly exposed to devastation. In a word: [the custom arose] when there was nothing to protect or keep in empty lands, and it was in everybody's interest to allow herds and flocks to roam in them. This situation prevailed in all of the flat country of León and Old Castile until the conquest of Toledo; in all New Castile, La Mancha and Andalusia down to Seville; and also in the frontiers of Granada, and even Navarre, Portugal and Aragon, until the union of these Crowns. The constant war in those ferocious times, notwithstanding whether they were Moors or Christians, reduced agriculture to burning down crops and farmhouses, felling vineyards, olive groves and orchards, and capturing men and herds in the frontier territories.

66. However, this custom, or this abandonment, to use a more accurate term, was the effect of temporary and fortuitous circumstances, and therefore it should not deprive proprietors of the right to enclose their fields. It was merely a discretionary act, unsuitable for serving as the basis of [juridical] custom. It lacked, moreover, all of the circumstances that could have legitimated it as such. It was not general, for it was never known in the mountainous or irrigated countryside. It was not rational, for it stood in conflict with all of the essential rights of property. Above all, it was contrary to the law, for neither the *Fuero* of León, the *Fuero Viejo* of Castile, the Alphonsine legislation or the general orders that were contemporary with its origin and development, and which were full of rustic norms, contain a single piece of legislation that forbids enclosures. Therefore, enclosures, which upheld the rights of domain over a property, were in keeping with the law. How, then, amid the silence of all these laws, could such a pernicious abuse prevail?

67. The Society, after much meditation and investigation into this matter, has found two laws that might have provided a pretext for jurists [*pragmáticos*] to attribute a legal basis to it, and the wish to banish such a harmful error from agriculture obliges the Society, guided by the torch of history, to expose them.[15]

68. The first of these laws was proclaimed in Cordoba by the Catholic Monarchs after the conquest of Granada, that is, on 3 November 1490. The new settlers wanted to enclose the farms and estates that they had obtained with the *repartimiento*, or distribution of the conquered lands. But the great number of livestock found in that country, where the herds of both frontiers were kept, meant that the threat of

---

tremis (que era la tercera parte de un sueldo) por cada estaca que quebrantase, y además en el resarcimiento del daño."

15 E. N.: "Pragmático. adj. for. Que se aplica al autor jurista, que interpreta, o glosa las leyes, para remediar algún exceso, abuso, o daño, que se experimenta en la república." Real Academia Española, *Diccionario*, 1803, 677, 1.

a sudden lack of pastures was felt by the local people. Enclosures were at that time unknown in those days in those frontier territories, for the reasons we have already detailed above; livestock farmers protested, and the contemporary notions, more favorable to the freedom of herds or flocks than to that of cultivation, dictated a law that prohibited enclosures; a law fatal for agricultural property, insofar as the fertility and abundance of water sources in that country invited a continuous reproduction of excellent crops. Such is the spirit of the thirteenth law, seventh title, seventh book of the *Recopilación*.[16]

69. But no one should think that this was a general law: it was a municipal ordinance, confined to the territory of Granada, and, indeed, only to the farms and estates distributed after its conquest. It was, so to speak, a condition attached to the legislation that regulated the lands distributed after the conquest, and in that sense it did not repel national property, but simply limited that which was by royal grace distributed in [Granada] at that time. It is therefore clear that this law could not establish a general jurisprudence for the rest of the territories in the realm, nor did it alter the natural right that every landlord has to enclose his lands.

70. The same goes for the next law, the fourteenth of the same book and title. Although identical ideas and principles that dictated the law in Córdoba presided over the revocation of the famous Ávila ordinance, all in all, their spirit was quite different. Both were contemporary, for the laws [*pragmática sanción*][17] contained in law fourteenth were proclaimed by the same Catholic Monarchs in the plains of Granada on 5 July 1491, five months after renewing the Córdoba law in Seville, but with a different object, as we explain below.[18]

---

16 E. N.: "*Lei XIII. Para que no se puedan dehesar los heredamientos i Cortijos del Reino de Granada. D. Fernando, i D. Isabel en Córdoba año 490. à 3 de Noviembre, i en Sevilla año 91.à 26. de Enero.* Mandamos que ninguna, ni ningunas personas à quien nos avemos hecho, ò hiciéremos merced de cualesquier cortijos, i heredamientos i tierras en los términos de las Ciudades, i Villas, i Lugares del Reino de Granada, que sin nuestra licencia, i especial mandado no los puedan dehesar, ni dehesen, ni defender, ni defiendan la yerba, i otros frutos, que naturalmente la tierra lleva, ni lo puedan guardar, ni guarden, salvo que libremente, para que todos los vecinos de las dichas Ciudades, i Villas, i Lugares, i sus términos lo puedan comer con sus ganados, i bestias, i bueyes de labor, no estando plantado, o empanado; sò pena que qualquier, que lo dehesare, ò defendiere, ò en los tales términos prendare, pierda cualquier derecho, que à los dichos términos tenga, i queden por términos comunes de las dichas Ciudades, i Villas, i Lugares." *Tomo Quinto de Recopilación que Contiene los Libros Séptimo, i Octavo* (Madrid: Imprenta Real de la Gazeta, 1776), 110–111.

17 E. N.: "Pragmática. s.f. La ley, ó estatuto, que se promulga, ó publica para remediar algún exceso, abuso, ó daño, que se experimenta en la república." Real Academia Española, *Diccionario de la Lengua Castellana* (Madrid: Joachin Ibarra, 1783), 756, 1.

18 E. N.: "*Lei XIV. Que pone revocación de la Ordenanza de Ávila, en que permitia dehesar las heredades, i las hacían con términos redondos, i que queden libres para las poder pacer, como se hacia antes de la dicha ordenanza. Los mismos en la Vega de Granada año 1491. à 5 de Julio, Pragmática.* Por quanto la Ciudad de Avila, Justicia, i Regidores della hicieron una Ordenanza, el tenor de la qual es este, que se sigue [...] la qual dicha Ordenanza parece ser hecha en grande agravio, i per-juicio de los vecinos, i moradores de la dicha Ciudad, i su tierra, i contra derecho; porende, como Ordenanza en perjuicio de la Repùblica, por la presente la revocamos, i anulamos, i

71. The aim behind the revoking of the Ávila ordinance was to forbid circular grounds, not enclosures. The latter were inherent to the right of property, while the former were conspicuously external to it: they were unequivocal usurpations. The latter favored agriculture, while the former were positively contrary to it. Therefore, the decree in question did not establish a new right nor did it impinge on the right to property in any way. Instead, it confirmed an old right, ending the abusive ways that landlords were using their freedom.

72. In this sense, revoking the Ávila ordinance could not have been more just. This ordinance, which authorized circular enclosures, favored the accumulation of property and intensification of labor, and hampered the division of property and cultivation. It therefore benefited large farmers and landowners, and harmed small ones. Moreover, it established a town monopoly of territory more advantageous to the rich than to the poor, and that was particularly pernicious to newcomers, whose animals were excluded from the watering places and drinking troughs, and even from passage, elements provided by providence without distinction. In short, it conspired against the integrity of the public domain, encompassing parts of it in private grounds, abrogating the rights of *monte y suerte*, so appreciated in our ancient legislation, and encouraging the establishment of large domains, manorial descents, privileged jurisdictions and noble entails, which have caused so much harm to the progress of our agriculture and to the liberty of its agents. Such was the famous Ávila ordinance, and such the fair pragmatic that revoked it. But the latter was reduced to the prohibition of circular grounds and this in the territory of Ávila alone, so how could it have been the basis for a general prohibition of enclosures?

73. And yet our jurists have made this opinion prevail, and the courts have adopted it. The Society cannot ignore the influence that the Honorable Council of the *Mesta* has had on one and the other. This body, always vigilant in its efforts to claim privileges, and always powerful enough to obtain and extend them, was the one that most firmly resisted land enclosures. Not content with the right of possession that permanently forbade cultivation in lands once under pasturage; not satisfied with the defense and extension of its immense drovers' roads [*cañadas*]; not satisfied with its right of continuous access to all public pastures; nor with the right of itinerant local entitlement [*vecindad mañera*] that is contrary to the spirit of the old laws, the *Mesta* also wanted the right to invade private properties.[19] The shepherds, crossing

---

mandamos que ningún Cavallero, ni Escudero, ni otra persona vecino de la dicha Ciudad, i su tierra, no use de ella: i damos licencia, i facultad a los vecinos de la dicha Ciudad, i su tierra, i Pueblos de ella, que puedan pacer, i rozar en los dichos términos, que assi por virtud de la dicha Ordenanza están dehesados, como lo hacían, quando los dichos heredamientos eran de diversos dueños, i antes que la dicha Ordenanza fuesse hecha, i por ello no sean prendados, sò pena que los que lo contrario hicieren, sean ávidos por forzadores, i como contra tales se proceda contra ellos." *Tomo Quinto de las Leyes de Recopilación que contiene los Libros Séptimo i Octavo*, 111–115.

19 E. N.: *Vecindad mañera* is based upon that of *vecindad*, which might be translated as "local citizenship." To be a *vecino mañero* was to be itinerant and yet to have the rights attached to *vecindad*, which included allowing the resident *vecinos'* herds to pasture in communal lands

from León to Extremadura with their immense flocks in the season in which most of the arable lands traversed were covered in stubble, and returning from Extremadura to León when they were lying fallow, looked upon the fallow lands and the stubble as resources at their disposal to continue expanding their enormous profits. This invasion delivered the final blow to property rights. The prohibition of enclosures was consecrated by the livestock laws of the *Mesta*; the transhumant tribunal of its so-called *entregadores* made it the object of its zeal. This tribunal legitimated the violations, perpetuating the lands' accessibility, and the liberty of landlords and tenants perished at its hands.

74. But Sire, regardless of the rights involved, reason calls for the repeal of such an abuse. The principles of natural justice and social rights, which precede all law and all custom and are superior to them, cries out against such a shameful violation of individual property. Any access granted to a stranger against an owner's will is an infringement, a true offense against his rights, and is therefore alien to that very character of justice without which no law, no custom should survive. Forbidding a landlord from enclosing his own lands, forbidding a tenant from defending his lands, is depriving them, not only of the right to enjoy their lands, but also of the right to guard them from usurpation. What would be said of a law that forbade farmers from locking the doors of their granaries?

75. At this point, the principles of justice are in agreement with those of political economy and are confirmed by experience. The care bestowed upon a property is always commensurate with how much it is appreciated. Man loves it as a precious guarantee of his subsistence, because he lives off it; as an object of his ambition, because he is its lord; as an insurance of his longevity, and, so to speak, as a sign of his immortality, because he passes it to his descendants. For this reason, this love is the source of all good industry; and all the prodigious advancements developed by genius and work in the art of cultivating the land are based upon it. This is why the laws that protect the exclusive utilization of property fortify this love; those who make it common reduce or weaken it; the former spur individual interest, the latter hinder it; the former are favorable, the latter unjust and detrimental to the progress of agriculture.

76. This influence is not confined to land ownership; it also affects labor. The tenant farmer of a plot of enclosed land, standing in for the landlord, feels its stimulus. Certain that his voice is the only one heeded within the precinct, he waters the land with the sweat of his brow; and his pains are alleviated by the enduring hope that his work will be rewarded. After harvesting a crop, he prepares the land for another, plowing it, fertilizing it, clearing it and forcing it into continual germination, thus expanding his property without extending the field's boundaries.

---

simultaneously in various towns and villages. Historian Gonzalo Anes says that the *mañero* was "the person who, without having goods or residing in a place, achieves *vecindad*, and therefore, the right to take advantage of communal pasture." See Anes, *Cultivos, Cosechas, y Pastoreo en la España Moderna* (Madrid: Real Academia de la Historia, 1999), 409.

Is there indeed any other cause behind the flourishing agriculture enjoyed in some of our provinces?

77. Your Highness acknowledged this great truth when, by the Royal *Cédula* of 15 June 1788, you protected the enclosures of orchards, vineyards and other types of cultivation [*plantaciones*].[20] But, Sire, are other crops less worthy in your eyes? Could it be that grain, which is the main staple of our public subsistence and the core of our agriculture, is less deserving of protection than wine, fruits and vegetables, which are mainly luxury goods? From whence does such a monstrous and harmful distinction arise?

78. It is time, Sire, it is high time, that the barbarous customs that so weaken individual property were abolished! It is time for Your Highness to break the chains that so shamefully oppress our agriculture, hindering its agents' self-interest! Or are not the spontaneous grasses that grow on the fields when they are left fallow or with stubble; the [cereal plant's] ears and grains that have fallen upon them; the residue from threshing and harvesting, are not all of these also part of their owners' land and of labor? A portion of the product wrought by the landlord's capital and the farmers and laborers' sweat? Only a misunderstood piety and a kind of Judaic superstition can leave all this to the voracity of the flocks, to the appetite of the traveler, and to the craving of the lazy and the idle who justify their indolence with the right to gleaning [*derecho de espiga y rebusco*].[21]

---

20 E. N.: The Royal *Cédula* referred to in this paragraph line is actually from 15 July 1788. The conflation with "June" is present in the original printed edition, and repeated throughout. The Royal *Cédula* established that: "Se permite a los dueños, y arrendadores de ellas [tierras], la facultad de cerrarlas y cercarlas. Por lo tocante a aquellas que se destinen para la cría de árboles silvestres, y la prohibición de entrar ganados, por la Instrucción de Montes, y Plantíos solo debía durar seis años desde el de 48, se amplía, y manda durar por 20, que se reputan necesarios para la cría de tales árboles. Aquellas en que sus dueños hubieren hecho plantíos de olivares, viñas, ó huertas de hortaliza con árboles frutales, deberán permanecer cerradas perpetuamente, y mientras se mantengan con dichos árboles, ó legumbres. Contra este permiso no prevalecerá uso ni costumbre en contrario. *Real Cédula de 15 de Julio de 1788.*" Severo Aguirre, *Prontuario Alfabético y Cronológico por Orden de Materias de las Instrucciones, Ordenanzas, Reglamentos, Pragmáticas, y demás Reales Resoluciones no Recopiladas, que han de Observarse para la Administración de Justicia y Gobierno de los Pueblos del Reyno* (Madrid: Oficina de Benito Cano, 1794), Tomo 2, 216. From this, we can draw the conclusion that Jovellanos referred to this sort of agricultural holdings when he used the term *plantaciones* in the text.

21 Whoever doubts this, see our very own Herrera (bk. 1, ch. 17): "Chickpeas should be planted far from roads or passersby between the wheat, or in closed places, because when they are ripe, there is not a single passerby who will not take a handful, even if it happens to be a fasting friar. Shepherds and the like are particularly troublesome. And if a group of women were to find them? No amount of hail could cause chickpeas as much harm! This is why it is better to plant them in places that are so closed off or hidden, that the first knowledge of their having been planted at all comes with the sound of them being picked."

The usefulness of enclosures

79. Your Highness will see that upon the repeal of such abuses, all of the estates in Spain will be enclosed. Irrigated lands as well as those in cooler climates will be enclosed with hedges, which are as beautiful as they are inexpensive and as effective in defending the lands as they are useful for sheltering and fertilizing them and increasing their production. In dry lands, walls and fences will be the preferred means [of enclosure]. The wealthy will enclose their fields with walls; the poor with ditches and turf. Wherever stone and lime are abundant, fields will be enclosed with masonry or stone; and where they are scarce, with adobe walls. Each country, each owner, each tenant will adapt to what climate, resources and ability allow, but they will enclose their lands, and this alone will improve cultivation. This was the rural order that characterized Spain under the Romans, and it still characterizes our well-cultivated provinces and the European nations that deserve the epithet of "agricultural."

80. Enclosures will be immediately followed by an increase in the number of trees planted, encouraged in vain until now. The efforts of those who have zealously and constantly demanded this important object are laudable, but who can deny that forbidding enclosures has frustrated these efforts and the many decrees dictated to promote it? Indeed, trees can grow anywhere; they can be watered by rain or irrigation; they can adapt to the hottest and driest climates; in conclusion, nature, always prone to this type of production, readily gives itself to the art of whosoever requires it. But which landlord, which tenant would dare plant the boundaries of their fields while fearing that the teeth of hungry herds and flocks would destroy in a day the hard work of many years? When everybody knows that their trees and their crops are protected, everybody will plant trees, at least where trees are known to be useful.

81. For although trees are under the protection of the law, and those who cut them down or destroy them are punished, this is not enough. There are also laws against theft, and nobody leaves their goods in the middle of the street. Man places his trust more in precautions than in laws, and in this he does well, because the former prevent evil while the latter punish it after the fact, and even though they include redress for damages, they can never repay the diligence, the anguish and the time spent in procuring it.

82. A decrease in the amount of labor expended will be another effect of enclosures, because exclusive access to the land will provide laborers with the possibility of collecting a greater proportion of produce and keeping more livestock with greater freedom and security, so that their industriousness will be rewarded with greater benefits. The ability to employ more labor in a smaller portion of land and yet procure greater rewards will invariably lead to the perfection of cultivation.

83. The Society will not attempt to give a definitive answer to that formidable question that has so divided modern economists, whether large-scale or small-scale agriculture is preferable. Although extremely important, this issue does not belong directly to the purview of legislation, because the division of holdings is a right that derives

from property, and laws should limit themselves to protecting the latter, letting the [respective] interest of agriculture's [various] agents determine how such division will be accomplished. In any case, once this interest is protected, it will invariably lead to smaller holdings.

84.   It is only natural that small-holding agriculture is preferred in countries where water is abundant, where the climate or the possibility of irrigation provides for continuous harvests, because, forced to multiply and repeat their operations, tenant farmers reduce the sphere of their work to smaller extensions. Along with this reduction, the farmer's interest will be more active and diligent, and also better focused and directed, and he will therefore know how to obtain greater yields out of a smaller space, and this is what will determine the reduction and subdivision of holdings. What else has led holdings in Murcia, Valencia, Guipúzcoa and in many parts of Asturias and Galicia to be as small as they are?

85.   But it is also natural that extensive farms are preferred in hot, dry areas. The lands of Andalusia, La Mancha and Extremadura could never yield two harvests a year. Therefore, with less employment for labor, its size must be increased. Even for a single, annual harvest, farmers have to alternate weak and strong seed, the neediest and the least demanding plants. Commonly, planting takes place in biennial rotation, with only part of the land planted while the remainder is reserved for pasture, which without irrigation is necessarily limited. It is therefore necessary for tenant farmers to have greater extensions of land in order to secure their subsistence. And this is why, in hot and arid climates, labor and lands are always on a large scale.

86.   Otherwise, acknowledging the specific advantages of each agricultural model as well as the fact that large farms might be beneficial for rich countries and small ones for poor countries, it is undeniable that agriculture based on immense estates, such as those that characterize Andalusia, are always evil and ruinous. Even when tenants and landlords have invested heavily, it is characterized by scant and bad cultivation. Because work is always directed and carried out by too many hands, all of them mercenary and brought from afar; because cultivation is always hurried, forcing time and season in all its operations; because it is always imperfect: the immensity of the object allows for neither proper fertilization, nor weeding, nor gleaning. In a word, immense farms are incompatible with the economy and diligence necessary for successful cultivation, because these are attained only when the sphere of the tenant's greed is proportional to his capacity or strength. Is it not painful to see how in the best estates of the realm a third of the land is sown once in three years while the other two portions lie fallow? Virgil's wise maxim indeed applies to such farms:

>   … *laudato ingentia rura:*
>   *Exiguum colito.*
>   *[Bestow your praise upon great estates:*
>   *Cultivate the small one.]*

87.   In any case, this equilibrium, this appropriate distribution of farmlands, their proportion and adaptation to climate and soil, to their owners' capital and to their

tenant's strength, are incompatible with the prohibition of enclosures. The liberty of erecting them is what leads temperate and humid, or water-rich, countries to witness the division of lands into small farms, subdivided into prairies, crops and orchards, with cattle raised alongside cultivation, and thus with fertilizer multiplied, work facilitated, cultivation perfected and agricultural production increased to the utmost.

88. The Society should also point out that enclosures and the proper division of land-holdings will also promote an increase in the rural population. A well-divided field, enclosed and well planted, perfectly suitable for the subsistence of a rural family, naturally beckons one to settle it, bringing one's herds and implements. This is how the tenant's interest, perpetually excited by the presence of its object and enlightened by the continual observation of the good effects of his toil, grows in both knowledge and activity, and is led to execute the most useful labor. Always working the land, and always with support at hand, always vigilant and ready to supply the exigencies of his crops, he is aided in his diligent and strenuous effort by the members of his family, and so the tenant's strength doubles and the product of his diligence increases and multiplies. Herein is the answer to what seems an incomprehensible enigma to those who have not been enlightened by experience: the immense production of the lands of Guipúzcoa, Asturias and Galicia is caused by the proper division and population of their farmlands.

89. Putting aside the many advantages that the increased population of its farmlands would generate for our agriculture, the Society cannot but pause to consider something that is even more worthy of Your Highness's paternal attention: the prospect of an immense rural population, spread out over the countryside, would guarantee that the country would have not only a laborious and wealthy people, but also a simple and virtuous one. The tenant farmer who makes his land his homestead is free of the stirrings and passions that agitate townsmen, and will be more distant from that ferment of corruption that luxury always instills, with more or less intensity, in all men. Committed together with his family to his labor, he can follow without distractions the object of his interest. And he will be more ardently driven to it by the feelings of love and tenderness that are so natural to men in domestic society. It will then be reasonable to expect both dedication and frugality from our farmers, along with abundance, which is their daughter; and, furthermore, the peace that is fostered when families are ruled by conjugal, paternal, filial and fraternal love, as well as concord, charity and hospitality. Our farmers will then possess those social and domestic virtues that constitute familial happiness and the true glory of states.

90. If these advantages were limited to the small-holding rural populace, it would be no less estimable in Your Highness's eyes, but enclosing great estates would also lead to their settlement. The benefits enjoyed by a tenant who resides on the land he works are the same in small and large properties, and perhaps even more secure in the latter, because, after all, the greater capital that is invested in large estates in the form of improvements means that farm operations can be carried out with greater and better assistance. And could the government find a simpler, more efficient, more natural

way to have the mass of landlords of middling and large estates move and settle in their lands, instead of living bunched up in the court and in the great capitals, where they languish in the hands of luxury and corruption?[22] This mob of miserable and foolish men who, running away from the happiness that calls to them on their estates, search for it where it does not exist; and, by competing in ostentation with opulent families, in a few years bring about their ruin and that of their innocent families. The Friends of the Country [*Amigos del País*], Sire, cannot look upon this with indifference nor refrain from appealing to Your Highness for a remedy to an evil that has a greater impact than it might at first appear on our agriculture's backwardness.

91. The foregoing observations naturally lead to the following conclusion: without the proper division and population of agricultural lands, any support offered for the improvement of our agriculture will harm it. Proof of this truth is found in a very recent example.

92. No complaints are more common than those of tenants and farmers whose lands are traversed by irrigation sluices and canals. Not only do they complain of the contribution that they must pay for the maintenance of the recently inaugurated irrigation system, but they also insist that irrigation makes their lands sterile. Is there any truth behind this paradoxical claim? The Society believes that there is.

93. What advantage is provided by irrigation? To make dry and arid land capable of producing continual harvests. But is this really a benefit for large and open estates that are situated a league or half a league away from tenants' households? Not at all. Does a resident of Frómista or Monzón with a farm of this type on the banks of the Canal of Castile, who rotates his crops biennially, derive from irrigation enough benefits to compensate for the increased expense and work that the canal requires? Here is the simple and natural explanation behind the appeals that have generated so many imprudent invectives against the supposed ignorance and laziness of our farmers.

94. It is undeniable that irrigation leads to a prodigious rise in land's productivity; but does that not lead to a proportional rise in labor and [other] costs? Artificial irrigation is costly because it must be purchased: nobody can use it without compensating the owner of the water, and compensation is even more reasonable the more costly that resource is. Irrigation is costly indeed, for the opening, closing, cleaning and maintaining of the piping system demands great effort and care, as do the taking and distributing of the water and its diversion and defense, all of which requires considerable time, and in this as in all activities, time is money. It is costly because the reproduction of produce that it facilitates demands more and continuous labor as well as abundant fertilizers to return to the soil the heat and salts that are consumed by continuous germination. In a word, it is costly because to increase the labor and the fertilizers that will be necessary, farmers will need more livestock,

---

22 We can apply what M. Varro (bk. 2) said of the Romans: "Omnes enim patresfamiliae, falce, & aratro, relictius intra murum correpsimus, & in circis potius, ac teatris, quam in segetibus, & vinetis manos movemus." Later we will indicate some of this evil's causes and effects.

taking land away from cultivation and destining it to pasture. So, why would a tenant desire irrigation, if the distance from his land, its extension, and its openness do not allow him to suitably adapt cultivation to irrigation?

95. This last article constitutes an even more urgent appeal for enclosures. Herds and flocks are at the basis of all successful crops, and it is impossible to increase them without increasing pasture, which demands the formation of well irrigated or rain-fed prairies. "Prata irrigua," said M. Porcio Caton, "si aquam habebis potissimum facito; si aquam non habebis sicca quamplurima factio." But this wise precept assumes that lands are enclosed and protected, for it cannot be realized in open lands. In some French provinces, particularly Anjou, dominated by great estates, farmers are not content with the good prairies that abound, and they grow their crops in thirds, to make good use of the fresh pastures in the fallow fields. This method is definitely far from being the most perfect, but even then it is worlds apart from the system that characterizes Andalusia, where the fallow fields, abandoned to the pillaging of loose herds, provide no sustenance for the tenants' own herds. How many costly disputes and struggles has Seville seen because the custom of enclosing *manchones*, patches of pasture land, that are absolutely necessary for the maintenance of tenants' work animals, is brought to court, even though these occupy only one of the three uncultivated fields, that is, a ninth of the entire farm, and are undertaken only from the feast of San Miguel (29 September) to the one of Cruz de Mayo (3 May)?

96. Finally, Sire, enclosures would bring to an end the incessant and futile disputes regarding whether mules or oxen are better for plowing.[23] After examining this matter and acknowledging that the quality of the land and the ease with which it can be plowed are influential factors, the Society believes that the decision depends very much upon whether the lands are open or closed. Thus, it considers it impossible for a large, unenclosed farm, without grass, and distant from the tenant's homestead, to be worked well with an animal whose progress is slow and is ill at ease in a stable, and even less so eating only hay; in the same way that it considers it quite difficult for a tenant who lives on his land, and who has good pasture land, to prefer the imperfect and unsteady work of a sterile and costly beast to the continuous goods and services of a docile, sober, fertile and steady animal, which ruminates rather than eats, and which, dead or alive, brings wealth to its owner, and seems destined by nature to aid cultivation and to increase the wealth of the rural family.

97. When the Society recommends that enclosures be allowed by law, it does not distinguish between any type of property or crop. Whether they are farmlands,

---

23   Varro and Columella assume that oxen are better suited for plowing, but they do not disapprove of the use of cows, mules or even donkeys, depending on the soil's characteristics. Columella notes that some lands in La Betica could be plowed with donkeys. But nothing is more decisive than what Pliny says (Hist. Nat., bk. 17, ch. 3) regarding what he saw in Africa: "In Byratio Africae, illum centena quinquagena fruge fertilem campum nullis cum siccus est, arabile tauris, post imbres, vili asello, & a parte altera jugi anu vomerem trahente vidimus scindi."

pasturelands, orchards, vineyards, olive groves, forests or woodlands, all are to be included in this policy [*provisión*], and all must be enclosed, because their exclusive and careful utilization will attract individual interest and encourage its action: all can be improved by this means and dedicated to more abundant production.

98. Perhaps the fortunes of the forests, which in the last three centuries have so aggrieved the government, will be improved with enclosures. It is astonishing just how many laws, ordinances, appeals and projects have been unable to achieve their objective. But by establishing as a general policy the enclosure of our forests, their conservation will be assured.

99. Nothing is truer or more constant than the fact that forests reproduce naturally, for once one exists, it demands nothing for its continuance other than protection and opportune exploitation. There are lands where enclosures alone have procured excellent woodlands, whether because the soil conserved the stumps and roots of ancient trees; or because the wind, waters and birds carried seeds and seedlings to them; or because nature, more prone to this than to any other production, nurtures in the earth's bosom the ancestral seeds of the trees that it destined to each climate and land.

100. But the truth is that, regarding this issue, lifting the ban on enclosures will not be sufficient redress: other usurpations that legislation has effected must be reversed. The general ordinances on woodlands and planting must be revoked along with the many municipal ordinances of provinces and towns [*provincias y pueblos*]: in a word, all that has been ordered until now regarding forests. If owners have the free and absolute right to exploit their wood, the nation will have great and plentiful forests.

101. This liberty will naturally awaken owners' self-interest and restore the activity and movement that these laws deadened by obliging owners to suffer by way of their trees the mark of slavery that subjected them to another's judgment; to ask and pay for a license to cut down a trunk; to follow rules that limited when and how to carry out cutting and pruning; to sell against their will and according to official appraisals; to admit procedural visits and inspections; and to provide information on the number and condition of his trees. How can we expect these owners to be diligent and effective in caring for their forests? If official interest meant to provide the greatest stimulus to this industry, by what aberration of ideas did it settle for the vile stimulus of fear, of forcing owners to act in order to avoid punishment?

102. Wood and timber have become so scarce in some provinces, Sire, that this issue deserves Your Highness's full attention. But the cause of this scarcity is to be found in the very policies destined to prevent it. Revoke them, and abundance will follow. Scarcity raises prices, and this alone will be the greatest attraction for interest, which, animated by liberty, will turn to care for the woodlands, because nobody cares little for that which is worth very much. Is it not true that all owners try to obtain the highest possible utility from their properties? Thus, where lack of fuel makes wood expensive, forests will not be felled, but rather protected and expanded; where luxury and industry increase construction, trees that provide the appropriate

timber will be grown; and trees that provide appropriate materials for naval and shipping construction will be planted near ports. Is this not the natural progress of all cultivation, all crops, all good industries? Is it not always consumption that encourages it and interest that determines and increases it?

103. The Society very well knows that, in Europe's present state, our Royal Navy is a crucial element of public defense. But will restrictive ordinances safeguard timber for ships' construction better than the private interest of the owners of forested land? It is certainly not the case that the timber needed for this branch of construction is among that which is scarce in Spain. The wild woodlands of the Pyrenees that stretch as far as Finisterre in one direction, and Cap de Creus in the other, are dense enough to secure the supply the navy for centuries. The forests of Asturias alone, despite having long supplied the timber for the great shipyards of Guarnizo and Esteiro, still hold enough wood to build many powerful squadrons of ships. What, then, causes the fear that has produced the many violent precautions and shameful laws that hurt this precious property, and thus the very objective of the laws? Municipal woodlands are protected despite the lengthy experience that has shown that they are not only costly and useless, but harmful, because uprooted from their native forest, where they would grow high enough to touch the clouds, and transplanted in a foreign soil that cannot nourish them, trees go, so to speak, from the cradle to the grave; equally useless, forest nurseries are encouraged, when it is evident that forced and misguided labor cannot possibly make the land yield what the wise and vigilant efforts of a talented planter could obtain; inspections continue, though these have become pointless except insofar as they vex and afflict our towns; and, finally, laws and ordinances based on absurd principles lacking any spirit of equity and justice continue to be enforced. Would it not be better to hear the appeals that individuals, communities and public magistrates all make against a system that so contravenes citizens' sacred rights of property and liberty?

104. The Society cannot deny the praise that the present Ministry of the Navy deserves for its incessant efforts to animate and protect property containing trees and forests; for the severity with which it has repressed the *asiento* monopolies; in a word, for the zeal with which it has confronted the abuses of this system and tried to perfect it. But the evil, Sire, is in the very root, in the system itself, and as long as it is not extirpated, it will continue to sprout everywhere, and it will be beyond all the efforts of zeal and justice. Restore to property all of its rights, and the remedy will be secured.

105. What would happen were these rights fully restored? If the Navy were to buy the timber that it needs without recourse to any special privileges, drawing purchase contracts like any private citizen, should it fear that it would not obtain enough wood? Interest alone will spur its owners to supply as much as is necessary. Should it fear that sellers would force it to accept too high a price? Since the Navy is the only, or nearly the only, consumer of this type of wood, it is more likely to set the price rather than to accept it. Moreover, larger timber will always have a lower price [*precio vilísimo*] in any activity other than the Royal works; therefore, the timber's owners will preserve it for those constructions; all the wild forests in the

mountainous provinces [*provincias de sierra*] will be reserved for Royal works; and, with hopes of being useful to them, new forests will be planted in the maritime provinces. Thus liberty, awakening interest everywhere, will naturally increase the amount and decrease the price of quality timber, which is what today's ordinances vainly pursue.

106. Public forests should not be exempted from this rule. The Society, steadfast in its principles, believes that they will never be better cared for than when converted into private property, enclosed and exploited privately by their owners, because the interest that will be invested in them will safeguard their conservation. It is possible to preserve the wild forests located in high and remote areas, where neither care nor population are wont to be found, as public and open woodlands. But their very situation will make redundant any legislation dedicated to their protection, and if some were indeed necessary, it would be enough to dictate that their wood and pastures be freely exploited in thirds, fourths, fifths or sixths, depending on their extension, with the remaining parts properly delimited and enclosed, so as to ensure their reproduction. The difficulty of transporting this timber will ensure that it is sold exclusively to the navy, for none other would find it worthwhile to pay what it would cost to surmount the heights of the precipices and the depths of the rivers that obstruct that timber's way to the sea. Were Your Highness to adopt these principles, converting forests to private property; making their exploitation and use exclusive; and freeing everywhere the planting, cultivation, exploitation and the trading of timber, the abundance and low prices that have until now been sought in vain would finally grace urban and mercantile construction, arts and industries, and homes and furnaces.

4th. Partial protection of cultivation

107. Such would have been the effect of liberty in all branches of cultivation, if all had been equally protected. But in protecting them unequally, the laws have promoted the backwardness of some, with very little advantage for the rest. Instead of proposing and constantly pursuing a single, general end, the growth of agriculture in all its variety, since legislation cannot aspire to anything but to increase public wealth through it, it protected or gave preference to those branches that momentarily promised more benefits. This gave birth to so many systems of particular and exclusive protection, so many preferences, so many privileges, and so many ordinances, that they have only served to thwart cultivation's activity and progress.

108. But could things have been different? Interest, Sire, knows more than zeal, and seeing things as they are, it surpasses whatever vicissitudes it encounters; it adapts to them; and when its liberty of movement is absolute, it secures without uncertainty the object of its desires. Zeal, given to abstract meditations and seeing things as they should be, or as it wishes they were, makes its plans without taking self-interest into account and obstructs its action, distancing it from its object, and thus greatly harming the public cause.

109. In view of this reflection, how should we judge the many municipal laws and ordinances that have oppressed the liberty of landlords and tenants in the use and destination of their lands? Those that forbid substituting pasture with crops or crops with pasture? Those that limit plantations or forbid uprooting vines and forests? In a word, those that intend to stop or to encourage or to direct through legislation and policy the tendencies that agriculture's agents should follow toward one branch or another? Do the authors of all these rules and regulations perchance know the various possible products that each land can yield better than those who would procure them? Will the state not obtain the greatest possible wealth from the land when it permits each individual to obtain the greatest possible utility from his own property?

110. This utility always depends on circumstances that change rapidly and continually. A new branch of commerce encourages a new branch of cultivation because the utility that it offers, once known, attracts agriculture's agents. When meat becomes expensive, everybody wants to raise livestock and, needing forage, all diligent husbandmen convert part of their land into pasture. Where internal consumption or exportation keeps the prices of wine and oil high, everybody plants vineyards and olive groves; and everybody extirpates them when their prices decrease and that of grain rises. Far from preventing it, legislation should encourage this ebb and flow of self-interest without which agriculture cannot grow or survive.

111. If examples were needed to confirm this doctrine, would we not find plenty of these in the ancient and modern history of all peoples? The introduction of luxury in Rome after the conquest of Asia entirely transformed cultivation in Italy. One need only read the old agronomic texts to see that near that great capital, farmers' attention was devoted primarily to fruits, orchards and the raising of birds and other animals. The benefits obtained from keeping and selling pigeons and thrushes, farming fish and other activities of this type were immense. Why? Because, on the one hand, legislation facilitated these activities; and, on the other, the banquets held for celebrating triumphs and feasts were such that there was never enough, not even to sate Lucullus's appetite for luxury.

112. A curious story provides more evidence for this argument. Sallust cautions that the Roman soldier, formerly frugal and virtuous, took to wine and pleasures when Sulla relaxed the discipline of the armies.[21] As a consequence, the returns provided by vineyards grew to such a degree that the Latin agronomists thought them agriculture's most lucrative branch, which explains why all of them recommend the planting of vineyards more than that of any other fruit or produce.

113. Rome's food policies may have had a great deal to do with this preference. The wheat sent by the tribute-paying provinces, which was freely distributed, naturally lowered the price of grain, not only in their territory but in all of Italy, and diverted cultivation to other products. And, so, the Roman and Italian countryside as well

---

24 Ibi primum insuevit exercitus PR. *Amare, potare,* signa, tabulas pictas. Vasa celata mirari (Catil. II.)

as that of the provinces became so filled with vineyards that Domitian not only forbade the planting of new vines in Italy, but he also ordered that half of the empire's
vineyards be uprooted.[25] This edict, in fact, was not only unfair but also futile: the
excess of vineyards themselves would have lowered the price of wine, reestablishing that of grain: however, it conclusively proves that laws can do nothing when
faced with the natural vicissitudes that affect crops and that only by submitting and
adapting to them will they bring about general well-being.

114. But we need not search for eccentric examples. Nor must we travel to remote times or
countries. What has become of the abundant vineyards of Cazalla? There is hardly
a vineyard in that territory, which was formerly well known for them: they have
all been uprooted and turned into olive groves or other crops, after the [Spanish]
American market, which had revealed a preference for those wines and encouraged
their plantations, awakened the interest of landlords closest to the coast. All around
Seville, Sanlúcar and Jerez, the countryside was covered with vines, and these were
favored by the market because they were more accessible, and the vineyards of
Cazalla were thus eclipsed.

115. The same cause, along with Portugal's severance [*desmembración*] [from Spain
after 1640], filled that coast with plantations of lemons and oranges, while Asturias,
Galicia and Montaña, which until midcentury had supplied England and France
with these fruits, saw their commerce dwindle. In the meantime, many of the former orange groves of Asturias were turned into apple orchards following the rise in
the price and consumption of cider. And in Galicia, [farmers] were destined to cultivate other, more useful products, without the intervention of laws that, regardless
of their intent or substance, can never animate or direct cultivation as powerfully as
the stimulus provided by interest.

116. Legislation's intervention is not less ruinous for cultivation when, to favor tenants,
it oppresses landlords, limiting their rights, regulating their leases and destroying
the object of their interest. Are there not a great many [draft] laws of this sort proposed to Your Highness in the Agrarian Law dossier? If such dreams were heeded,
neither time nor price nor form would be freely agreed by tenants and landlords;
everything between them would be regulated by law. And under such conditions of
slavery, what would become of property? What of cultivation?

117. Among the many such laws proposed to Your Highness is one that would fix and
limit rents in favor of tenants in relation to land values measured by appraisals. But
this law, presented along with others like it as a matter of equity, would in fact be
unjust. They all generally presume that the only factor behind an increase in rent

---

25 Ad summam quondam ubertatem vini, frumenti vero inopiam existimans nimio studio negligi
    arva edixit: *Nequis in Italia novellaret, utque in provintiis vineta succiderentur relicta, ubi plurimum dimidia
    parte.* (Sueton in Domic.) This barbarous law was revoked during Probus' government (M.
    H. E. bk. 4, ch. 2). "To win the will of the provinces," says the author, "he revoked and left as
    naught Domitian's edict in which those of Gaul and Spain were forbidden from planting new
    vines."

is the landlord's greed [*codicia*]; but is the greed of the tenant not a factor as well? Is there any doubt that rents would be more stable and fair if the latter's concurrence, their bidding and their competition for land, did not encourage the former to raise the rents that they charge? Land rents never rise without the combination of these two interests, just as they never decrease without this same combination, because if competition among tenants encourages landlords to raise their rents, its absence moves them to lower rents, and the only factors that set prices are markets and leases themselves.

118. It is true that in some areas, land rents have risen a great deal. Some would say too much; but increases are justified in their principles and causes. No price that is fixed through the mutual and free concurrence of all parts and is set on the basis of the natural elements that regulate its commerce can be described as unfair. It is natural that, where the rural population is abundant and there are more tenants than lands to be rented, landlords set the price; just as it is natural that the price is set for them where lands are abundant and men who want to rent them few. In the former case, the landlord, wanting to obtain the highest possible rent for his property, will increase it to the highest level, and the tenant must content himself with making the smallest possible profit; but in the latter case, the tenant's aspiration for profit means that the landlord must content himself with the lowest possible rent. If a law that increased rent to favor landlords were considered unfair, why would it be fair to lower rent in the tenants' favor?

119. Another attempt to prevent rents from increasing was to fix prices in rental agreements [*manteniendo á los colonos en sus arriendos*]. Such policy was a result of a momentary sense of equity after many attempts in vain to achieve this measure. The Royal *Cédula* of 6 December 1785 granted tenants this privilege by preventing them from being bearers of the *imposición de frutos civiles* imposed on landlords by the royal decree of 29 June of that same year. But the Society cannot refrain from observing that this policy will prove to be futile or unfair; futile, because wherever lands are leased according to tenants' terms, landlords are unable to increase rents; therefore, they are unable to pass on the weight of the new contribution to their tenants even if they want to. And it will be unfair wherever landlords set the terms of the leases, because if, as we have shown, any rent agreed to by tenants and landowners in a freely negotiated lease is fair, then a law that deprives the landowner of that liberty, and of the utility associated with it, cannot be fair.

120. Aside from the fact that the effect of such a law can only be secured momentarily, landowners, indeed, as a consequence of the prohibition imposed upon them, will suffer at their tenants' hands by not raising the rents. But there is no doubt that they will raise the rents they charge once a new lease is negotiated with new tenants. This is something that the law does not forbid, nor could it do so without causing even greater injustice. Then, viewing it as a unique or at the very least an uncommon opportunity, landlords will be more anxious to increase rents to the highest level, so that eventually rents will reach the level that the circumstances of each province permits and the law will have failed in its object, but not before causing all the harm

that its intervention was destined to cause. Has the effect of the tenancy privilege granted to the court's residents been any different?

121. Your Highness has received proposals that, following these same principles, would prolong the terms of all leases in order to favor cultivation. But the Society believes that such a law would be neither useful nor fair: it acknowledges that long leases are generally favorable to cultivation, but not always to property, and that justice is owed to all. Where the value of rents decreases, and even where it is stable, landlords are naturally inclined to prolong their leases without the need for legislation's intervention; but where value rises, they prefer shorter leases, to increase rents upon their renewal. In this way, the landlords of Seville have doubled their rents in the short period from 1770 to 1780. A law that prolongs and fixes lease periods would therefore be contrary to justice because it would defraud landlords of this just utility.

122. On the other hand, it is worth noting that rent increases have taken place only where they are paid in money, which suggests that rents have increased either because the rural population has increased, or because the price of grain has increased, or both. In contrast, where rents are paid in grain, some have remained permanently the same and others practically unaltered; henceforth an equally favorable price alteration to landlords and tenants does not affect the combinations of this interest. Justice is to be found only in the liberty of these combinations.

123. Another of the laws proposed to Your Highness would be unfair for the same reason: that all rents be paid in grain or in proportionally equal shares of produce. Certainly, there is no better means to assure the reciprocal proportion of interests of landlords and tenants, not only in every climate and every soil but also in every accident suffered by cultivation due to the vicissitudes of the seasons and the years. However, any such legal imposition would be harmful to property and therefore unjust. A lease of this sort demands continuous vigilance, a large number of controllers, long and prolix inquiries and accounts; collecting, conducting, storing, conserving and selling the grain and produce entail a great expense; and it also entails cares that are not ordinarily assumed by landlords.[26] In places where cultivation is more prosperous, such a lease would be very difficult to arrange, and almost impracticable given the variety and multiplication of produce. What is indeed fair is for each party to freely choose how to pay or collect rents, combining by this means the interests of both tenants and landlords. Is it not this liberty that has, since time immemorial, made portions of grain constitute the preferred rent in our

---

26 The observations made by Pliny the Younger regarding this point are curious indeed. In Book 9, Ep. 37 to Paulinus, he notes, "Nam priore lustro quamquam post magnas remissiones, reliqua creverunt; inde perisque nulla jam cura minuendi aeris alieni, quod desperant posse persolvi, rapiunt etiam, consumuntque quod natum est, ut.qui jam putent se non sibi parcere, occurrendum ergo augescentibus vitiis, & medendum est Medendi una ratio, *si non nu?memo?, sed partibus locem,* atque deinde ex meis, *aliquos exactores opera, custodies fructibus ponam,* & alioqui nullum fidem, acres oculos, numerosas manus poscit; expediendum tamen, & quasi in veteri morbo quaelibet mutatiouis auxilia tentanda sunt."

Northern provinces; half the produce in those of Aragon; and money in Andalusia and in much of Castile and La Mancha?

124. Finally, Sire, various proposals made to Your Highness regard the establishment of *tanteos* and privileges; the prohibition of subleases; and the limitation or the extension or the reduction of holdings and other such dispositions, which are as derogatory to property rights as they are to freedom of cultivation. But the Society has developed extensively enough its basic, general principle, and it therefore does not consider it necessary to debate each of these individually. It will never find justice where it does not first perceive this liberty, which is the only object to be protected by the law; it will never believe liberty to be compatible with the privileges that counteract it; it will never, in conclusion, expect prosperity in agriculture from systems of partial and exclusive protection, but only from the just, equal and general protection that, granted to both landed property and labor, excites at all times the interest of agriculture's agents.

5th. *The Mesta*

125. The clarity and conviction shed by this luminous principle should be enough to strike down this most perverse agrarian system [*sistema agrario*]. Can the monstrous privileges of transhumant herding be sustained when judged in this light? The Society, Sire, guided by the spirit of impartiality that necessarily reigns in a community of friends of the public good, and free of the conflicting passions that have so far characterized discussions of the *Mesta*, will neither defend it as the greatest of services nor combat it as the worst of all public evils. Instead, the Society will limit itself to applying its principles to it. The laws, the privileges of this body, whatever is marked by monopoly's seal or derived from exclusive protections will receive a just censure: but by no means will it look upon this branch of agriculture as unworthy of the vigilance and fair protection that the law should grant equally to all agricultural activity that is useful and honest.

126. The unremitting zeal with which all nations employ the most exquisite means to secure the growth and improvement of their wool is truly worthy of admiration; yet we wage war against our own. The English have made excellent and very fine fleeces by crossing their sheep with those of Castile under the reigns of Edward IV, Henry VIII and Queen Elizabeth. After establishing their republic, the Dutch also improved their breeds, adapting sheep brought from their Oriental lands to their climate. The Swedes, since the reign of the celebrated Christina, and later, Saxony and Prussia, have sought this same advantage, taking rams and ewes from Spain, England and even Arabia to their frozen climates. During the last few years, Catherine II has been promoting this same result by awarding honors and prizes in the St. Petersburg Academy. And, finally, France has just committed great sums to breed Arabian and Indian sheep in its lands. And, in the midst of all this activity, will we, who at some point did not disdain breeding our sheep with those of England, and through this means produced unequaled

wool whose excellence other nations strive to emulate; will we now become our wool's worst enemy?[27]

127. It is true that this farming activity represents only one branch of agricultural commerce for us, while foreigners try to improve their wool to increase industry. It is true that they come to buy our wool with more avidity than that with which we sell it to them, for they sell it back to us manufactured, and thus we pay the total cost of their manufacturing, including the price of the wool we sold. And it is also true that the value of their industrial production is four times the value of the raw material that we provided, according to Don Jerónimo de Uztáriz's calculations, and therein lies the most formidable argument espoused by the enemies of sheep rearing.

128. The Society, however, will not be dazzled by so perfect [*especioso*] an argument [*raciocionio*]. Inasmuch we [Spaniards] cannot be, ignore how to be or do not want to be industrious, should we not pay with the price of our wool the part of manufacturing costs of foreign industrial production, even when such consumption causes our poverty, ignorance and sloth? Manufactures which, when consumed, impose poverty, ignorance, and sloth upon us. If we ever can, know how and want to be industrious, will it be an evil to have the best raw material in abundance, and at an affordable price, in order to develop [*fomentar*] our own industry? If we were industrious, one day, would it not be the case that the abundance of this material would assure us an infallible preference? Would it not be the case that foreign industry would become precarious, and even dependent upon us? Are we still so longing for the desire of what is right that we confuse what is wrong for what is good?

129. But if it is remarkable that such reasoning has not convinced everyone that wool production is worthy of legal protection, it is even more remarkable that such protection has been used to maintain the unfair and exorbitant privileges held by the *Mesta*. Nothing is as dangerous, both in morality and in politics, as going to extremes. Protecting a branch of industry with monopoly and privileges positively discourages and harms the rest, because forcefully pushing interest toward one object steers it away from the others. Let us aspire to wealth through our wool production; should we not also strive to do the same, or more, for grain cultivation, upon which the preservation and growth of states' power depend? And if livestock

---

27 Old Columella bought some wild rams that had been brought from Africa to Cádiz, according to his nephew, and crossed them with his sheep, obtaining a better breed. He then crossed these new rams with sheep from Taranto, and the wool of their offspring had the fineness of their mothers' fleece with the excellent color of their fathers'. The Taranto wool's excellence, to which we probably owe our own, is evidenced in the following excerpt of M. Varro (bk. 3, ch. 2): "Plaeraque similiter facienda (speaking of transhumance) in ovibus pellitis, quae propter lanae bonitatem, ut sunt tarentinae, & attica, pellibus integuntur, ne lana inquinetur, quominus vel infici recte possit, vel lavari & purgari." It seems that this operation was renewed in the time of King Don Alfonso XI, when in the *old ships, sheep from England were brought to Spain* for the first time (*naves carracas las pécoras de Inglaterra España*). See the Centón del bachiller Cibdad Real, epist. 37. Father Sarmiento believed that that was why our finest sheep were called *marinas* (from the sea), which then became *merinas* (merino).

were to deserve privileges, would not stationary flocks deserve them more? They not only provide support for cultivation, they also represent an infinitely greater mass of wealth and are more closely linked to public happiness. Let us examine these privileges in light of these sound economic principles.

130. The laws that forbid the cultivation of lands once used for pasturage have been approved thanks to *mesteño* machinations, which obtained the aforementioned prohibition by arguing that fertilizer and meat were scarce, even though transhumant herds contribute the least to agriculture and meat products. Regarding this law, we repeat what we already stated concerning the prohibition of enclosures, not only because both limit landowners' free use of their land, but also because they oppose the procurement of the greatest possible production from the land. The moment that the landowner decides to plow a pasture, we can assume that he expects to obtain more utility from cultivation than from pasture, and, therefore, the laws that bind his liberty act not only against justice, but against the general aim of agrarian legislation, which is to ensure that land yields the greatest possible production.

131. The same can be said of the right of *mesteño* shepherds to the pastures owned by others. Besides violating the same right and liberty mentioned above, it deprives the landowner of the right and liberty to choose his tenant farmers. This choice is an important one because the landowner, even at the same price, may prefer one tenant over another for reasons of affection or charity, or even for reasons of gratitude or respect; and the satisfaction of those feelings is indeed worthy because in the social state we consider as more just a man who measures his utility by his moral good rather than by his physical one. Therefore, taking away this choice from the landowner means diminishing the most precious part of his property.

132. This reduction of his rights is contrary to justice when the privilege is exercised by one sheep farmer over another, but it is even more so when a sheep farmer exercises it over a plowman, and it is at the pinnacle of injustice when exercised by the sheep farmer over the landowner. If in the second case it foils the growth of grain cultivation, tying the land to a more meager production and, in general, of a lesser value, in the latter case, it places before the landowner a difficult choice: that of becoming a sheep farmer without having the calling for it, or that of abandoning the cultivation of his property and the fruit of the toil and industry exercised upon it.

133. The privilege of the *tasa*, which is antieconomic and antipolitical in its very essence, is even more so when combined with the rest of the privileges usurped by the *mesta*.[28] The law that prohibits the breaking up of pasturelands, whose sole aim is to support the superabundance of grass and hay, necessarily leads to the absolute debasement of pasture's price. The right of *mesteño* shepherds to the pastures owned by others conspires to this same end, insofar as it banishes tenant competition, one of the primary elements of price changes. What can be said of the *tasa* but that it

---

28 E. N.: The *tasa* here refers to the *tasa de las hierbas*, which is the set of privileges enjoyed by transhumant livestock owners and that had deleterious effects in enclosures, and curtailed the property rights of landowners. For a full characterization, see Anes, *Cultivos*, 156.

has been invented to avoid an equilibrium in prices? This strives from the fact that the *tasa* takes as an established value as a standard, and not those that were in place at the moment at which the lease was agreed on.

134. And what of the laws that have inexorably tied the values of pasture grass [*hierbas*] to those of a century ago? Has this done anything but debase property, whose value, which changes over time, cannot be determined by legislation, but by its products? Why should the price of grass be fixed when that of wool is not? And, considering that the vicissitudes of trade have raised the price of wool to staggering levels, would it not be an enormous injustice to fix the price of grass according to these rates?

135. The same can be said of the *tanteos*, or the possibility for a party to ask a seller for a price given to another, which dispensed by our laws is an open offense to justice. Its effects are also most pernicious to property because, destroying the concurrence [of buyers and sellers when negotiating a price], they stop the natural change in, and, consequently, the fairness of, prices, which is only attained through the bargaining of interested parties. To the *tanteos* must be added the *alenguamientos, exclusión de pujas, fuimientos, amparos, acogimientos, reclamos* and a plethora of exotic terms coined by the *Mesta*, jargon—most of which is known only to its members—that define the many tools used to lower the price of grass and hay, transforming these into a horrendous monopoly in favor of transhumant sheep owners. In light of all these privileges, it is difficult to decide whether one should admire the ease with which such absurd measures have been obtained or be astounded at the obstinacy and gall that have underpinned them for two centuries.

136. The Society, Sire, could never reconcile these practices with its principles. The very existence of this pastoral council, in whose name such privileges are possessed, is in the Society's eyes an offense to reason and the law, and the privilege that allows it to exist is the most harmful of all. Without this fellowship that gathers the power and wealth of the few against the helplessness and need of the many; that supports a body capable of challenging not only the provinces' representatives but also those of the whole kingdom; and that for nearly two centuries has frustrated the efforts of their zeal, futilely aimed at freeing agriculture and stationary flocks from oppression, we cannot understand how such odious and exorbitant privileges could have been maintained. How dare they defend these? They are as harmful to Your Highness's authority as they are prejudicial to the public good. If Your Highness were to repeal such privileges, it would remedy the depopulation of the frontier provinces, the decline of stationary flocks, the lack of cultivation in the most fertile provinces of the kingdom and, what is more, the offenses against the sacred right of public and private property.

137. Please devote your worthy reflection, Your Highness, to the fact that the *cabaña real* was created for no other purpose than to welcome all of the kingdom's flocks under the protection of the law, and that the union of the *sierra* shepherds had no other object than to secure this benefit.[29] The residents of the *sierra*, who, starting in the

---

29 E. N.: *Cabaña Real* was an alternative term for the *Mesta* and it was named after the extension of the rights of the "royal herds" (*cabaña real*) to the *Mesta*: "El conjunto de ganado

Pyrenees spill into the interior of our continent [*nuestro continente*],[30] were forced to move their herds to lower lands in search of pastures and shelter during the winter, when the snow banishes them from the peaks, and they felt the need to unite, not to obtain privileges, but to secure those protections that the law offered to others and that the wealthy owners of the stationary herds [*riberiego*] had begun to appropriate only for themselves.[31] Thus rural history presents these two groups, *sierra* [itinerant] and *riberiego* [stationary] shepherds, in continuous conflict, and the laws always in favor of the former, who deserved their protection precisely because they were weaker. Therein we see the origin of the *Mesta* and its privileges, until greed and the desire of partaking in them led to that famous coalition, the solemn guild that in 1556 gathered the *sierra* and *riberiego* sheep owners into a single body. This league, albeit unequal and unfair for the former, who thereafter saw their interests diminish, while those of the latter grew, was even more unfair and ruinous for the public good, because it combined the wealth and authority of the *riberiegos* with the industry and numbers of the sierra sheep farmers, producing a body of livestock farmers so enormously powerful that, through sophisms and clamor, it has managed not only to acquire the monopoly of all the pastures of the kingdom, but also to transform the best arable lands into pasturelands, ruining stationary shepherding and cultivation, along with the rural population.

138. It was well deserved and admirable that the law allowed and protected this shepherding fellowship in those unfortunate times when citizens were forced to join forces in order to grant their properties a protection that they could not expect from deficient legislation. Then, the union of the weak against the strong was nothing other than the exercise of the natural right of self-defense, and its legal sanction was a fair and legitimate act. But when legislation has already forbidden such fellowships as contrary to the public good; when the law is respected across the land; when there is no individual, no group and no class that does not bend to its sovereign authority, in a word, when reason and mercy oppose the odious privileges that they entail, why should the union of the strong against the weak be tolerated? Why should an association devoted solely to the defense of a certain class enjoy a type of protection that the law gives to everyone?

139. Alas, Sire, let us stop here; this is enough light and reason for Your Highness to declare the complete dissolution of this arrogant fellowship, the abolition of its exorbitant privileges, the repeal of its unfair ordinances and the suppression of its oppressive court of law. This council of men and monks turned shepherds and livestock farmers must forever disappear from the sight of our plowmen and

---

trashumante que tienen los ganaderos que componen el Concejo de la Mesta. *Greges region conssesui super re pecuaria subjetae.*" Real Academia Española, *Diccionario*, 1783, 181,1. Anes, *Cultivos*, 396.

30 E. N.: This reference to the interior of the Iberian Peninsula as *continente* in the eighteenth century was a consequence of a definition of continent as a "great extension of territory that is not isolated." Real Academia Española, *Diccionario*, 1783, 282, 2.

31 E. N.: "*Riberiego,ga*. Adj. Applied to the livestock that is not transhumant." Ibid., 820, 2.

laborers; and the same with the entire host of *alcaldes, entregadores, quadrilliers* and *achagueros* that at all times and in all places afflict and oppress them in the name of the Council of the [*Mesta*]. And, once and for all, restore to stationary flocks their means of subsistence; to cultivation its liberty; to property its rights; and to reason and justice their jurisdiction.

140. The evil of which we speak is as urgent as it is notorious, and the Society would violate all of its own purpose if it did not make it clear to Your Highness that the moment has arrived to remedy it, and that delay would be as contrary to justice as to the well-being of agriculture. May transhumant herds enjoy the equal and fair protection that the law provides to all branches of industry, but may self-interest guide the direction of individuals' actions toward the objects that in each country, in each period and in each set of circumstances offer the greatest profit. Then all will be ruled by principles of equity and justice; that is, by the desire for utility that is inseparable from them. As long as the demand for wool is high, pastures will be rented at high prices and sheep farmers will find and afford grass and hay for their herds, because pastureland owners will obtain more profit in renting them as pasture than in cultivating them. If, on the contrary, cultivation were to offer higher returns and pasturelands transformed into croplands, pasturelands for livestock [*dehesas*] would break down, leading to a decrease in transhumant herds, and perhaps even of fine wool; but at the same time, cultivation, stationary flocks and the rural population would grow. This growth would more than abundantly compensate for that loss, and public wealth would also increase, gaining as much as private interest with the change. We need not be afraid of losing our superiority in wools: their excellence, and the dependence of the national and foreign industries on them, firmly secure their conservation, as does the interest of landowners; because when the scarcity of pastures leads them to raise the prices of grass and hay, the scarcity of sheep will lead sheep owners to raise the price of their wool. In this way, a fair equilibrium between cultivation and livestock will be reached, one that safeguards the public good, and that absurd laws and odious privileges do nothing but alter.

141. The Society considers only one of these privileges as worthy of exception, if indeed one should use the term "privilege" for a custom that precedes not only the *Mesta*, but also the *cabaña real*, and even the establishment of cultivation. And that is the use of *cañadas*, or pastoral roads, without which transhumant livestock would indeed perish. The periodic migration of its numerous flocks, repeated twice a year, in autumn and spring, over the great expanse that separates León from Extremadura, requires the freedom and amplitude of the *cañadas*, more so since in the protective system that we are establishing, enclosures will fence in every stretch of countryside except for the royal roads [*caminos reales*] and those that branch off from them, as well as the public and private rights of way that are indispensable for the use of estates.

142. The Society will not justify this custom by arguing, as the *Mesta's* protectors and those who would emulate it agitatedly do, that transhumance is necessary to produce fine wool. In accordance with its principles, such a necessity, if it were indeed true, would not be enough to justify the creation of a privilege, because no

encouragement of a particular interest can justify the repeal of the consecrated principles of public well-being, and the need for transhumance for our fine wools would not lead directly to a defense of *cañadas*.

143. Transhumance was indeed necessary at some point in the past for the conservation of the herds, and therefore the establishment of *cañadas* was fair and legitimate. The indispensable need to maintain the flocks led to the establishment of transhumance, and to it alone does Spain owe the rich and precious quality of its wools, long-celebrated throughout our history. It is as evident that the high mountain passes of León and Asturias, covered in snow during the winter, could not sustain the numerous and large flocks that graze the fresh and delicious grass that covers them in the summer, as it is that the lush meadows of Extremadura, scorched by the summer sun, could not maintain in that season the immense herds that graze upon them in the winter. Make only one of these flocks remain for an entire summer in Extremadura, or an entire winter in the mountains of Babia [Northern León], and it will inevitably perish.

144. This difference in pastures led to the establishment of transhumance, naturally and thoughtlessly, though not to make fine wool, but rather to conserve and multiply the herds. After the Saracen invasion, the Spaniards who had found shelter in the mountains, which today are the home of most of our transhumant herds, [and they] preserved in them the only source of wealth [imaginable] amid so much confusion; and as they expelled the Moors from the lowlands [*tierras llanas*], they settled there with their herds, extending the limits of property along with those of the empire [*imperio*]. The differences in the seasons taught them to combine the advantages of both climates, and thus the use of summer pastures and winter pastures was born; and perhaps the direction of the conquests was tied to this movement, for they penetrated Extremadura first, instead of Guadarrama. And so, once that fertile province was added to the kingdom of León, the heat and aridity of the new territory were combined with the coolness of the older kingdoms, and transhumance was established between Extremadura and Babia, and between the sierras and river valleys, long before cultivation began anew. Therefore, when agriculture was restored and extended across the fertile gothic fields [*campos góticos*], the right of way of the *cañadas* was respected.

145. It cannot be surprising, then, that conceived in times of a preponderance of transhumance, Castilian legislation should respect the *cañadas*, a custom established both by need and by nature. In this, it followed the example of wiser peoples. Roman laws, which also recognized transhumance, protected pastoral roads. In Cicero, we see that this public right of way was established across Italy under the name *calles pastorum*.[32] The *cañadas* were also mentioned by Marcus Terentius Varro, when he recalls the transhumance of Apulia's sheep to the peaks of Samnium, many miles away, for their summer grazing.[33] He also states that his own sheep went to the peaks of Reatino to graze during the summer, and writes of the transhumance of

---

32 Pro. Sextio, Italicae calles, atque pastorum stabula.
33 Bk. 2, ch. 2.

horse herds. Thus we see that interest everywhere has led to the fruitful combination of climates and seasons, and that laws devoted to protecting this combination have secured the wealth of their states.

146. Though other peoples also permitted transhumance and protected drovers' roads [*cañadas*], none that we know of protected or held a congregation of shepherds [the *Mesta*] united under the authority of a public magistrate to make war on cultivation and stationary flocks, and ruin them with graces and exemptions. None allowed the enjoyment of privileges of dubious origin, abusively observed, pernicious in their aims and destructive of property rights. None erected tribunals in their favor and sent them out across the realm, armed with an authority that was strong enough to oppress the weak, but not strong enough to restrain the powerful. None legitimated its meetings, sanctioned its laws, authorized its representation nor opposed it to the defenders of the public. None ... But this is enough: the Society has revealed the evil; to evaluate it and repress it is in Your Highness's hands.

6th. Mortmain tenures [La amortización]

147. Another, graver, more urgent and more pernicious threat to agriculture claims your supreme attention: there would not be so much anxious running to join the confraternity of the *Mesta* among us if, while our laws facilitated the accumulation of livestock-related wealth in a reduced number of powerful bodies and persons, they did not also favor the accumulation of landed wealth in the same class of persons and bodies, dividing individual interest from cultivation and stationary herds, and directing the nation's wealth and industry toward other aims. Examining this new evil in light of its principles, the Society will present to Your Highness its widespread consequences as an effect of the inequality with which laws have bestowed their protection.

148. It is certainly impossible to favor individual interest with equality, granting individuals the right to aspire to landed property, without at the same time favoring the accumulation of landed wealth; and it is also impossible to abide this accumulation without acknowledging the inequality of fortunes that is its foundation and the true origin of the many vices and evils that afflict the body politic.[34]

---

34 The primary object of all agrarian laws established or proposed in Rome was to prevent this accumulation and preserve some equality. Romulus determined that each citizen was to enjoy a patrimony of 2 *huebras* of (M. Varro, t. 10); once the kings were expelled, this sum was extended to 7 *huebras*. Curius Dentatus was content with that, for when the people conferred upon him 50 *huebras* as a reward for his victories, he refused them as an excess that did not behoove a Roman. But accumulation continued to make great progress and, to contain it, in the Roman year of 385, Gaius Licinius Stolo distributed 7 *huebras* of the republic's lands to each plebeian and fixed at 500 *huebras* the legal maximum that a citizen could hold. But the evil was so irredeemable that Stolo himself was condemned for possessing more than 500 *huebras* in his name, and quite a few more in his son's name. Long after this, attempts to put these laws into execution were followed by a terrible sedition that for the first time spilled the blood of Roman citizens in the city, and in which the Gracchi fell. Sulla's conquests and proscriptions

149. And so, we cannot deny that the accumulation of wealth is an evil; but since it is a necessary evil, the remedy is closer at hand. When every citizen can aspire to wealth, the natural vicissitudes of fortune will make it go quickly from one to another: therefore, it can never be both immense and long lasting for any one individual. The same tendency that moves all persons to this object, acting as stimulus for some, is an obstacle for others. If the natural progression of liberty does not lead to equal wealth accumulation, at the very least it will be equally a reward for industriousness and a punishment to the idle.

150. On the other hand, when equality of rights is safeguarded, inequality of conditions has very salutary effects. It puts the different classes in a necessary and reciprocal dependence; it unites them with the strong ties of mutual interest: it calls the less fortunate to the place of the wealthiest and most graced; in a nutshell, it awakens and incites personal interest, arousing it more powerfully when equality of rights harbors in all the hope of attaining wealth.

151. It is therefore not these laws that will uselessly occupy the attention of the Society. Its reflections are directed toward those who continually take property out of circulation and commerce; who tie it to the perpetual possession of certain individual or familial bodies; who forever exclude the rest of the individuals from the right to ever aspire to it; and who uniting the indefinite right of increasing it with the absolute prohibition of decreasing it, facilitate indefinite accumulation and open up a dreadful abyss that can swallow the state's entire territorial wealth.[35] Such are the laws that favor mortmain and entailment [amortización].

---

and his mad profusion increased the evil even more, and made a remedy impossible. It was not enough to execute the Agrarian Law with all the zeal of Tribune Servilius Rullus, who faced [Marcus Tullius] Cicero as his rival in the year of the latter's Consulate (see his sentences on the Lege Agraria), but Tullius himself stated that accumulation was so heinous that there were barely 20 landowners in a city of nearly 1,200: "Non esse," he says, "in civitate duomillia hominum, quei rem haberent" (De oficiis 2 and 21). We have seen, in Pliny's testimony (sup. n. 8 innot.), that during Nero's rule, all African property belonged to only six citizens, and in Ammianus, we read that this situation continued worsening until late in the fourth century. In such a state lay Rome when Alaric sacked it (Gibbon, vol. 5, ch. 31, pp. 268–279). What can we infer from all of this? That in the progress of the human spirit toward perfection, it is more reasonable to expect that man will embrace primitive communal ownership than that he will succeed in reaching equality once property has been established. If accumulation is, then, a necessary evil, should the laws conspire to augment it, or should they strive to reduce it as much as possible?

35 We will be excused for citing the excellent treatise *Regalía de la Amortización*, on the rights of the Crown over entailed property, that our wise associate, [Pedro Rodríguez] the Count Campomanes, published in 1765, where with copious references to authorities on the subject and abundant arguments, he shows the justice of the law that he proposes; and the need for it with a massive number of testimonies that reveal the excesses to which land entailment has reached in our time. However, to verify this need we will only copy the notable expressions with which the defender of the kingdom of Galicia opened his allegation (in the question on primogeniture, or *majorat*), printed in Madrid with the title *La razón natural por el reyno de Galicia*: "Almost all of the surface of Galicia," he says, "under lower courts' jurisdiction, has been alienated from the crown: it is almost all in the hands of communities, churches,

152. Oh, the things the Society could say about them if it considered them in all their relations and effects! But the object of this Report obliges it to circumscribe its reflections to the evils that they cause upon agriculture alone.

153. The worst of these is the rise of property prices. Land, like all goods, registers in its price the alterations that come from its abundance or scarcity, and is worth more when less is sold, and less when more is sold. For this reason, the amount of land that is in circulation and the market will always be a key element in determining its value, and more so since the particular appreciation men feel for this kind of wealth makes them prefer it to all others.

154. That land in Spain has reached scandalous prices; that these prices are a natural effect of its scarcity in the market; and that this scarcity is derived mainly from the large amount of land that is entailed, are statements of fact that do not need to be proven. It is a notorious evil, and what we must do is show Your Highness its influence on agriculture, so that you may see fit to apply a remedy.

155. This influence will be easily demonstrated with a simple comparison between the advantages that the acquisition of landed property has for cultivation, and the disadvantages that result from when its acquisition is difficult. Compare the agriculture of countries in which the price of land is low, countries in which it is moderate and countries in which it is high, and the demonstration will be complete.

156. The United States of America [*Provincias Unidas de América*] is an example of the first [case].[36] There, wealthy persons invest their capital in land: a part of which is used to purchase a lot, another part to procure its population and enclose it and the final part to cultivate it, selecting a crop that will make the land as profitable as possible. Thus, agriculture in that country reaches a growth so prodigious that it seems almost incalculable, but their rural population, doubled in a space of a few years, and their immense exportations of grain and flour, give us a fair enough idea.[37]

---

monasteries and pious institutions, and the rest is attached to grandees, titles and gentlemen from within and without the province." This evil is even greater in a province that houses and feeds a tenth of the kingdom's population—a judgment on the rest of the country's fate can be formed accordingly.

36 A foreign *Gaceta* of the past 1792, which calculated the progress made by American agriculture, indicates: from August 1789 to September 1790 the United States exported 900,156 barrels of flour and crackers; 1,124,458 bushels (*boisseaux*) of wheat (that is nearly a third of a *fanega*); 21,765 of barley; 2,102,137 of corn; 98,842 of oats; 7,562 of *morisco* wheat; 38,752 of peas and beans; 5,318 barrels of potatoes; 100,845 *tercios* of rice; and 118,460 sacks of tobacco; moreover, around 2 million units of grain were destined for distillery production. And yet the population of that republic was no more than 4 million during that time.

37 The low price of land naturally lowers the price of its produce, and this encourages trade, placing products in the most faraway markets. If this were not the case, how could the rice of Philadelphia sell in Constantinople for a lower price than that of Italy and Egypt? See the *Madrid Gazette* of 11 February of the current year.

157. Such extraordinary cheapness was caused by fortuitous and temporary circumstances, but as long as land circulates freely, a fair limit on its price is always set, so that prosperity in agriculture is guaranteed. The consideration with which territorial wealth is held; the dependence, so to speak, of all classes in relation to the propertied class; the security with which it is possessed and the comfort with which it is enjoyed; and the ease with which it is transmitted to remote descendants, make land the prime object of human ambition. A general tendency moves all desires and fortunes toward this object, and when laws do not destroy it, the impulse of this tendency is the first and most powerful stimulus for agriculture. England, where the price of land is moderate, and where agriculture flourishes nonetheless, offers the best example and the greatest proof of this truth.

158. But that tendency has a natural limit: property's dearness. When land is excessively costly, the production of the land will infallibly decrease, along with the desire to acquire land. When the capital invested in land delivers a high return, investing in land is a useful and profitable speculation, as it is in North America; when the return is moderate, it is still a prudent and safe speculation, as the English case shows; but when the return is small, nobody pursues such an investment, or invests solely as a speculation out of pride and vanity, as happens in Spain.

159. The events caused by this situation ordinarily proceed in the following manner: first, capital flees from landed property to be employed in livestock, trade and industry, or in other, more profitable enterprises; second, nobody sells their land unless they have an extreme need to do so, because nobody harbors the hope of ever being able to acquire it again; third, nobody buys except in the extreme case of safeguarding a part of their fortune, because no other stimulus can move one to buy that which is very costly and gives low returns; fourth, because safeguarding their fortunes is the buyers' object, they have no incentive to improve the land they acquired, and the more they spend to acquire the land, the less they have to improve it, or because the incentive to safeguard their fortunes makes them buy even more land leaving less to improve their previous acquisitions; fifth, the desire to accumulate is naturally followed by the desire to make what has been accumulated inalienable, because nothing is closer to the desire to safeguard property than that of entailing it to posterity; sixth, as this increases the power of mortmain corporations and families, it increases the number of lands lost to entailment, because the more they acquire, the more means they have of acquiring, and, unable to sell what they once acquired, the progress of their wealth must be indefinite; and, seventh, this evil embraces large as well as small saleable lands—the former, because they are only accessible to the power of opulent bodies and families, and the latter, because since the number of people who have access to them is larger, competition makes them even dearer. Such are the factors that have led the nation's property to be possessed by a small number of individuals.

160. And in such a state, what can be said about cultivation? The first effect of its situation is to be forever separated from property, because it is not possible for large proprietors to cultivate all of their land; and, if it were, they would probably not

want to cultivate it all; and, if they did, they would not be able to do it well. If at some point necessity or whim moved them to cultivate a part of their property, they would either establish immense farmsteads, of imperfect and weak cultivation, as we see in the estates and olive groves planted in Andalusia by lords or monasteries; or they might prefer what is pleasant to what is useful, and like those powerful Romans against whom Columella so justly declaimed, they would replace with hunting grounds, horse pastures, orchards of trees valued for their shade and beauty, gardens, lakes and fishing ponds, fountains and waterfalls, and all the beauties of rustic luxury, the simple and useful labors of husbandry.

161. As a consequence, landlords, content with living in luxury and comfort derived from their rents, will expend their energies on increasing them, and rents will rise, as they have already done among us, to the highest possible level. Since agriculture does not offer it any utility, capital will flee from land and from cultivation, which, abandoned in the hands of weak and impoverished men, will be as weak and poor as they. For it is true indeed that the land produces in proportion to the funds that are invested in its cultivation, and, therefore, what product can we expect from a tenant farmer, whose only capital are his hoe and his own labor? Finally, instead of putting their capital toward improving and cultivating their lands, wealthy landowners will invest them in other enterprises, as so many grandees [*grandes títulos*] and monasteries already do, maintaining immense herds while their properties remain open, their enclosures broken, depopulated and imperfectly cultivated.

162. These are not, my Lord, exaggerations of zeal; they are certain, although sad, deductions that Your Highness would make by only directing your gaze at our provinces. In which of them is the best and largest portion of the landed property not entailed? In which is the price of land not so high that its yield barely reaches 1.5 percent? In which have rents not risen scandalously? In which are estates not unenclosed, depopulated, without trees, without irrigation or improvements? In which is agriculture not abandoned to poor and ignorant tenant farmers? In which, alas, does money not flee the countryside to find employment in other professions and enterprises?

163. Certainly we can cite some provinces where the fertility of the soil, the mildness of the climate, the proportionality of irrigation or the laboriousness of its inhabitants has sustained cultivation against this powerful and harmful factor. But these same provinces will give Your Highness the most conclusive evidence of the unfortunate effects of entailment. Let us take Castile as an example, which is still referred to, and for good reason, as the granary of Spain.

164. There was a time when this province was the center of Spain's wealth and trade. When the Moors of Granada disrupted the navigation and commerce of the Andalusian coasts, and those of the east belonged exclusively to the kingdom of Aragon, Castilian navigation spilled out of the northern ports that go from Portugal to France, directing all activity and all relations into the interior of Castile, as its cities grew into emporia. The conquest of Granada, the union of the two Crowns and the discovery of the Indies gave Spanish commerce the most prodigious extension,

attracting all felicity and wealth; while the money that was concentrated in the Castilian markets was spread out along with abundance and prosperity. Arts, industry, commerce and navigation were greatly encouraged; but while the population and the opulence of the cities increased dramatically, the desertion of the countryside and the weakness of cultivation revealed the fragile and unworthy foundation of so much glory.

165. If we look for the cause of this phenomenon, we will find it in entailment and mortmain. Most of the landed property of Castile had passed to churches and other religious institutions, whose endowments initially were moderate, but in time became unreasonably immense. Castile also harbored the oldest and wealthiest estates entailed by primogeniture [*mayorazgos*], erected by *ricos-hombres* in their estates.[38] Most of the lands granted by King Henry [of Castile]—the so-called *gracias enriqueñas*—were in Castile, and they were turned into *mayorazgos* using the same laws that sought to circumscribe them. At that time, the foundation of new and immense *mayorazgo*s was very common in Castile, for the easy acquisition of rights to found them, even though they went against the well-being of so many sons, and the cruel Toro law that authorized entailing improvements caused more ravages where opulence was greatest. This very opulence opened wider the doors of further land entailment in Castile through the founding of new monasteries, schools, hospitals, confraternities, patronages, chaplaincies, *memorias and aniversarios*, which are but the reliefs of dying souls, always generous, whether moved by impulses of piety, the counsel of superstition or the remorse of a life of avarice.[39] What, then, was left in Castile of landed property that could be invested in industrious production? How did such prodigious wealth come to be buried in the properties of the idle?

166. The glory of this province passed like a streak of lightning. The commerce that had first spread over eastern and southern ports and was later fixed in Seville, thanks to the fleet system, drained Castile's wealth, ruined its factories, depopulated its villages and resulted in the poverty and desolation of its countryside.[40] If

---

38 E. N.: "Mayorazgo" was "the right that the firstborn had to inherit goods with the added quality that they shall remain perpetually within the family." Real Academia Española, *Diccionario*, 1783, 626, 1.

39 E. N.: *Memorias* and *Aniversarios* were religious services (masses) offered in suffrage of a deceased person's soul. The former could refer to any *obra pía* (religious institution) founded in memory of the deceased; the latter referred to the mass or other services offered on the yearly anniversary of the death.

40 We can get some idea on the progression of this depopulation from the words of the illustrious Manrique (cited by Mr. Campomanes), who says that in the last 50 years convents had been trebled; many families had emigrated; the priesthood had grown; and chaplaincies and convents had multiplied, and the number of their residents increased. He calculates that the population decrease was approximately seven-tenths, and he pointedly says that Burgos went from 7,000 to 900 families, and León from 5,000 to 500, while many small towns were entirely deserted. He adds that Valladolid was sustained by its High Court (*Chancillería*), Salamanca by its schools and Segovia by its cloth mills, but this was written in 1624, and from then until the end of the century depopulation continued unabated.

during its prosperous period Castile had established a rich and flourishing cultivation, agriculture would have retained its abundant wealth within the province,
and this abundance would have nurtured industry, industry would have sustained
commerce, and, despite the distance between its diverse places, wealth would
have flowed, at least for a longer time, through its old channels. But without agriculture, other economic activity crumbled in Castile [*sin agricultura todo se cayó en
Castilla*], along with the fragile bases of its precarious felicity. What has remained
of that old glory but the skeletons of its cities, formerly populous and full of mills
and factories, shops and warehouses, and today occupied by churches, convents
and hospitals that have survived the misery they themselves caused?

167. If commerce and industry in other provinces gained in this revolution [*revolución*]
what Castile lost, its agriculture, subject to the same evils, suffered the same fate. It
is enough to cite those territories in Andalusia that during a period of more than
two centuries were at the center of American commerce.[11] Is there by any chance a
single rural establishment in them that proves that their wealth was directed toward
agriculture? Was a single forest cleared; a single irrigation channel constructed?
Can one find a ditch, a machine, an improvement or a single monument that gives
evidence of the effort expended in favor of cultivation? Such works are found only
where land circulates; where it offers utility; where it passes from poor and sluggish
hands to rich and risk-taking [*especuladoras*] ones; and not where it is stuck in perpetuity in families dissipated by luxury; or in permanent bodies distinct in their very
character from all activity and good industry.

168. The present state of our provinces' agriculture should not be attributed to their
respective climates. Cultivation in Hispania Bætica [Andalusia] flourished under
the Romans, as Columella, the first of the agronomists who was originally from
there, testified; it also flourished under the Arabs, despite being governed by des-
potic laws, because neither the former nor the latter knew entailment or any of
the other obstacles that tie down property and constrain the liberty of cultivation
among us. These provinces have barely advanced since they were reconquered;
in fact, their production of oil and grain has decreased, and almost all of their fig
and silk production—which were among the goods traded most efficaciously by the
Moors—has disappeared. But is that all? Are not the irrigation systems in Granada,
Murcia and Valencia, practically the only ones that remain today, also the product
of African industry [*industria africana*]?

169. Let us once and for all sever those bonds that so shamefully stymie our agriculture. The Society knows very well the fair concerns that it must take into account
in reaching its judgment. Entailment, both ecclesiastical and civil, has interwoven
causes and reasons, which should not be lost sight of. But, Sire, asked by Your
Highness to propose the means to reestablish cultivation, would it not be unworthy
of your trust, if detained by absurd preoccupations, were the Society to abstain
from applying its principles to agriculture's restoration?

---

41 E. N.: *Revolución* is synonymous with change in this context.

1st. Ecclesiastical

170. If ecclesiastical mortmain is contrary to all the principles of civil economy, it is no less contrary to those of Castilian legislation. It was an old maxim of this legislation that churches and monasteries could not aspire to landed property, and a fundamental law followed from this maxim's prohibition. This law, solemnly established in the Cortes of Benavente for the Kingdom of León, and in those of Nájera for Castile, was extended with the conquests to Toledo, Jaen, Cordova, Murcia and Seville in their *fueros*.[12]

171. All general Castilian codes sanctioned this law, as we can see in the primitive *fueros* of León and Sepúlveda; that of the *fijos-dalgo* or the old *fuero* of Castile; the decree of Alcalá; and even the *fuero real*, although contemporary to the *Partidas*, which instead of consecrating these and other maxims of national rights and discipline, simply transcribed the ultramontane maxims of Gratian. There was no municipal *fuero* that did not adopt it for its territory, either, as we can see in those of Alarcón, Consuegra and Cuenca, Cáceres and Badajoz, Baeza and Carmona, Sahagún, Zamora and many others, granted or confirmed in their most part by the piety of [King] Saint Ferdinand [III] or the wisdom of his son [Alfonso X, the Wise].

172. So, what if greed overcame this healthy barrier? Politics always reestablished it, not out of hatred for the church, but to favor the state; and not so much to hinder the enrichment of the clergy, but to prevent the impoverishment of the people that so generously made donations to it. From the tenth until the fourteenth century, the kings and the Cortes worked together to fortify this barrier against outbreaks of piety; and if after that time, in the shadow of the convulsions that agitated the country, this venerable dam was broken and left unprotected, the government, in the midst of its weakness, took great pains to restore it. King John II of Castile taxed mortmain donations to a fifth of their value, exclusive of the *alcabala* sales tax. And the Cortes of Valladolid of 1345, of Guadalajara in 1390, of Valladolid again in 1523, of Toledo in 1522 and of Seville in 1532 clamored for a law to contain mortmain and received one, albeit ineffectual [*en vano*]. The Cortes of Madrid, in 1534, sought to erect another dam to keep this enormous evil at bay. But what dams, what barriers, could contain the efforts of greed and devotion, joined together in a common purpose?

Regular clergy

173. If one were to study the particular origin of monastic possessions, one would find that the regular clergy's possessions are more a patrimony of the nobility than of the clergy, and that it belongs more to the state than to the church. Most of the old monasteries were founded and endowed as retreats for families, who remained the

---

42 E. N.: "Fuero. s.m. Ley, o estatuto particular de algún reyno, ó provincia. *Forum*. [Law or statute specific to a kingdom or province]" Real Academia Española, *Diccionario*, 1783, 498, 2.

titleholders.[13] When the only profession known to the nobility was that of arms, and the only wealth was that of spoils, stipends and rewards obtained in war, the noblemen who were unfit for warfare were condemned to celibacy and poverty, and they dragged along with them an equal number of damsels [*doncellas*] of their own class. So that these victims of politics could subsist, an incredible host of monasteries were founded called *dúplices* because they took in individuals of both sexes; they were also called *herederos*, or heirs, because they were part of families' estates and inheritances, and they were not only inherited, they were also split, sold, exchanged and leased through contracts or testaments from one family to another. They were filled more by necessity than by religious vocation, and were more havens from misery than for devotion, until finally the laxity of their discipline made them disappear, and their buildings and goods were incorporated and merged into churches and free monasteries, whose flourishing observance made them a living argument against the vices of their previous constitution.

174. Thus, free monasteries became wealthier and wealthier, and at the same time, the corruption and ignorance of the secular clergy led these monasteries to attract the trust and devotion of towns and people, and such is origin of their proliferation and aggrandizement in the tenth, eleventh and twelfth centuries. But as the laxity of the clergy led to the proliferation of monasteries, that of the property-owning monks led to the emergence and multiplication of mendicant monks. These monks also relaxed their rules and became property owners, motivating reforms of one and another, which was the origin of the many institutes and religious orders and of the portentous multiplication of convents, which were supported by alms and thereby decreased the common people's means of subsistence.

175. God prevents the Society from directing its pen to the deprecation of institutions whose sanctity it greatly respects, and whose services to the church, in its worst moments of affliction, it knows and recognizes. Yet, forced to reveal the evils that afflict our agriculture, how can it remain silent with regard to truths that so many saintly and pious men have already denounced? How can it ignore that our regular clergy is neither corrupt nor ignorant, as it was in the Middle Ages? That its enlightenment [*ilustración*], its zeal and its charity are greatly commendable? And that nothing could be more injurious to it than the notion that it needs so many and so diverse assistants to perform its duties? Be it then left to the secular ecclesiastical authorities to determine the most appropriate existence, number, form and functions of these religious bodies, and we will limit ourselves to proposing

---

43 Friar Prudencio de Sandoval and chroniclers Yepes and Manrique have much to say about such monasteries, whose abundance would be incredible if it were not recorded in so many archives. There is particular information on those in Cantabria in Fr. Sota (*Príncipes de Asturias y Cantabria*, bk. 3). Those in Asturias are recorded by Fr. Carballo (pt. 2, tit. 19, chaps. 13 and 14), and he seemingly accurately calculates the number of churches and monasteries founded in Galicia at more than 400, for 18 were added to that of Samos only, 35 to that of San Martín de Santiago, and more than 40 to that of Celanova. See the *Alegación por el Reino de Galicia* cited above.

to Your Highness the influence that, as landholders, they have in our agriculture's fortune.

Secular clergy

176. The acquisition of land by the secular clergy was more legitimate and useful in its origin, but it was also terrible for agriculture. Acquisition began in great part as private foundations of churches that, like monasteries, remained the property of the founding families, of which there are still a great many relics in the host of ecclesiastical rights secularized in our northern provinces, most pointedly in the *prestamerías* of Biscay. At that time, these possessions were a sort of offering to the clergy, presented on the altars of religion to sustain its cult and its ministers. By this means, the state, freeing the clergy of the first of its cares, that is, procuring its own subsistence, secured for the people in its holy duties the first of all its succors, and this is why the law forbade churches and monasteries from obtaining landed property while securing their possession over *mansos* and dowry properties against any other claim or pretension.

177. With the passage of time, the constitution became consolidated, the clergy was regarded as one of its hierarchical orders and its members justly aspired to more wealth. Concurring with the nobility in the people's defense at war and in its government at the Cortes, the clergy also earned and was dignified with the graces that rewarded such services and encouraged their continuance. And, thus, while the law sought to keep the clergy from acquiring properties via contracts or wills, the monarchs, as a consequence of the conquests [of the Islamic territories in Iberia], granted them villas, castles, lordships, rents and seigneurial jurisdictions to compensate and honor them.

178. But when the old laws were forgotten, and the way to ecclesiastical mortmain was cleared, how swiftly the piety of the worshippers increased it! How many benefices, vicarages, *aniversarios* and pious establishments [*obras pías*] were founded following the promulgation of the Toro laws, which authorized indefinite entail and presented testators with the opportunity of entailing their property in mortmain as an act of sacrificial expiation? Perhaps the host of goods entailed this way is much higher than those acquired through the above-mentioned glorious titles, and perhaps the ills that this new type of mortmain caused agriculture, were also more severe and fatal.

179. It is certainly beyond the scope of the Society to determine whether the accumulation of titles, invented to keep within the church some ministers without clear function or office and henceforth disregarding the ancient discipline, have been more harmful than beneficial to the clergy, whose ranks kept increasing.[11] Moreover, it is

---

44 The 1787 Spanish census shows that we have 22,460 parish priests and vicars, and another 47,710 individuals in the regular clergy. Supposing that half of the 23,692 individuals who constitute the class of the beneficed clergy have a residence, assignation or office in the church (which is supposing a lot, for this class includes those graced with sinecure benefices, *prestamerias* and endowed vicarages), we can estimate that our number of ecclesiastical functionaries is 34,360, while 35,844 individuals are free from offices or functions.

certainly not the Society's intention to rob the moribund of the solace and consolation that these pious acts of fervor and devotion bring. If there is any abuse or evil in them, it is up to the church to find a remedy, and to Your Highness to promote it as its natural defender and protector of its canons. But in the meantime, can it be considered unbecoming to propose a means that reconciles the regard that such a pious and legitimate custom deserves, with the well-being and preservation of the state? Preserve the liberty of establishing these foundations, but forbid henceforth endowing them with landed property, ordering instead that the lands consecrated to them be sold within a given period by the very executors of the will, and that the endowments be fulfilled with *juros, censos,* stock in public funds and other such instruments. Proceeding this way we would respect the old laws without offending piety and close a large avenue through which land impetuously flows toward mortmain.

180. And why should other available avenues that funnel landed property to the ecclesiastical bodies not be closed? After the clergy is separated from wars and tumultuous public gatherings, it will be left to the holy and peaceful exercise of its ministry. Furthermore, its allowance will be sustained superabundantly by the state, in a way that has no precedent in Catholic countries. It will be relieved from its worldly needs, alleviating the people's burdens and enabling the state to redirect civil contributions to them. After all of this occurs, will the church have a fair and decorous reason to persist in entailing the remainder of the kingdom's territorial property?

181. It may well be that this effort is neither as certain nor as great as it is supposed; or that only a small and concerned portion of our clergy is embarked upon it. At least, this is the view of the Society, which has seen how over time many wise and pious churchmen have spoken against the excess of wealth and the abuse of their orders' acquisitions. Why is it not possible that in a time in which so many learned and zealous prelates, following the footsteps of the holy fathers, struggle tirelessly to reestablish the pure and ancient discipline of the church; in a time when so many pious churchmen renew the examples of moderation and ardent charity that used to illuminate it; in a time when so many religious men edify us with their spirit of humility, poverty and abnegation, some of us may share the same desires manifested by the Márquez, the Manríques, the Navarretes, the Riberas and so many other venerable churchmen?

182. The Society, Sire, animated by respect for, and trust in, our clergy's wisdom and virtue, is so far from fearing that an entailment law could be repugnant to it, that it indeed believes that if Your Highness were to charge the reverend prelates of the church with disposing of their landed property themselves so that it may return to the hands of the people, whether by selling them and transforming their product into *imposiciones de censos* or public funds, or by giving them in perpetual emphyteutic leases with the right of redemption, they would hasten to render this service to the country with the same zeal and generosity with which they have always succored it in all its troubles.

183. Perhaps this sign of trust, so worthy of a pious and religious monarch as well as of a wise and charitable clergy, would be a better remedy against mortmain than all of

the plans that politics can devise. Perhaps all the reforms attempted in this respect have failed solely because dictates were preferred to counsel, authority to suggestion; and because we expected from the laws what should have been expected from the clergy's piety and generosity. Whatever else can be said of the old institutions, the clergy certainly enjoys its property with legitimate and fair titles; it enjoys it under the protection of the law; and it cannot look at the designs bent upon the violation of its rights without feeling apprehension. But the clergy understands better than we do how much the upkeep of all this property is a hindrance and distraction, and how easily it can become a lure for the greedy and a danger to the pride of the weak. It also knows that, transferred into the hands of the laborious people, its true bequest—tithes—will grow, and misery and poverty will diminish. Given the clergy's generosity, is it not fairer to expect a decorous resignation of its lands that will earn it the people's gratitude and veneration, than its acquiescence to a despoilment that will vilify it in their eyes?

184. But if such a hope unfortunately turned out to be vain; if the clergy insisted on keeping all of the territorial property it now holds in its hands (something that the Society does not fear), then at the very least preventing the clergy from holding even more land seems indispensable, and so the Society will close this article with those memorable words pronounced 28 years ago before Your Highness, by the wise magistrate who at that time was promoting a law that would limit mortmain, with the same ardent zeal with which he later promoted the Agrarian Law: "The public is too enlightened," he said, "to admit new contradictions to this prerogative. The need for a remedy is so large that it seems regressive not to seek it: the whole kingdom has demanded it for centuries; and it expects that the magistrates' intelligence will propose a law that conserves landed property for the people, and prevents the ruin that threatens the state if properties continue to be placed in mortmain."

2nd. Civil: mayorazgos *[primogeniture entail]*

185. The situation of civil entailment is of greater urgency still, because it progresses more rapidly, since the number of families is larger than that of ecclesiastical bodies, and because the tendency to accumulate is more active in the former than in the latter. Accumulation necessarily enters into families' plans, because wealth is the chief support of their splendor, whereas in the clergy, accumulation can only enter accidentally, because the church's permanence rests on incontestable foundations and its true glory can only derive from the clergy's zeal and its moderation, which are independent from, and perhaps even foreign to, wealth. For concrete evidence of this truth, one need only to compare the number of entailed properties in secular families to the number held by ecclesiastical bodies to see that the former is much larger, even though *mayorazgo* began centuries after the clergy's first acquisitions.

186. The term *mayorazgo* [primogeniture entail] epitomizes all of the difficulties of the matter at hand. There is barely an institution that is more repugnant to the principles of a wise and just legislation, and yet there is hardly another that deserves

greater regard in the eyes of the Society. If only it were able to present it to Your Highness in its true perspective, and reconcile the consideration that it deserves with the great object of this report, which is agriculture's well-being!

187. It is necessary to confess that the right to pass on property after death is not contained either in [God's] designs or in the laws of nature. The Supreme Maker assured men's existence by the following means: the child's is based upon fatherly love; the elderly's is founded upon filial care; and that of the robust man is founded on the need to work, which flows from the continual excitement of his love for life. Hence, [the Supreme Maker] liberated men from taking care of posterity, calling them entirely to the incomparable reward of their ultimate end. Therein, men in their natural state have a very imperfect idea regarding property; oh, if only they had never developed it further!

188. But gathered in societies, to secure their natural rights, they carefully established [*cuidaron de fijar y arreglar*] the right of property, which they saw as the most important and the one most linked with their existence. First they made it stable and independent of its holders' occupation, and from this, dominion was born; then they made it commutative, and this gave origin to contracts; and, finally, they made it transmissible in the event of death, and opened the door to wills and successions. Without these rights, could they have cherished or improved properties that were constantly vulnerable to the greed of the most astute or the strongest?

189. The ancient legislators gave this transmissibility the greatest possible extension. Solon consecrated it in his laws, and following his example, the Decemvirate included it in the Twelve Tables. Though these laws identified the intestates' progeny as the rightful, compulsory heirs, they did not limit the freedom of bequeathing assets in their favor, thinking that good sons did not need this legal protection and bad sons did not deserve it. While Rome was virtuous, this liberty prevailed, but when corruption began to weaken sentiments and dissolve the links of nature, these limits were set in place. Children expected from the law what they should have expected from virtue alone, and what was done to stop one corruption, became a stimulus for another.

190. Yet, how far from these principles is our present legislation! Neither the Greeks nor the Romans, nor any of the ancient legislators, extended the faculty of bequeathing outside one line of succession. Such an extension would not have perfected, but destroyed, property rights, for in granting a citizen the right to dispose of his property forever, the entire series of owners who could have benefited from that property is forbidden from holding it.

191. And, despite this, our plebeian jurists, superstitious devotees of Roman institutes, justify the existence of *mayorazgos* with them, using the cases of common entails and guardianships or legacies in trust. But how are these things similar to *mayorazgos*? Roman common entail was none other than the conditional identification of a second heir if the primary heir did not inherit, and the guardianship referred to designating the heir of a child who should die before coming of age. Neither one nor the other hinted at the possibility of extending the final will to successive

generations, but to other ends, worthy of a fair and humane legislation: the first to avoid the stain that sullied the memory of the intestate; the second, to secure the rights of pupils from their relatives' scheming.

192. Similar observations can be made regarding trusteeships, which were simply confidential charges through which the testator transferred the inheritance to one who could not receive it directly through a will. At first, they were not legally binding. During the Republic, the fulfillment of trusteeships was left to the faithfulness of the trustee. Augustus, whose name is implored by some fiducial commissioners, made fulfillment obligatory and was the first who turned this duty of piety and appreciation into a civil obligation. It is true that there were also family trusteeships among the Romans, but these were used not to prolong, but to divide successions; not to fix them upon a series of persons, but to extend them across a family; not to take them into posterity, but to distribute them among a limited and existing generation. Finally, Emperor Justinian, expanding this right, extended the effects of trusteeships to the fourth generation, but without altering the nature and succession of assets, nor without consolidating them forever in one scion. Who can actually recognize in such moderate institutions the slightest outline of our *mayorazgos?*

193. Certainly, granting a citizen the right to transmit his fortune to an infinite series of owners, leaving the conditions of this transmission to his will alone, independently of the successors but also of the laws; removing forever property's commutability and transmissibility, which are its most precious attributes; and trusting the preservation of a family to the endowment of one individual in each generation at the expense of the poverty of the rest, while binding this endowment to the accident of birth [order], disregarding virtue and merit, are repugnant not only to the dictates of reason and to the sentiments of nature, but also to the principles of the social pact and to the general maxims of legislation and politics.

194. Vain is the attempt to justify these institutions by linking them to the monarchical constitution, because our monarchy was founded and rose to its greatest splendor without *mayorazgos.* The *Fuero juzgo,* which regulated public and private law in the nation until the twelfth century, does not contain a single trace of them. Moreover, though it is full of maxims that come from Roman law, and is quite concordant with it in matters of inheritance, it does not include a single reference to substitutions and trusteeships. Nor do the codes that preceded the *Partidas* mention them except to indicate they were recognized by civil law. From what source, then, could such a barbaric institution have been derived?

195. Undoubtedly, [it derived] from feudal law. The law that prevailed in Italy in the Middle Ages was only one of the primary objects of study of Bolognese jurists. Our own legal scholars drank from the doctrines of that school, planted it in the Alphonsine legislation, cultivated it in the schools of Salamanca, and there lie its truest seeds.

196. If only, having admitted this destructive doctrine, they had molded the succession of *mayorazgos* on the succession of fiefs! Most of the latter were transferable, or at

least only lifelong, and they consisted of personal services, or rents in money, that they were called *de honor y de tierra* [of honor and land]. When there were landed and inheritable assets to be divided among the descendants, these did not go beyond an individual's grandchildren. Yet the great and pernicious evil of *mayorazgos* was derived from this weak principle.

197. The oldest record of *mayorazgos* in Spain dates from the fourteenth century, but they remained extremely rare. The need to moderate the *mercedes enriqueñas* reduced many great estates to *mayorazgos*, albeit of a limited nature. But others aspired to perpetuity, and the Crown opened its doors to them by setting down conditions that enabled such *mayorazgos*. Lawyers then sought to surmount the barriers that the laws placed on entailments; the Cortes of Toro finally lifted them at the end of the fifteenth century; and, from the early sixteenth century, the law placed no limits or restraints on *mayorazgos*.[15] Already in this period, holders of entitlements regarded and defended them as if they were indispensable to the reproduction of the nobility and insepara-ble from it. But did the constitutional nobility that founded the Spanish monarchy, in battle against Spain's ferocious enemies for centuries, gloriously expanding its limits, defending their *patria* with the force of arms while governing it with good counsel, whether fighting in the battlefield, debating in the Cortes, upholding the throne, or defending the people, that nobility which has always been the shield and support of the state, did it require *mayorazgos* to be illustrious or wealthy?

198. No, indeed: the nobility was wealthy and owned great swathes of land, yet it did not inherit its fortune, but rather acquired and won it by the strength of its sword, so to speak. The rewards and recompenses of their valor were lifelong and reli-ant on merit, and when they were bequeathed as inheritance, they were divided among all the children, who were permanently charged with the kingdom's public defense, and dependent upon it. If cowardice and idleness excluded them from this defense, they also led to the dissipation of the fortune that came with it in a single generation. Does not history present us with many illustrious names that in less than a century are eclipsed by others that burst onto the scene in splendor, and are

---

45 It is certainly noteworthy that Spanish law [*el derecho español*] has been subverted by the very legislation that is supposed to uphold and improve it. Our jurists, exclusively devoted to the study of Roman jurisprudence, flooded the judicial arena [*foro*] with a host of conflicting opin-ions that constantly perturbed the judges. In the hope of fixing the legal truth, the Cortes of Toro gave sanction to [*canonizaron*] the most disastrous opinions. Expanding the doctrine of trusteeships and fiefs, their laws gave shape to the first type of *mayorazgos*, although that name had as yet to tarnish our legislation. By countenancing the perpetual entailment of property, which the testator might leave to whom he pleased, to the prejudice of his legitimate heirs, celibates were encouraged to leave the whole of their property in mortmain. By admitting proof of immemorial possession as akin to titles, against the presumption of the most rightful laws, which assume that all property is free, communicable and transmissible, they changed the free property of families into property entailed in perpetuity. And, by extending the right of representation from the lineal descendent to the collateral relatives, and from the fourth generation ad infinitum, they opened that unfathomable chasm into which landed property falls and is buried everyday.

laureled thanks to their prowess and services?[46] Such was the effect of graces earned by personal merit, and not by the accident of birth; such was the influx of reputations attached to persons and not to families.

199. But let us concede that *mayorazgos* are indispensable for the preservation of the nobility: what justifies them beyond that? What reason can legitimate the unlimited liberty of establishing them, granted to whomever has no heirs, whether he is noble or plebeian, rich or poor, with little or great wealth? And, above all, what justifies the right to entail the third, and the fifth parts, that is to say, the moiety of all the land in the kingdom at the expense of blood relatives?[17]

200. The law of the *Fuero* granted the right to improvements, so that good parents could reward the virtue of good children. Toro's law, which allowed entailing improvements, deprived both parents and children of this recourse and this recompense, and robbed virtue to satisfy the vanity of families' future generations. What, then, was the favor that the nobility obtained from this law? Did not this law open wide a door that since the sixteenth century has allowed many families that amass a moderate fortune to burst into *hidalguía*? Are we to consider favorable to the nobility the institution that has most contributed to vulgarizing or debasing it?

201. The Society, Sire, always will look upon the nobility's *mayorazgos* with the utmost respect and indulgence, and in this delicate matter it will yield its opinion in their favor. If their institution has changed much in our days, it is not the nobility's fault, but the effect of the instability that invariably accompanies politics when the latter deviates from nature. The nobility is no longer entrusted with the charge of governing the state in the Cortes, nor defending it in the battlefields, it is true: but can it be denied that [*mayorazgos*] have brought it nearer to these glorious tasks?

202. Modern history always represents the nobility as assiduously performing such glorious tasks. Free from the care of procuring its own subsistence; obliged to sustain a favorable reputation worthy of its class; pushed by its education toward the recompenses of honor and distanced by it from those related solely to interest, where could nobility find a more worthy employment for its lofty ideals if not in the careers associated with fame and glory? Thus, we see the nobility anxiously running toward

---

46 Already in the sixteenth century, the Bishop of Mondoñedo observed that many illustrious lineages that had in other times been renowned and admired were buried in obscurity and poverty, citing, among others, the Albornoz, Tenorio, Villegas, Trillo, Estevanez, Quintana, Viedma and Cerezuela families, etc. Guevara, epist. Fam. pt. 1. Letter of 12 December 1526.

47 The *Real Cédula* of 1789 has limited entailments by way of improvement, and certainly remedied a very grave ill, because although entailments are generally harmful, small ones are even more so, not only because of the disorders that they cause in families and the public, but also because the ease with which they can be produced increases entailment. But what is the cause of the indulgence with which this law regards large entailments? Would it not be better to close this door completely, leaving in its stead the *Fuero*'s law? Permit parents to recompense their children by a third or fifth part, whether their fortune be large or small, but do not let them add the charge of entailment to improvements, depriving their descendants and the country from the influx that this healthy law can produce by reforming public customs.

such careers. A noble portion of youth consecrates part of their families' subsistence and the solace of the years of its bloom to the arid and tedious study that obligatorily precedes civilian and ecclesiastical employments. But, besides these, many illustrious young men are called to the army and the navy: by what vocation? Who sustains them in the long and painful transit to their first ranks? Who enslaves them to the most exact and rigorous discipline? Who makes them suffer gladly its difficult and dangerous obligations? Who, finally, enlarges before their eyes the hopes and illusions of rewards, and thus drives them to arduous undertakings in search of the smoke and mirrors of glory that will be their only recompense?

203. It is undeniable that neither birth nor class carries with it virtue and talent, and that therefore it would be a grave injustice to close the path to the armed services and their rewards to some classes and persons. However, it is as difficult to find the valor, the integrity, the elevation of spirits and the other great qualities that great employment demands among those who have received a poor or obscure education, or among those who engage in activities whose continuous exercise reduces the spirit by presenting to it no stimulus beyond necessity and no motivation beyond interest, as it is easy to find them in the midst of abundance, splendor and even the very concerns of those families that are used to preferring honor to convenience, and that do not seek fortune, but fame and glory. Confounding these ideas that are confirmed by the history of nature and society would be the same as denying the influence of the opinion of others on a man's conduct; it would be like expecting that the same principle that produces the material exactitude of an attorney's clerk begets that holy inflexibility with which a magistrate turns a deaf ear to the demands of friendship, beauty or favors; or resists the violent hurricanes of power. It would be like supposing that the blind and mechanical obedience of a soldier's disposition is what gives serenity and composure in battle to a general, when the latter alone assumes the responsibility for his troops' obedience and valor, and in one transient action risks his reputation, which is the most precious of his possessions.

204. It is fair, then, Sire, that since the nobility can no longer win estates or wealth in battle, that it be supported by those won and bequeathed by its ancestors; it is fair for the state to secure the honor and gallantry of its magistrates and defenders by elevating their ideas and sentiments. Let the nobility keep their *mayorazgos*, but since entitlements are an evil that is indispensable to generate this good, let them be treated as a necessary evil, and reduce them to a minimum. This is the golden mean found by the Society that avoids two equally dangerous extremes. If Your Highness looked upon its maxims in light of the old ideas, they would certainly seem harsh and strange; but if, by an effort as worthy of your wisdom as of the importance of the object at hand, these maxims were elevated as principles of the legislation which you know so profoundly, Spain would be free from the evil that most oppresses and weakens it.

205. The first policy that the nation demands of these principles is the repeal of all laws that allow the entail of landed property. The entailments carried out until the present under your authority should be respected; but there have been so many of

them, and they are so harmful to the public, that their pernicious influence must be limited as soon as possible. Therefore, entailment celebrated by contracts among the living must cease, along with that of entailments in wills via improvements, trusteeships, legacies and all other means, so that, acknowledging all citizens' faculty of disposing of their property in life and death according to the law, they are not allowed to enslave landed property by forbidding its sale or by imposing duties that are so high that they amount to the same thing.

206. Preventing the creation of new *mayorazgos* as necessary, as we have shown, is at the same time fair, because the faculty of bequeathing their property through testaments is granted to citizens by laws, not by nature, and if laws grant it, laws can undoubtedly modify it. And what modification would be fairer than that which, conserving the spirit of our old legislation, the right to transmit property after death, circumscribes it to one generation, to save the rest?

207. It may be said that by closing the door to entailments, a path to nobility is closed, and a stimulus to virtue is therefore removed. The first part is true, but it is also convenient. The actual nobility, far from losing out, will benefit from this, because its good reputation will grow in time, and it will not be confused nor debased by the increase in its numbers. But the nation will benefit even more, because the more avenues it closes to the sterile classes, the more it will have opened to the useful professions; and because nobility that has no other origin than wealth is not the one the nation needs.

208. The second part is not as formidable an objection. Besides the glory that invariably accrues to illustrious actions, and that constitutes the best and most solid nobility, the state can grant titles, personal or hereditary, to those who deserve it, without necessarily granting the faculty to entail. If the children of a citizen [*ciudadano*] so distinguished were to follow his example, they would turn a lifelong title of nobility into a hereditary one; but what would be lost if they were unable to do so? There can never be more valuable titles than those whose conservation depends on merit.

209. Above all, the sovereign can make exceptions to this general rule as he sees fit. When a citizen, renowned for his great and continued services, is elevated to that level of glory that carries with it the people's veneration; and when the rewards given for his virtue increase his fortune along with his glory, the capacity of founding a *mayorazgo* to perpetuate his name can be the ultimate recompense. These exceptions, dispensed sparingly in deserving cases, far from damaging, would be quite fruitful examples. But let us be careful, because justice and circumspection are absolutely necessary to prevent the debasement of these graces; for, Sire, if favor or importunity wrest them for those who have grown rich in the Indies, through *asientos* [monopoly contracts], or mercantile or industrial activities, what reward will the state reserve for its benefactors?

210. The evil caused by *mayorazgos* is so great that it will not be enough to stop their progress: other solutions must be applied. The most evident, if not the worst of all ills, is caused to every family in whose favor a *mayorazgo* was founded. Nothing is more

repugnant than seeing individuals of noble families whose elder sons enjoy great and profitable *mayorazgos*, without estates or careers, condemned to poverty, celibacy and idleness. The supreme equity of the Royal Courts of Justice, endeavoring to reconcile the rights of entailment and the privilege of rank, with the rights of blood, taxes these primogenitures with annuities in favor of these ill-fated siblings. But this remedy creates another evil, for annuities hurt the entailed property by diminishing its returns; they therefore weaken the tie between self-interest and the land's production, and exacerbate the principle of ruin and abandonment that is inherent in unalienable properties. It would therefore be more just to allow heirs to sell entailed estates rather than to burden them with paralyzing annuities.

211. It is true that by these means some *mayorazgos* would be diminished and others extinguished: well, let it be so! After all, the immense entailments that foment excessive wealth, and the corruption that invariably comes with it, are as pernicious to the state as those that, too small to be productive, feed the pride and idleness of a great number of poor *hidalgos*, who are lost to the useful professions that they disdain and to the illustrious careers that they cannot follow.

212. But this is no reason to fear that our nobility would diminish. Nobility is a hereditary quality and, therefore, perpetual and inextinguishable. It is also divisible and multipliable ad infinitum; because communicated to all the branches that descend from the noble trunk and seed, its progression through time knows no end. It is true that it is sometimes lost or confounded in poverty [*se confunde y pierde en la pobreza*]; but if this were not the case, what would become of the state?[48] What of nobility itself? Would there be a single non-noble family in the kingdom? And if it were enjoyed by all, how could nobility be a quality that distinguished and conferred privileges upon some families from all others?

213. The public cause also demands that *mayorazgo* holders are allowed to give the entailed property in emphyteusis. They are now legally forbidden from making such a contract because it is regarded as equivalent to selling the property's possession. But why not allow a transaction that, on the one hand, conserves the entailed property within the family by reserving its dominion and, on the other, secures the improvement of rents by making a co-participant responsible for them?

214. Fraudulent operations might be concealed in the design of certain emphyteutic leases, but it would be easy to prevent them by requiring that the necessary information be delivered to the competent territorial authorities and, if necessary, with the sanction of the superior magistrates of the province. The participation of the *mayorazgo*'s immediate successor in the inquest, or of the syndic if the successor were underage, would be enough to prevent the inconveniences that could accrue in the granting of such a power.

---

48 The rule established in Castile that made those who could not sustain its luster and functions relinquish their *hidalguía* proves the degree to which our elders conciliated the cruel concerns of politics with the rights of humanity. See the *Fuero viejo* or the treatise on the *fijosdalgo*. Bk. 10, tit. 5, n. 16, p. 27 of the Aso and Manuel edition.

215. Agriculture, Sire, justly demands this policy, because the interest of tenant farmers will never be more active than when they are coproprietors, and when the sentiment that they work for themselves and their children encourages them to improve their lands and perfect their crops. This coming together of two interests and two capitals over the same object will constitute the greatest of all the stimuli that can be offered to agriculture.

216. Perhaps this might be not merely the only, but the fairest and most direct means to banish immense estates from our midst; to secure the diversification and population of our countryside; to link cultivation with property; and to make land productive all year, so that what today is achieved as a result of fallowness and down times can be multiplied with nourishment and labor.

217. A doctrine derived from Roman law, introduced in the *foro* by our *mayorazgo* holders and their supporters, and sustained more by their opinions than by the authority of the law, has deprived the nation of these assets, and therefore deserves Your Highness's disapproval [*censura*]. According to it, the successor of a *mayorazgo* has no obligations regarding the lease agreements celebrated by his predecessor because, says the doctrine, he is not properly an heir, and therefore, he does not inherit these obligations along with the property. This interpretation has given rise to the maxim that leases expire with the lessor's death. But such a doctrine seems contrary to reason and equity because, details aside, one cannot deny that *mayorazgo* holders have the absolute domain of the entailed assets, as an heir would, lacking only the faculty to sell them or alter their succession. In any case, the notion of "administrator" that dogmatic jurists attribute to *mayorazgo* holders is enough to make contracts and other obligations binding and transmissible.

218. Moreover, such opinions cause irreparable damage to our agriculture, because they reduce tenancies to brief periods, and through this, discourage the cultivation of entailed estates. Since through their education, their class and their habitual residence, the owners are far removed from the countryside and rural professions, one cannot readily expect them to work the land; but if tenants are to have three- or four-year leases only, or other uncertain arrangements, how can we expect them to clear, enclose, plant and improve their plots? Is it not only natural that, under these circumstances, tenant farmers will only care to work the present crops, plundering so to speak the already cultivated areas, instead of caring for the land such that it gives future yields that they may not enjoy?

219. Another policy is therefore necessary, one that banishes that opinion from our courts of law; reestablishes the reciprocal rights of property and cultivation; allows holders of *mayorazgos* to enter into long-term leases, as long as 29 years; and guarantees that the terms set in tenancy contracts will hold firm. Economists attribute England's flourishing agriculture to a similar policy introduced there to secure the terms of tenancies in feudal estates.[49] Why, then, do we not adopt it in order to reestablish

---

49 Smith, bk. 3, ch. 2.

our own? Forbidding the collection of anticipated rents, so that the tenant who pays them has to assume their loss, would preclude a profligate landowner from cheating his successors, and thus prevent the only fraud that could be produced under the protection of this permission.

220. But though this liberty conforms to the principles of justice, nothing would be more repugnant to them than to turn it into a general, heavy-handed rule. The Society defends *mayorazgo* holders' right and capacity to grant long leases, but it is far from recommending a law that would fix the length of time of their leases, taking from them the liberty of abbreviating them, believing instead that such a law would be unjust. Its reflections elsewhere on this point prove just how much it disagrees with those extreme parties [*partidos extremos*] that, proposed to Your Highness to favor cultivation, would only serve to ruin it.

221. Finally, Sire, the repeal of the law of Toro, which prevents the children and heirs of a *mayorazgo*'s successor from deducting the improvements made to it, seems indispensable.[50] This law, which according to Mr. Palacios Rubios's testimony was approved hastily and without the proper counsel, was rendered more fatal by our jurists' ignorant application and interpretations than by its original disposition. Moreover, it should not exist at a time in which Your Highness is trying to purge our legislation of its vices. The Society does not need to demonstrate the damage done to cultivation by this law, nor even to show the injustice of the doctrines that founded upon it distract the care and concern of good and diligent parents from improving cultivation; because this law rewards those who under the shadow of authority sacrifice—out of pride and vanity—the sentiments of nature, and those who to aggrandize their names condemn their posterity to misery and helplessness.

222. Such are, Sire, the policies that the Society expects from Your Highness' supreme wisdom. There is no doubt that when you examine *mayorazgos* in all their linkages, you will find that many other policies are also necessary to prevent other evils, but the present ones are centered on succoring agriculture without depriving the state of the political advantages that it may derive from the institution of *mayorazgo*. Acknowledging the nobility as necessary to the conservation and splendor of the monarchy, these policies will add to the brilliant and stable regard with which the public regards its nobles. By shutting the avenues of obscure wealth that lead to

---

50 This law, which our lawyers and jurists label unfair and barbaric, is made even more so by the extension that they gave it in their commentaries. It strictly applied only to the repairs done to urban buildings [*edificios urbanos*], but they extended it to all types of improvements. The more you read the law, the further you are from grasping the reasons that could have prompted its writing. Is it possible that when it was no longer legal for individuals to build castles and strongholds; when repairing those that were falling apart was expressly forbidden; when the destruction of those still possessed by lords was ordered; when, finally, the government was struggling to take these bulwarks of feudal despotism from the nobility, which harbored insubordination and disregard toward justice and the law; is it possible that improvements and expansions of castles and forts were entailed by some lords? This should lead us to realize how far were sound political principles from the minds of the legal experts of the time.

noble titles, they open them only to glorious and worthy merit; and by calling upon noble youth to go down the paths of honor, their nobility will be committed to honor without expelling virtue and talents. Above all, Sire, these policies will place an insurmountable barrier to the mad rush to establish new *mayorazgos*; they will reduce within reasonable limits those immense estates that feed enormous and contagious luxury; they will dissolve without injustice or violence, but by a sort of attrition, those that undeservingly bear the *mayorazgo* distinction and serve as incentives to idleness; they will not allow the enslavement of property to hinder the liberty of cultivation; and they will reconcile the principles of politics that protect *mayorazgos*, with those of justice that condemn them, thus being as favorable to agriculture as they are glorious to Your Highness.

7th. Circulation of agricultural produce

223. Up to this point, the Society has examined the laws related to land and labor ownership; it still has to address those laws that address the property of the products begotten by the former two, for these influence cultivation quite powerfully by affecting the interest of those most immediately concerned with its prosperity.

224. Being the direct product of labor and constituting the tenant farmer's only property, the fruits of the earth must be regarded as sacred and worthy of the law's protection, for they represent on the one hand the subsistence of the most numerous and most precious portion of the individuals of the state, and, on the other, the only reward that their sweat and fatigue receive. None owes this property to fortune or the accident of birth: all derive it immediately from their ingenuity and dedication; moreover, it is precarious and uncertain, because it is greatly dependent upon the weather. These reasons make the fruits of the land deserving of the justice and the humanity of the government.

225. Tenant farmers are not the only group interested in this property's legal protection; landlords are as well. The products of the land are naturally divided between proprietors and farmers, so that they simultaneously represent the fruit of land and labor ownership. Thus, any law that undermines the property of these products will harm individual interest across the board, which is not only unfair, but also contrary to the object of agrarian legislation.

226. These thoughts should be enough to make a general qualification of all the laws that somewhat circumscribe the free circulation of the land's produce. From here forward, the Society will attempt to make general observations about these laws, since it would be impossible to comment on them one by one given the immense succession of laws, ordinances and regulations that have diminished the free circulation of produce.

227. Fortunately, the Society does not have to combat the most repugnant of all, because Your Highness's enlightenment has forever banished the grain tax from our legislation and policies. That law, born in a time of confusion and problems, which was

later repealed as often as it was reestablished; it was as feared by the weak agents of cultivation as it was disregarded by the rich landlords and merchants; and it was therefore as harmful to agriculture as it was a failure.

On fixed prices [De las posturas]

228. But while this law was repealed and the grain tax forever abolished, other agricultural goods are still burdened by an even more pernicious tax, one that is not regulated by legislators' equity and wisdom, but rather by the decisions [*arbitrios*] of municipal judges [who fix prices].[51] But why? If the price of grain, considered a basic necessity, is not determined by anyone, why are other fruits of the earth not treated similarly with regard to the setting of their price?

229. This alone reveals the carelessness with which legislation has addressed the food policies [*policía alimentaria*] of our towns, entrusting them to the prudence of governors, and approving or tolerating municipal ordinances far too easily; for taxes and *posturas* on foodstuffs are not derived from a general law, but from some of these principles.

230. With these in place, it was inevitable for the property of food produce to be exposed to arbitrariness, and therefore injustice, and this not only at the hands of municipal magistrates but also of their subalterns. Since both conducted themselves according to the ordinary rules of prudence, it was only natural for them to concern themselves only with the urban population's well-being, the only object of the *posturas*, and to forget that of the people who are the owners of the produce [*propietario de los frutos*]. Such is the origin of the food market's enslavement.

231. In the final analysis, however, this policy is no different from the other laws that harmed individual interest. The wellspring of abundance is not found in the town plazas, but rather in the fields; only liberty can open them and direct them toward the points where self-interest calls. Therefore, obstacles to the exercise of that interest detain or misdirect this abundance, and food scarcity is generated, not only despite of the *posturas*, but because of them.

232. It makes little sense, Sire, to expect that anything other than abundance will generate low prices; and it makes scant sense to expect this abundance from anything other than the free negotiation of the price of products. Only the hope of self-interest can excite the farmer to multiply his produce and bring it to market. Only liberty, by feeding this hope, can produce competition, and through it, the equity of prices that is so justly desired. Taxes, prohibitions and other precautionary rules do nothing but dampen that hope; they therefore discourage cultivation, diminish

---

51 E. N.: "Postura. El Precio que por la justicia se pone a las cosas comestibles [The price assigned by the justice to edible goods]. *Pretii præscriptio.*" Real Academia Española, *Diccionario*, 1783, 754, 3.

competition and abundance, and, in an inevitable reaction, cause scarcity by the very means devised to prevent it.

233. Among these rules, those that limit the liberty of food-market intermediary agents, such as hawkers, street vendors, mongers, etc. deserve special attention. These people are regarded with horror and treated harshly by ordinances and municipal judges, as if they were not necessary instruments, or, at least, useful in this commerce; or as if they were not to farmers what shopkeepers and merchants are to manufacturers and tradesmen.

234. An ignorance that is unworthy of our century is what inspired in our ancestors this unjust preoccupation. They claimed that these agents bought low to sell high, as if this is not inherent to all trade [*tráfico*]. It is notorious that advantageous differences in prices [*ventajas*] represent the value of the trade [*industria*] and the earning [*rédito*] from the trader's capital. Legislators did not calculate that the surcharges set by sellers on food prices compensated the time and labor that they had to spend seeking out the products in the roads and villages, bringing them to market, retailing these goods and assuming the losses and accidents that characterize this small trade. Our ancestors did not calculate that if farmers took these labors upon themselves, prices would also rise, for they would need to take into account the value of the time and work robbed from their profession and spent on these tasks. Otherwise, they would be sold at a loss, in which case farmers would rather consume them than sell them, or they would stop cultivating them altogether, and the market would be undersupplied. [Our ancestors] did not calculate that this division between farmers and middlemen, far from raising prices, keeps them low: first, because it economizes time and labor; second, because it increases the dexterity and knowledge of those involved, turning this trade into a profession; third, because the acquaintance of neighbors and clients it provides facilitates consumption; and, fourth, because by multiplying sales, a series of small gains become in fact a large and composite gain that benefits the classes that cultivate as well as those that consume.

235. All of this reveals that the countless regulations that fill the municipal records, such as those that prohibit sales outside the city; or oblige vendors to sell only at certain times, in certain places and following certain norms; those that privilege certain consumers—such as innkeepers and pub and tavern owners, who can provision their establishments before the general public, as if they were not at the service of the people—and that grant certain preferences and delays to particular individuals and corporations for their purchases, etc., like taxes and *posturas*, keep markets ill-supplied, because they too dampen self-interest and produce food shortages by decreasing competition and abundance.

236. Similar restraints are being devised to ward off monopolies, those monsters that municipal policy makers see hiding behind liberty everywhere. They do not seem to contemplate that although freedom may give rise to monopolies, it also reins them in, for in exciting general self-interest, it naturally produces competition, the mortal enemy of monopoly. They do not seem to consider that precisely because all of the agents involved in commerce aspire to be monopolists, none of them can achieve

this goal, for the competition among them places the power of fixing the price in the hands of the consumer. They do not appear to grasp that monopoly rears its ugly head only in the absence of competition, which is driven from the market by municipal regulations and vexations. And, at that moment, necessity makes consumers cast over it an accommodating veil, so that the vigilance and precaution of policy makers is not enough to unmask monopolist activity or defeat it. Finally, they do not seem to realize that monopolies occur frequently among goods that are subject to *posturas* and prohibitions, and not among those that are freely exchanged; in the latter, experience shows that vendors, far from hiding in the shadows, openly seek consumers, calling them, shouting for them or knocking on their doors to invite them to purchase all that they may need.

237. Regulations such as these are partly responsible for the shortage of certain goods that are both easily produced and widely consumed. Since farmers do not find it in their best interest to sell their goods at a fixed price in distant markets that vex them with formalities and aggravations, they simply stop cultivating them. And two or three who arrive at this same decision are enough to fix a general opinion in an entire province. Or can anybody find another origin to the shameful situation in which we recently found ourselves, having to import eggs from France in order to supply the markets of Madrid?

238. One should not make the mistake of regarding these goods with indifference, as if they were accidental to cultivation or had little to do with agriculture's general prosperity. There are countries where tenant farmers subsist thanks to them, for without their support they could not overcome the increase in rents caused by population growth on the one hand and land scarcity on the other. There are countries where fruits, vegetables, chickens, eggs, milk and other such products constitute husbandmen's only source of wealth. These goods are totally theirs, because the main crops are destined to pay for the expenses of cultivation, seeds, tithes, first fruits [*primicia*], offerings of St. James [*Santiago*], taxes and, above all, rent, calculated according to actual or presumed volume of the annual produce. They therefore constitute a worthier object of legislation's protection than so far has been acknowledged. Any person can easily demonstrate this by calculating what a rural family earns with an orchard, a pair of dairy cows and four or six goats for milking, a sow, a dovecote and a good poultry yard. Certainly, the estimated contribution made by this obscure source of public wealth, which is as little known as it is unappreciated in most of Spain, would prove great.

239. There is no doubt that there are other factors at play in the shortages of this type of goods. As long as lands remain unenclosed and poorly divided, and as long as estates are depopulated, we cannot expect an abundance of these goods, for this would require the multiplication of families and livestock, and their dispersion across the countryside; and the diligence, the economy, that no other scenario can provide. But even if this scenario existed, as it surely will, as a result of sound agrarian legislation, we cannot expect these goods to be produced until the principles that have thus far animated our towns' food policies are repealed.

240. Abundance and cheapness can only come from a series of reforms. The farmer will be inclined to multiply his livestock and fruit when he can sell them freely from his very own farm, at the roadside or at the first market that he happens upon; when anybody can act as the intermediary between the consumers and him; when the protection of these liberties animates the agents involved in this production and commerce. Then foodstuffs will be as abundant as permitted by the territory's given conditions of cultivation and consumption. With their self-interest thus excited, the former agents will strive to increase their production, and the latter to increase their sales; thus, competition in each sector will produce abundance and drive out monopoly, and by this simple and fair means, so much better than those generated by municipal prudence, we will have achieved the cheapness that is its first object, as well as a primary element of a flourishing urban industry.

241. This general doctrine is applicable to every kind of supplies, including those considered as indispensable for human subsistence. Certainly meat would be much cheaper if all cattle brought to the slaughterhouse for consumption were admitted, instead of being entrusted to a monopolist contractor. These, in turn, compensate for the low prices of the meat sold at auction by sacrificing the safety of the supply. A similar fate would befall wine and oil, if the *millones* and the ensuing precautions brought about by such a harsh tax were not abetted by municipal policies to keep them perpetually and necessarily scarce, without the least advantage for their cultivation.

242. The Society would deviate too far from its main purpose if it traced and described every relation that exists between the population of the countryside and that of the cities, and between urban and rural policies; and, therefore, it will close this article with a discussion of bread, which is the primary reason for the connection between them.

On general domestic trade

243. Bread, like all other tradable goods, is cheap or dear depending on whether it is abundant or scarce; and if we were to dispense with the alterations introduced in its trade by laws and public opinion, its price would be perfectly proportional to that of grain. Let us see, then, if this essential item, so delicate and worthy of the government's concerns, can regulate itself with the same simple principles that we have outlined. And in order to apply them with more certainty, let us begin by addressing the domestic grain trade.

244. There is a notable difference between this trade and that of other foods, and it undoubtedly gave rise to the various modifications with which the law has limited it. This difference is born from the fact that grains are considered a basic staple, or better yet, from townspeople's continuous demand for grain. The increase and decrease in the price of grain is not so much caused by the volume of the harvest; that is, by its actual abundance or actual scarcity; but rather by the public's perception regarding its abundance or scarcity. This perception is based not on

the amount of grain in vaults and storehouses, but on the amount for sale in the markets or stored in public granaries. Hence, any policy that addresses the grain trade would be fairer and more prudent if it bridged the gap between the public's perception of grain supplies and reality.

245. This reflection should enable us to understand that if free negotiation is useful in other food items, in grain it is both absolutely necessary and preferable to any other system, for none can be established without recourse to partial precautions and policies, and it is clear that these means influence public opinion on this basic good, heightening perceptions of fear regarding grain's scarcity or perceptions of security regarding its abundance.

246. This alteration, which in times of abundance can harm farmers and landowners by lowering the price of grain below the actual value given by the harvest's volume, is calamitous in times of scarcity, because fear acts upon the imagination more vividly than hope, and apprehension leads to rash conclusions more quickly than hopefulness. In such a situation, any measures implemented to remedy scarcity serve only to augment apprehension, and the magistrate's very solicitude will double the people's anxiety, depriving it of the rays of hope that are inseparable from desire, and condemning it to the anguish and agitation of fear, which are never more acute than when subsistence itself is threatened.

247. Therefore, since a free domestic grain trade is most favorable for consumers, and since the sole objective of the limitations that have been imposed on this trade is the relief and security of consumers, it is not without reason that freedom for agriculture should be claimed as well, a freedom that is indispensable for its prosperity and growth.

248. On the other hand, this freedom is founded on the most rigorous principles of justice. If it is an established truth that in some provinces of Spain grain harvests are insufficient to meet demand, while in others the harvest exceeds it, the liberty of domestic trade will justly favor both: the former by supplying what is indispensable for their subsistence; and the latter by the no less important compensation for their work and sustenance of their agriculture. Agricultural yields can fall beneath the level of consumption in each province, even amidst great freedom, because many other factors influence its destiny and can hinder its prosperity. But without this freedom, regardless of all else, it would never prosper nor exceed the consumption in each territory, because a relentless economic axiom, confirmed by experience, is that consumption is the measure of cultivation; and, so, if one province produces more than what it can consume, it will simply cultivate less, until production equals consumption; and, therefore, the excess will disappear, harming not only the fertile and abundant province, but also the sterile ones that could have benefitted from it.

249. This reasoning is sounder still when we consider that our agricultural provinces, being less industrial, must consume the manufactures of other provinces that are, for their part, less agricultural. These manufactures are therefore more expensive in the former, where their value is always proportional to salaried work, and this salary must

always be higher in the latter, because it is proportional to the price of bread. Besides, agricultural provinces pay for all the duties and risks that make industry dear in its development and commerce. Supposing, then, that in agricultural provinces the value of wheat is extremely low precisely because there is a surplus: neither the farmer nor the landowner will have enough to pay for the value of foreign manufactures, and not being able to subsist without them, since they have no industry of their own, their capital will constantly dwindle, and they will be impoverished; their agriculture will decline; and their population, which is sustained by it, will be on the path to ruin.

250. There are those who abuse these arguments when analyzing the existing relations between the sources of agriculture and industry, claiming that a ban on the commerce of grain will turn some provinces agricultural and encourage industry in others, making the former attracted to cultivation by the high prices of grain, and the latter to industry by manufactures' high prices. But these politicians [*politicos*] fail to grasp that nature has distributed its gifts differently; that agriculture and industry each require natural resources [*proporciones naturales*] not possessed by every province, and means that cannot be acquired all of a sudden; that the first requires extensive and fertile lands, funds and enlightenment [*luces*]; while the second requires capital, knowledge, activity, spirit of enterprise [*espíritu de economía*] and means to be communicated [*comunicaciones*]; and that it is as impossible for Castile, without these aids, suddenly to become industrial as it would be for Catalonia to become agricultural without the aforementioned attributes.

251. If something can overcome this inequality, it is without a doubt the domestic grain trade. Through it, agricultural provinces sell their surplus, increasing their annual wealth; and they will make that surplus larger by improving their agriculture, so that they might at last use part of that wealth to establish manufactures. And this progress can only be achieved through the free commerce of their grains, and not in accordance with any other principle. At the same time, the more industrial provinces will obtain the grain they need at a lower price, and thus they will be able to devote their wealth to increasing their industrial surpluses, and using the wealth thus obtained to improve their territory's agriculture to the level that their soil permits. Is this not demonstrated by the example of Catalonia, where agriculture and industry are constantly growing, as well as by the example of Castile, where they are constantly declining?

252. In an effort to reconcile the utility and risks of free domestic trade, peddlers, or *trajineros*, have been allowed in all provinces, while grain traders have been forbidden. But what is this measure, if not an attempt to turn into traders what are merely instruments of trade? Peddlers are a poor lot, with no other capital besides their labor and their pack animals, and if domestic trade is reduced to what they can buy and sell, the amount of tradable grain will be necessarily low, so that while many provinces will be condemned to hunger, others will be ruined by their very abundance. It is therefore impossible to succor one or the other without the intervention of more powerful commercial agents.

253. There is no reason to trouble ourselves over this matter: these agents will only be found in commerce because only the existing commercial capital can be dedicated to this object. On the other hand, only traders are capable of engaging in profitable and useful speculation with an article with so many and such complex relations; they alone, through their connections and correspondents, can combine the abundance of some provinces with the scarcity of others; they alone can transport great stocks of grain over long distances, overcoming all kinds of difficulties and risks; they alone can bear the odiousness that is associated with this trade thanks to the preoccupations of the people and the laws that foment them; finally, they alone have the foresight [*previsión*], constancy and diligent completion of intermediate tasks and operations, without which circulation is always limited, uncertain and sluggish.

254. Nevertheless, some will insist that a monopoly will destroy everything that freedom has created; and exerted by peddlers, such a monopoly might not be frightful, but it will inevitably be so if it is held by grain merchants. Indeed, the superiority of capital, understanding and means that the latter possess does not exist among the former. Peddlers are many; they are dispersed across limited spaces; and they are not inclined to great calculations. Accustomed as they are to compete against one another through transportation prices, they are incapable of coming together to undertake a common enterprise, and, therefore, they can only exercise limited and individual monopolies, that is to say, inconsequential ones. In contrast, merchants, established in the capital cities, which are the centers of the circulation of the provinces' money and grain, are informed of the circumstances of all the other corners of the land by their correspondents. Furthermore, naturally united by the common interests and relations of their profession, they are as willing to unite when self-interest pushes them to a common point as to wage war against each other when it divides them. What horrible monopolies over grain would they not seek to establish if unlimited freedom protected their dealings? In a single week, their operations could place the supplies of a whole province in their hands, and the towns' subsistence, peace and happiness would become mere playthings of their greed.

255. Herein, Sire, is all that can be said against freedom of the grain trade; herein the basis of all the restrictions imposed by the law. It would not be difficult to respond with reasoning as abstract as those who champion such a restriction. But the Society, which avoids dogmas and is not interested in anything other than the public's well-being, shall limit its arguments to the present state of our provinces, and examine power and influence of monopolies in them: perhaps this will indicate the way to an important and desired truth.

256. If the power of the law were enough to intimidate monopolists; if their operations were evident or easily discoverable; if interest did not multiply their artifices and resources, and the law would not increase their cautions, then the laws that forbid or restrict the domestic grain trade would be comparable to those that protect freedom. Knowing the effects of these types of law in the circulation of this precious merchandise, the simple comparison of their advantages and shortcomings would provide a true and constant result, and legislation could embrace them

both without a second thought. Yet sad experience often has demonstrated that the opposite is true; and the insufficiency of the laws against the maneuvers of greed is as notorious as the irresistible strength of interest against the power of the law.

257. Who would dare to guarantee that the most severe prohibitions are adequate to eliminate monopoly? Who can ignore that the very restrictions imposed by law have often favored and encouraged them? If evidence were necessary to prove this truth, would we not find it in the laws themselves? Reading their preambles, one perceives that monopolies have existed at all times and in all states, and also that it was the failure of the cautions against it contained in previous laws that prompted the promulgation of others. And if one were to continue this investigation up until the times when not only the legislator but even the municipal magistrate policed this branch of commerce, one would discover that monopolies in Spain were most frequent and scandalous under those restrictive laws.

258. And how could it be otherwise, if it was nurtured by unyielding necessity? Whatever legal system is adopted, should it not permit the trading of grain, so as to prevent some provinces from starving while others feed their excess grain to their pigs? And regardless of the conditions set for this trade, whatever its limitations, whatever agents are allowed to carry it out or whatever instruments they can have at their disposal, is there any doubt that need and self-interest will eventually place all of these elements in the hands of traders? Who but they would hazard their capital? Moreover, if other affluent persons did it, would they not do it as traders, with the same spirit, the same aim and even the same greed? How, then, can we repress a monopoly that is encouraged by so many factors, and that necessity itself foments?

259. Knowledge and experience show us beyond any doubt that monopoly multiplies its ploys at the same time as the law multiplies cautions against it. "Law does, deceit undoes," the saying goes. What happens when only peddlers are allowed to trade? Peddlers, muleteers, drivers: they are all the trader's confidants, his factors, his front men. And what is the effect of policies mandating the products in warehouses to be registered and labeled? Warehouses are transformed into granaries, and granaries into warehouses: the merchant does not store, but buys; and the owner who sells him the grain does not deliver it, but keeps it at the merchant's disposal, becoming his agent and charging him for the grain's storage. And what is the consequence of forbidding private transactions of grain outside the market? Fifty bushels are taken to market, while 500 bushels are sold privately! Only an Argus-eyed official could penetrate these simulated contracts, these obscure confidences, secured by a combination of interests! In the end, whether the government wants to see it, intervene in it and regulate it; or whether it trusts in the force of commerce and leaves the provisioning of the markets to God, everything is lost. Cries to heaven are heard, confusion grows, fear is awakened and, taking advantage of the situation and under the pretense of providing relief, monopoly arrives to procure its own enrichment as it destroys all prosperity. If only the history of our food shortages [*carestías*] had not confirmed this sad deception so recently and so often!

260. From this alone, one could conclude that freedom should be favored, because in multiplying the number of suppliers and facilitating sales, it is the sole obstacle standing in the way of monopolies. But two elements that are unique to our situation, and, for that very reason, powerful, prove even more conclusively that liberty would nowhere be more advantageous, nor mercantile monopolies less feared, than among us.

261. The first is that grain monopolies in Spain are established naturally, at least up to a point. In whose hands does most of the grain end up? Undoubtedly, churches, monasteries and wealthy primogeniture entails [*mayorazgos*]. What has been said above regarding the enormous accumulation of entailed property proves it. Let us see, then, if these landholders are, or are not, monopolists.

262. Without intending to offend anyone, and acknowledging that these classes have shown ardent proof of charity in times of need and trouble, it is undeniable that the common aim of all owners of grain is to sell at the highest possible price; that this aim makes them hoard until the so-called *meses mayores*, those months that precede the next harvest; and that this hoarding is never as certain as when it is most harmful; that is, when early evidence of scarcity awakens the hope of even higher prices. Dispensing with the deliberate manipulations, the obscurity, the hidden operations, which are always frightening, because the ways of interest are slippery, by what other name can we call our present distribution of grain if not legal and authorized monopoly?

263. Now, given this state of affairs, freeing up our domestic grain trade appears to be indispensable. The intervention of traders, their very monopolies, if we want to use that term, will be favorable, because in confronting the landowners' monopoly it will weaken it. By multiplying the number of grain depositories, and therefore of sellers, it will increase competition and lower prices, which are always regulated by these factors; and, grain holders and producers, aiming at destroying each other, will be in constant competition and the public will feel its benefits.

264. This reflection is more powerful when you consider the nature of each of these monopolies, or, shall we say, commercial ventures. By the spirit of their profession, merchants are invested in the number, rather than in the result, of their speculations: that is, they prefer to obtain a higher profit generated by many small operations than a smaller profit obtained by a single, large operation. Hence, they are content with making a given profit in each speculation [*especulación*] rather than holding out for the maximum profit possible. They do obtain the highest possible profit in each operation, in a respective, not absolute way, regulated not by the hope or limits of that one operation alone, but by their hopes regarding all the operations that they can carry out. Thus, this hope, along with the need to preserve their reputation, fulfill their contracts and pay their bills, and to prevent the interruption of their business, narrows the breadth of their greed and make available their goods when a favorable price comes along, instead of holding out for the highest price.

265. This is not the case with wealthy proprietors. Selling their grain at the highest possible price is the only transaction that they pursue. With this goal in mind, they keep their grain stores until they can make that profit, and they almost infallibly do, depending on the circumstances, the times and the crops involved. They are not motivated by this design only in years of dearth, but also in the abundant ones, and even from one crop to the next, for, as the political writer Zabala has remarked, in the abundant years of his era, proprietors sold what they had, became indebted and mortgaged their estates to prevent the price of grain from falling. Is this, one might ask, the conduct of merchants?

266. Suppose that domestic trade were to be liberated [*la libertad del comercio interior*]: the merchant would buy grain at the time of the harvest and, since large landowners never sell at that time, it is clear that smaller growers would supply it, increasing competition during this period. Therein lies the one good that agriculture can receive from trade: a price that is proportional to the costs incurred by its immediate agents, so that the difference between the first and last period of each crop is not too large or harmful to the unfortunate tenant farmers. The same merchant, continuing his business, would sell the moment an opportunity for earning a decent profit presented itself, increasing the competition of sellers in the second period and compelling landowners to match his price, thus making it possible for consumers to obtain more benefits from this competition than from the most well-conceived restrictive laws.

267. The second reason favoring the domestic grain trade is the difficulty of transportation. Our most fertile provinces are distant from our less abundant ones, and without navigable rivers, canals or good roads, transportation is not only difficult and risky, but slow, and it has already been argued that only professional traders can overcome these difficulties. Small traffic, from town to town, is easily carried on without them, because growers and peddlers are able to supply these markets; but [Your Highness should remember that] the chief aim of this trade is to bring the surplus to the provinces where scarcity prevails. And should the government really leave this aim in the hands of those landowners who await shortages to bring consumers to their granaries? Should the government leave the matter in the hands of growers, who no longer have the grain when necessity rears its head? Should it leave it to peddlers, who see no other need than that which is at their own doors; who rarely leave their own province, and who cannot be expected to supply distant markets? Undoubtedly, a peddler will take his goods wherever they are needed, but only when a merchant hires him. However, to expect that peddlers on their own they would suddenly, without the requisite knowledge or experience, pass from one profession to the other, and turn into merchants while remaining peddlers; is this not trusting the very subsistence of our towns, the primary object of the government's concern, to a casual effect of an impossible hope?

268. It is therefore necessary, Sire, to establish the freedom of the domestic grain trade through a permanent law that, exciting self-interest, opposes one monopoly with another, and wards off the obscure negotiations that are carried out in the shadows

of restrictive legislation. This freedom, legitimated as much by the principles of justice as by those of sound economics [*buena economía*], indispensable in fecund as well
as in barren lands, and as beneficial to growers as it is to consumers, will constitute
one of the greatest stimuli that Your Highness can give to Spanish agriculture.

On foreign trade

1st. Of agricultural products

269. The arguments offered in favor of the free domestic trade of our agricultural
products are also applicable to external trade, and they prove that free exportation
should be protected by the law as a property right that accrues from both land and
labor, and as a stimulus for individual interest. Putting aside the trade in wheat and
other cereals, to which different principles should be applied, the Society harbors
no doubt that there is a need for a law that affords constant and unrestricted protection to our products' free exportation by land and sea. And since our legislation
already acknowledges the right to export, all that needs to be done is to combat the
principles that undergird the limitations and exceptions to the foreign commerce of
certain items.

270. These can be grouped in two sorts: the first includes items that, without being basic
necessities, are regarded as significant for public subsistence, such as oil, meat,
horses, etc. The belief that they should be kept within the realm to safeguard their
abundance has resulted in the outright ban on their exportation; or in the imposition of high duties or the requirement of certain licenses and other formalities that
for all intents and purposes amount to an export ban.

271. The Society has elsewhere combated the error that is behind this maxim, and it has
demonstrated that the best way to increase the products of both land and labor is
to stimulate individual interest by granting liberty of commerce [*libertad de su tráfico*].
Given this freedom to trade, products will abound wherever laborious men are
interested in cultivating and producing them, whatever they may be; for it is certain
that no system, no law, can secure abundance if man is not spurred by self-interest.

272. Furthermore, it is worth noting that such bans operate against their own expressed
aim and are doubly harmful to the nations that implement them, because not only
do they decrease the cultivation of products that could benefit from foreign consumption; they also encourage their cultivation in foreign nations, for the country
that cannot acquire them from the one that prohibits their exportation will seek
them elsewhere, and others will increase their cultivation to supply them, and more
so since the general policy in Europe favors the unlimited exportation of produce.
Export bans therefore discourage one's own agriculture while stimulating production in other countries.

273. We have too much faith in the excellence of our soil as singularly blessed by nature to
yield precious and valuable goods. But with the exception of wool, what do we have
that cannot be advantageously produced in other countries? If we discourage oil

production in Andalusia, Extremadura and Navarra, will not France and Lombardy foment theirs? Will animal husbandry in Portugal and Africa not grow and prosper as ours decays? And, furthermore, would Portugal, in fact, not stimulate the growth and recovery of its horse herds, raising its own foals, if we obstinately refuse to allow our breeders to sell horses in that kingdom? One should never lose sight of the fact that it is necessity that initially arouses interest, and interest is the spur to industry.

2nd. Of raw materials

274. This refers to the second type of goods produced by land and labor subject to restrictions and bans, encompassing those known as raw materials. Through these restrictions, the government hopes not only that they will be abundant and inexpensive among us, but that they will be expensive and scarce in other countries, and perhaps even altogether absent there. We already have shown that eliminating restrictions would achieve the first aim more surely and directly than banning [their export]. We will now demonstrate that restrictions will not help us achieve the second aim either.

275. Let us take the example of fine wool, a good that we regard as exclusively our own, inaccessible to the efforts of foreign industry. Let us suppose for an instant that we have irrevocably closed off its exportation, and that not a single fleece can leave the kingdom, neither by permit nor via contraband. Certainly, the French and the English would be unable to continue producing their luxurious woolen cloths [*paños*], for our fine wool is essential in their making. But would this weaken their industry? No, it would not. A nation's industry is based on more than a single material, and it is not supported by one but by many branches. The same capital, the same understanding, the same activity that is used to make those textiles that interest selects today, will be diverted tomorrow to elaborate another kind when necessity pushes them away from the former, and interest locates the latter. Do we not perceive this already in industry, which is daily altered by the vicissitudes of fashion and caprice? Do we believe the sphere of enterprise to be so narrow that it cannot direct its activity toward objects other than those dependent on foreign duties?

276. National industry, Sire, cannot grow at the expense of national agriculture or by means that are opposed to its own nature. If it did, nobody would surpass us in the manufacturing of woolen cloth. Is the scarcity or high price of wool the cause of our industry's languishing state? Is this industry not prosperous outside of Spain, where fine wool is sold at exorbitant prices, while we who can procure it for 100 percent less remain incapable of equaling foreign manufactures, whether the quality of their cloth or their price, which forces us to import them?

277. What would certainly happen in the hypothetical case described above is that our wool profits would dwindle in the same proportion as our wool extraction, for nothing is truer in economic science [*ciencia económica*] than the axiom that holds consumption as the measure of all cultivation, all husbandries and all industry. No one should believe that restricting our wool exports would augment our industry; no one should believe that we would produce those cloths

no longer produced elsewhere: these hopes, based only on the effect of regulations and biased legislation are nothing but illusions of zeal and reveries caused by ignorance. It is therefore obvious that the free foreign trade of agricultural products would prove as beneficial to our industry as it is necessary to our agriculture's prosperity.

3rd. Of grain

278. At this point, the Society must turn to the foreign trade of grain, and it is necessary to tackle this difficult and dangerous issue in spite of the conflicting doubts and opinions that it continues to harbor. The resolution of this matter seems beyond the scope of the principles and calculations of economic science, as if reality refused to confirm them, so that the advantages of freedom [*libertad*] are always accompanied by great evils or imminent risks. At every step, experience overwhelms theory, and facts belie reasoning, and whichever path is taken, whichever side is favored, drawbacks beset advantages, as people tend to envision the fear of the former rather than the hope of the latter.

279. But perhaps this perplexing situation does not derive from the principles' fallibility as much as from their misapplication. Men, whether due to sloth or pride, are prone to generalize abstract truths without pausing to consider carefully their application; and, as if generalizing ideas were not enough, they generalize from particular examples, being inclined to envy what is not theirs and to underrate what is. Politicians' most common obsession is trying to fit what seemed to work well in another time and in another country into their own time and country; and as if one free, wealthy, industrial, commercial and predominantly maritime country were the same as another with entirely different characteristics. The examples of Holland and England have been enough to convince them that the free trade of grain, so beneficial to those two countries, must be beneficial to all nations.

280. To avoid falling into such errors, the Society, which does not let abstract ideas or the experiences of others dictate its ruminations, will examine this matter as it concerns our situation and circumstances, taking into account the following questions: first, is the free exportation of grain necessary in Spain? And, second, would it be beneficial? Since these two questions are at the heart of any legislation concerning grain exportation, answering them will be enough to satisfy our doubts on this matter and those of Your Highness.

281. An affirmative answer to the first question would be true if in ordinary years our wheat harvests greatly exceeded our own consumption, for the free export of grain would only be necessary to export to the foreign markets that surplus of wheat that cannot be consumed in the kingdom. If this surplus were small, it would not influence grain prices, or do so nearly imperceptibly, which means that it would not discourage cultivation; therefore, the need for the free export of grain could only exist if considerable surpluses were a constant probability.

282. Does Spain enjoy such grain surpluses? Does it have a constant probability of its existence in ordinary years? Who would dare to answer yes? Who has calculated the average yield of our crops? Who has calculated our average consumption? Who has estimated this for each kind of grain? And who has calculated this estimate for each province and each territory? And without these figures, without establishing each of them, without comparing them, without deducting a common result, how can we predict that our yearly crops will constantly yield a considerable surplus?

283. It is certainly true that in some provinces ordinary harvests have produced surpluses annually, but we also know that in other provinces, which are both more numerous and more populous, there is often scarcity, not only in ordinary years but in abundant ones, too. This observation is enough to put to rest the argument that in ordinary years our crops will likely yield a surplus, and perhaps on the contrary to support the conclusion that there is no such surplus at all.

284. We can deduce the same evidence from a posteriori facts, for if, on the one hand, it is well known that in ordinary years some foreign wheat finds its way into the markets of various provinces, it is, on the other, also known that in such years no province exports national wheat. And this double argument, which is easily confirmed by looking at customs records, demonstrates that there is no surplus in ordinary years.

285. Grain prices in those years corroborate this conclusion, for they show no signs of falling across most of the kingdom. Although prices are somewhat moderate or even low in the provinces of León and Old Castile in ordinary years, this is not caused by the existence of a general surplus that is not absorbed by national consumption nor by the existence of grain surplus in these particular regions, but by the difficulty of selling their surplus to the needy provinces, because of the distance between them, complicated by the absence of proper communications, or because of the restrictions imposed on our domestic trade. The fact that the price of grain remains high in the remaining provinces and low in these two supports this argument; and ultimately, the increase in rents and the general eagerness with which lands are cleared so that cultivation of grain can be extended, despite the obstacles that legislation places on its progress, confirms that grain's price makes it a profitable product. We can therefore infer that Spain does not have a considerable surplus of grain in ordinary years; thus, the free export of grain is unnecessary.

286. But could it be beneficial? The reasons that we already have outlined should be sufficient to demonstrate that it is not, for though exports are undoubtedly capable of raising the average price of grain, and in this sense being favorable for agriculture, it is also true that depriving the national market of part of the grains that are regularly consumed necessarily implies causing shortages, which are very harmful to our industry and arts, and consequently damage our agriculture.

287. Fear of shortages suggested a happy medium that apparently reconciled liberty and risk. It supposed that if prices were an accurate indicator [*barómetro cierto*] of abundance or a shortage of grains, it regulated the possibility of their exports based upon prices: allowing to export when prices indicated abundance and restricting it when

they indicated the opposite. However, two reasons will unveil the fallibility and perils of this medium—which was also adopted in imitation of foreign countries.

288. Before revealing them, the Society will note that this strategy would work well only if we could fully expect a surplus. The freedom of exporting grain for foreign consumption then would be necessary, and limiting that freedom when the price indicated that this surplus no longer existed would be a reasonable precaution. But reestablishing free trade when the probability of a surplus has not been clearly ascertained would expose the kingdom to the export of grain that is not, in fact, surplus, but is actually necessary for the consumption of its inhabitants.

289. This is a very likely danger, and therein lies the first reason to reject the proposed strategy. The influence of opinion on prices tends to lower them when the harvest season is at hand, and raise them when it is distant. In the first of these periods, the sellers are many, and the difference between the available grain supplies and the grain demanded is large, so that the idea of abundance seems only natural. Equally natural is the notion of scarcity in the second period, when sellers are few and the difference between supply and demand is much smaller. It would therefore be quite possible for a portion of grain necessary for immediate consumption during the latter period to exit the kingdom during the first, precisely when traders are buying grain from growers and hastening to supply the needy markets before their competitors do so.

290. Furthermore, and here is the second reason, prices are a fallible index that can be greatly altered when a fear of scarcity looms. At that point, prices cease to reflect grain supplies, as they do in ordinary times, because perception, no longer governed by hope but by fear, looks further ahead in time and is more concerned with what is lacking than with what is present. Opinion based upon perception sets apprehension in motion; it anticipates and multiplies the horrors aroused by the fear of neediness. And how much worse would this situation become should the knowledge of exports become widely known and, in consequence, lead to a rise in prices? And would not the very act of closing the ports be interpreted by the public as a signal, a testimony, a proclamation that scarcity is imminent?

291. Some might argue that under a system that establishes freedom in the import and export of grain [*sistema de libertad*], the former will counter the damage of the latter. The high price level that discourages exports will encourage imports; and strengthened by the infallibility of reciprocal interest, this will not only repel the horrors of necessity, but also the fears out of apprehension. Beautiful reflections born from theory! Beautiful, indeed, if our imagination could remain as calm when fear and suffering plague us as when we write and ponder. But let their beauty be celebrated; let it be celebrated by those fortunate countries who, blessed with a superabundance of grain, find it necessary to export that surplus; and let them trust to this resource the supplement of contingent want. But exposing a people not so blessed to want, letting scarcity increase by purposefully trusting such a casual, slow and precarious device, would this not constitute temerity, or, at the very least, a politically imprudent act?

292. We conclude, then, that in our present situation the export of grain, regardless of whether it is absolutely free or its price is regulated, is neither necessary nor beneficial.

293. And what shall we say about imports? To be sure, if in ordinary years we were certain that our grain harvest could meet our level of consumption, it would harm our agriculture to allow the entry of foreign grain, which would necessarily lower the price of our own, especially if that price, for whatever reason, is normally high. But since we cannot be sure that our harvests will yield enough, it seems that closing the door to imports might be dangerous, for it would expose us to lacking the necessary grain to ensure public subsistence, with all of the evils and horrors that accompany this calamity. There is not much more to add regarding this subject. Having reached the conclusion that in ordinary years we do not produce more grain than what is necessary for our consumption, it should be evident that we do not produce, or at least, that we cannot be certain that we will produce, enough; and this should be sufficient cause for supporting the free importation of grain.

294. The Society's expert opinion is, therefore, that a law should ban the exportation of our grain and permit the importation of foreign grain, under the following conditions.

295. First: this law must be temporary, with a defined, relatively brief period of, for example, eight to ten years, for our agriculture is making great progress, and if this progress increases each day, as it shall if Your Highness removes the obstacles that constrain it, there is no doubt that soon enough our farmers will produce more than enough grain to fully supply our domestic consumption, and when that moment arrives, exports of grain must be permitted immediately.

296. Second: this ban should be limited to wheat, rye and corn, the types of grain that are considered basic staples, and should exclude rice, barley, beans and other types of grain, which should be legally exported at all times, without restrictions or limitations, including licenses, duties or other taxes, and subject only to customs registries, not only to prevent fraud, but to provide the government with exact records of their exportation.

297. Third: that the ban does not include the flour destined for our colonies [*nuestras colonias*], which must be allowed to be exported at all times and through all the authorized ports. This exception does not present any risk, for at present we have only one flour-making factory [*fábrica de harinas*], that of Monzón, which, located more than 40 leagues from Santander, in the heart of Castile, the country where grain is most abundant in the kingdom, can only export a small amount of its product. Moreover, this exception seems necessary to encourage our cultivation and commerce, and also to keep within the realm the funds we now spend to import flour from France and Philadelphia to send to our Windward Islands [*nuestras islas de Barlovento*].

298. Fourth: that if during the period established there were an especially bountiful year, the government could suspend the law, allowing the exportation of grain, or at least of the surplus, whether through all ports, or through those of the

provinces where the surplus was largest. This exception is more just, insofar as the product of a full harvest is twice as large or more as that of a common harvest, for since consumption would not grow in the same proportion to match supply, the ban would expose us to the possibility of losing the surplus yielded in such years.

299. Fifth: that, since the importation of foreign grain can hurt our agriculture in those years in which our production, although not superabundant, is larger than in ordinary years, it might be suitable to limit imports in those years, using prices as an index; for they are as accurate a measure in times of security as they are fallible in times of apprehension or actual scarcity; a given price can be used to determine the limit beyond which imports are to be generally suspended.

300. Sixth: that the grains imported can be reexported at all times. This policy, in addition to being fair, will be most adequate to encourage the importation of grains—as necessary to our internal supply as to vacate any domestic surpluses; these, in turn, would be put to the *comercio de economía*, which, as the example of the Netherlands shows, offers much utility and advantage.

301. Seventh: that the period during which this law is in force is used to acquire the knowledge necessary to decisively choose our final position with regard to this important matter, so as to establish a general and permanent law. The information to be gathered includes: first, the exact annual yield of each kind of grain in each of our provinces; second, the consumption in each province of each of these types of grains, estimating not only the overall consumption, but the consumption per district and per class of wheat and rye bread and cornbread, and, if at all possible, of fine breads and mixed-flour breads. This calculation, the most essential in political arithmetic, the most necessary to regulate the principal object of its concern, and the most useful given all the information that it comprises, is only accessible to the power of the government, for it has authority over the various depots, registers and public granaries and warehouses where grain is stored and sold; and it can command prelates and *cabildos*, courts and municipal councils, intendants and *corregidores* to provide it with further information. Therefore, since gathering this information is of primary importance, the government must urgently assign this task to persons capable of carrying it out promptly, exactly and completely, as befits the prosperity of agriculture and the public's welfare.

8th. On taxes examined in relation to agriculture

302. Before moving on, we will address the obstacles that fiscal laws place on agriculture's path to improvement, a delicate and difficult matter and one in which silence seems as dangerous as discussion. But although the Society can refrain from addressing the relations between these laws and industry, commerce and the other branches of public subsistence, who would forgive it for keeping quiet regarding those related to cultivation, which is what Your Highness engaged it to ponder and reform?

303. A well-established principle posits that agriculture is the chief source of individual wealth as well as public revenue, and from this principle we can infer that for the public treasury to be rich, the agents of agriculture must be rich. There is no doubt that industry and commerce open many and copious wellsprings of wealth of one sort or another; but these are derived from agricultural prosperity; they are fed by it and are dependent on it. The Society will have the opportunity to demonstrate this argument later; for the moment, it will only point out that nothing is better established by the science of government than the fact that fiscal laws in any country can be assessed according to whether they exert a positive or a negative influence on the fortunes of agriculture.

304. Our system of provincial taxation clearly disregards the aforementioned principle, not only because of the obstacles that it presents to the free circulation of the products of the land, but also because it generally thwarts the interests of landowners and tenants. We will say nothing of the first inconvenience, because its ill effects have been amply demonstrated in what was discussed previously regarding the free circulation of produce. With regard to the second, opinions vary, with some sustaining that our system of provincial taxes is quite favorable to agriculture. First: it is easy to assume that taxing consumption, which is generally proportional to consumers' purchasing capacity, meets the condition of equality in the exaction of tributes that justice so strongly recommends. Second: it would seem that this equality is even more securely achieved by taxing not only basic goods, which are subject to the *millones*, but all articles sold by trading houses, which pay the *alcabala*, since no article, whether consumed to meet a basic need or to satisfy a desire for luxury, could either be surcharged or avoid paying its fair share. Third and finally: taxing consumption goods at the time of their final purchase also seemed to ensure that the burden would fall not so much on tenants and farmers, but on consumers, a category that embraces all classes and all individuals. Therein are the illusions that led to the adoption of this system as if it were not only just, but also favorable to cultivation.

305. But a little reflection is enough to banish that impression. First: it is indeed true that tax-paying families are more or less numerous depending on their respective fortunes, and they consume more or less accordingly. But this proportion is far from being equal, for, notwithstanding the different nature of the articles consumed by richer or poorer families, there is a notable difference in the quantity of their savings. One should not and cannot suppose that every individual spends the whole of his income; on the contrary, we assume that some, particularly those who are better off, precisely because of their comfortable economic situation, save part of their annual income to increase their capital. Otherwise, no individual, and therefore, no nation, would ever become rich. And woe to those countries whose capital does not grow! Now, these savings are, in fact, free of the contributions levied on consumption. If all the individuals in the state saved part of their income (which is a very unlikely event), it is clear that there would be great differences between the savings of the rich and the savings of the poor, and, therefore,

between those portions of their individual fortune that are exempted from this kind of tax.

306. The inequality of the system is even more notable with respect to the nature of the articles consumed, for even if we supposed that they were relatively the same, there is no doubt that poor and less well-off [*menos acomodadas*] families spend most of their income to procure their own maintenance [*mantenimientos*]; that is, on goods that are subject to *sisas*, *millones* and import duties; even their dress and other domestic comforts are subject to these same levies, though indirectly, for they are usually made with elements produced nationally and transformed by other taxpayers, in whose salaries the same levy is embedded. The opposite is true for wealthy families, for whom sustenance [*sustento*] occupies the least part of their income and includes articles that are often foreign, such as tea, coffee and fortified wines; or that come from our colonies, such as sugar, cocoa and others. The greatest expenditures of the rich go to their dress and items of luxury or comfort, most of which are also foreign, given the furor with which fashion and those who follow it prefer foreign things, and this must make an enormous difference in the tax that they pay. It should not be thought that this difference is compensated with the taxes [*derechos*] that comprise the general revenues [*rentas generales*]. These are not very high in the times where there is fear of contraband [*contrabando*], and when they are actually increased they cause fraudulent importation.

307. Second: the taxes imposed on consumption do not always fall upon consumers. While this is the case whenever sellers are the ones who set the price to the buyers, for then the tax is embedded in the sales price, it is not the case when, instead of having this capacity, the seller accedes to the price imposed by the buyer. For is it not evident that the buyer will aspire to pay less, and the seller will have to content himself with the least possible profit?

308. The final case is the most frequent and usual among us. First, because in many provinces our rural population is more numerous than our urban population, and therefore, more provisions are offered at the market than are demanded. Second, because, as we have shown, our subsistence policies and municipal rules favor the urban population over the rural, and buyers over sellers. Third: because when there is a surplus, the difficulty of arranging its sale again favors buyers, especially if we consider the obstacles faced by sellers regarding the circulation of produce in other internal markets and its exportation outside the kingdom.

309. Third: notwithstanding the above, one fact alone should be enough to destroy the notion of fairness attributed to our duties on consumption. And it is that no one is exempted from paying them, especially the *millones*, not even the destitute class whose subsistence is reduced to the *bare minimum* and should therefore be exempt from all taxes. It is a true principle, or at least a very prudent economic maxim based on reason and equity, that all taxes should be paid with what constitutes the *unnecessary* [*superfluo*], and not the *necessary* [*necesario*] [portions] of the taxpayers' fortunes. Because anything that diminishes that which is necessary for a family's subsistence can precipitate its ruin, and along with it, the loss of a taxpayer—and of

the hopes of many. And when a large portion of the rural population finds itself in this state, laborers in particular, who are the driving force [*brazo derecho*] of cultivation in those regions where large holdings are the norm, it is evident that a tax on consumption is both unfair and unfavorable to agriculture, for it either decreases the number of laborers or else leads to a rise in their wages.

310. Fourth: Consider the influence provincial taxes have upon cultivation, embracing as they do so many of its products, from the most important and most precious, such as oils, wines and meats, subject to the *millones*; to the least valuable, such as fruit, legumes, vegetables, fowl, etc., subject to the *alcabala*. Reflect upon the fact that they are taxed repeatedly, here directly and there indirectly. Let us give an example. First, the hay consumed by cattle is taxed because pasturage rental is considered a sale, and therefore it is subject to the *alcabala*; then each animal fattened on that pasture is subject to a sales tax each time it is sold and resold at fairs and markets; and, finally, the meat sold for consumption is also subject to taxation. Thus, these kinds of taxes harass the products of the land from the very outset; they pursue them and bite them throughout their circulation, like a predator, without ever losing sight or hold of their prey up to the last instance of their consumption. This circumstance alone is enough to justify all of the reproaches that Zabala, Ustáriz, Ulloa and our other economists have leveled against such taxes.

311. Fifth: must we continue? Land, which produces so many goods, at least for that very reason should be respected in its free circulation. On the contrary, it is burdened by the present system. The Society cannot stop from petitioning [*representar*] Your Highness that, though it regards the *alcabala* as worthy of its barbarous origin, it is never as onerous as when it is imposed upon on the sale of land and real estate. Given that it is an indisputable principle that it is the same to tax what the land produces as to tax the rent collected on the land, as to tax its property, it seems that a system founded on the taxation of all products derived from the land, and even its rents, should at least refrain from taxing its property—the source of both products and rents. But we [the Spaniards], not content with imposing taxes on what the land produces, or in their seventh part as it happens in the goods included in the *millones*, or in a fourteenth part like in the *alcabala de hierbas*, or in a twenty-fifth part such as the supplies for ordinary consumption—which pay 4 percent–, we have taxed land ownership directly with a further fourteenth-part sales tax in its circulation—added to the tenth with which the property is taxed in favor of the church, without counting the *primacía*. All of these should make ostensible how stubborn fiscal legislation has been in its pursuit to make land ownership more expensive when, conversely, it should be made inexpensive in order to foster agriculture's prosperity—which should be a prime objective of this legislation.

312. The Society already demonstrated the pernicious effects that these high prices have had on agriculture; but it must add two further considerations that make even more evident the detrimental effects caused by the *alcabala*. First: since this tax is levied upon land sales, it exempts unalienable property and falls exclusively on free and commercial property [*propiedad libre y comercial*]; that is, on the most precious portion

of the kingdom's land. Second: it is more onerous with regard to the circulation of the land that is even dearer—small properties—and not only because these circulate the most, but because each sale involves the use of sealed paper; the recording of official deeds before a notary; and, sometimes, the procurement of appraisements and adjudication. These expenses, which are imperceptible in the sale of large and wealthy farms, represent a fortune for smallholders, and, added to the *alcabala's* fourteenth, make the barriers to such transactions practically insurmountable, to the ruinous detriment of agriculture.

313. Sixth: compare the condition of landed property vis-à-vis other types of property, and the sad impact of provincial taxes on cultivation will be fully unveiled. Is it not true that this system does not tax, at least not directly, the floating capital [*capitales que giran*] in commerce, nor the profits or revenues that it produces? Is it not true that the capital employed in factories or industrial enterprises is not taxed either? Is it not true that factories enjoy favorable tax exemptions, not only in the sale of their products but also in their purchases of raw materials, even when these are items subject to the *millones*? Are not guilds, banks and commercial houses exempt from paying taxes on their capital and revenues, even if these are generated by entailed properties, while emphyteutic leases, perhaps because they are identified as a sort of territorial property, are levied with an *alcabala* of fourteenth part [*catorcena*] in the imposition and redemption of their capital, and another twentieth part [*veintena*] in the *frutos civiles* tax on their annual revenues? In light of this, who would dare to trade in personal property or capital for an agricultural venture? Indeed, is it not more advantageous to exchange landed property for money—effectively ruining and discouraging agriculture?

314. Some might say that this last-mentioned evil is not universal, for it does not afflict the provinces of the kingdom of Aragon, with its cadastral levies; nor Navarre and the Basque Country, which pay according to their privileges; nor, finally, those Castilian towns that instead pay a certain annual redemption. But is this very difference not an evil in itself, as equally repugnant to the eyes of reason as to those of justice? Are we not all children of the same country [*hijos de una misma patria*], citizens in the same society [*ciudadanos de una misma sociedad*] and members of the same state? Are we not all obligated to contribute equally to the public treasury for the defense and protection of all? But how is this equality to be observed if the bases of taxation are not one and the same? Even if the final amount of the taxes raised were equivalent, would not inequality continue? Why should landed property and rents, and the labor employed on them, and the products obtained, be free in some provinces and towns and enslaved by oppression in others?

315. Seventh: having presented this reflection, the Society cannot remain silent concerning another notable inequality: the exemption enjoyed by the secular and regular clergy in terms of provincial taxes, which they either do not pay at all or they pay only to be reimbursed subsequently. Nothing is fairer in the Society's eyes than those personal privileges and immunities that are given to the respectable members of these orders so that they may conserve their decorum and need not be distracted

from the holy exercise of their duties. But when the matter at hand is the public revenue, to which all individuals, of all classes and of all orders must contribute, what justifies such an exception? Can such a privilege truly be granted to one class of persons without overburdening the others; and without destroying that fair equality beyond which taxation loses all possibility of being equitable and fair?

316. Some will say that the clergy contributes through other levies, and that is true; but what the Society has stated previously also exposes the error in this situation. If, for instance, the clergy contributes more through other channels, what reason is there for such a venerable and necessary class to be burdened by heavier taxes than the other classes that constitute the state? And if it contributes less, what reason is there for a wealthy and property-holding class, whose members are sufficiently endowed, to contribute less to the public revenue than the poor and laboring classes that support it?

317. Without counting the expenses incurred by the state in the [employment of] numerous legions of administrators, inspectors, commanders and guards that provincial tax collection requires, expenses paid by all taxpayers; without counting how much they vex the farmer and peasant who cannot take a single step with the fruits of their toil without finding themselves surrounded by ministers and satellites [*ministros y satélites*]; without counting the affliction caused by the odious regime of policing, visits, guides, register entries and other formalities; without counting the oppression and humiliation caused by the denunciations, detentions, legal proceedings and other such vexations that the smallest and sometimes most innocent fraud can produce; nor how much the freedom of our internal markets and trade suffers as a result of this system. Even without taking all of this into account, what has been said is sufficient to demonstrate that our fiscal laws, at least as they relate to agriculture, constitute one of the most powerful obstacles to the interest of the agents of cultivation, and consequently, to their prosperity.

318. Examining with the same thoroughness the system of general taxes would be too long and difficult an endeavor; but the Society will not proceed without making at least one observation: that in its design, the interests of commerce and industry are taken into account, but rarely those of agriculture. Our customs offices open or close their doors to national or foreign goods depending on the benefits trade or industry may receive, but never cultivation and its agents. By this principle, the export of raw materials is prohibited to keep their price low and thus favor industry, without considering the harm done to agriculture, which produces them; and with similar intentions, the importation of foreign raw materials to favor industry is permitted, regardless of the harm it poses to agriculture. The same principle is used when determining the taxes or exemptions and surcharges or reliefs that will be applied to the importation or exportation of certain items.

319. What is the origin of such an erroneous system? The Society will develop its answer to this question later, but in the interim it beseeches Your Highness to observe the following: first, that trade is carried out by wealthy people, knowledgeable in the calculation of their interests and united in their promotion; second, that industry is

usually located in the great cities, under the watchful eye of public magistrates and surrounded by passionate supporters and patrons; and, third, that agriculture, confined to the countryside and directed by uncouth and defenseless people, lacks the voice with which to stake claims, nor possesses the power with which to secure them. With these considerations in mind, the answer to the question just posed is obvious.

SECOND KIND

MORAL OBSTACLES, OR THOSE DERIVED FROM OPINION

320. Such are, Sire, the principal ways by which legislation hinders our agriculture's prosperity. Those obstacles that arise from opinion, and therefore pertain to the moral order, are no less substantial, nor is their influence less powerful. But since it is impossible for the Society to discover all of them and to track each and every one of them down, because the sources of public opinion are many and varied, and often also so deeply ingrained, it will content itself with pointing out those that are most susceptible to Your Highness's zeal and authority.

321. A nation's agriculture can be appraised according to two general features: first, public prosperity; and, second, individual welfare and happiness. With respect to the first, it is undeniable that large states, which, like Spain, enjoy an ample and fertile territory, should consider agriculture as the main wellspring of their prosperity, for wealth and population, which are the primary supports of national power, depend more immediately upon it than upon any of the other lucrative professions, and even all the others put together. With regard to the second, it is also undeniable that agriculture is the easiest, safest and most widespread means of increasing the number of individuals in a state, and the particular contentment of each, not only because of the great quantity of labor that it requires in its various branches and objects, but also because of the immense sum of employment that it provides for the professions dedicated to transforming or trading its products. And if politics were to turn to this sublime and lofty object that the wisest and most flourishing governments of antiquity promoted, and acknowledge that the felicity of empires [*imperios*] as well as of its individuals is found in the qualities of the body and the spirit, that is, in the valor and virtues of its citizens, then it would also acknowledge that agriculture, the mother of innocence and honest labor, and in Columella's words, wisdom's kin and companion, is the primary support of the strength and splendor of nations.[52]

322. It follows from these truths, for which there is much evidence in ancient and modern history, that opinion can oppose agriculture's progress in two ways: first, by casting it as a secondary object in the eyes of the government and calling the latter's attention to other sources of public wealth; and, second, by providing agriculture's

---

52 "Sola res rustica, quae sine dubitatione próxima, & quasi consanguínea sapientiae est, tam discentibus egeat, quam magistiris." Columella in praef.

agents with inefficient or erroneous means for the advancement of cultivation and for the personal fortunes that depend on it to grow. In both cases, the nation and its individuals would obtain fewer advantages from agriculture and, consequently, the prosperity of both would be diminished. This is the standard the Society will use to evaluate opinions related to agriculture.

1st. On the part of the government

323. One can see that the opinions that produced all of the political obstacles that we have identified and combated fall in the first category. Because all these laws, ordinances and rules to favor *baldíos*, plantations [*plantaciones*], wool production, the inalienability of estates belonging to particular families or the clergy, and urban industry and population, with the ruinous consequences that all of them have caused to cultivation, would not have been enacted if the government had always been thoroughly convinced that no sector was more deserving of its protection and solicitude than agriculture, and that it could not favor others at the latter's expense without obstructing in some way the chief and most abundant source of public wealth.

324. When one investigates the origin of this kind of opinion, one immediately stumbles upon a fatal preoccupation that has taken hold everywhere during the last few centuries, and which has infected every European government. All have aspired to base their power on commerce, and since then the balance of state protection has inclined toward it; and since its extension and advancement seemed to depend on the industry that supplied it and the navigation that undergirded it, the solicitude of modern states was entirely turned toward the mercantile arts. Their history, written since the fall of the Roman Empire, and markedly since the establishment of the Italian republics and the ruin of the feudal system, confirms this truth in each page. For centuries, horrendous wars, the scourge of humanity, and particularly of agriculture, have been waged for the sole purpose of promoting trade. For centuries, this system has presided over the peace treaties and political negotiations. Succumbing to the force of this contagion, Spain has implemented it as its own for centuries, such that, despite being destined by nature to be primarily an agricultural nation, its discoveries, its conquests, its wars, its peace negotiations, its treaties and even its laws have visibly tended toward fomenting and protecting the mercantile professions, usually at the expense of agriculture. Which privileges have not been enacted to favor the arts, whose practitioners are gathered in guilds, who have succeeded in monopolizing labor's inventiveness, skill and even liberty? Which graces were not conceded upon trade and navigation, since they also gathered in great bodies and employed their power and cunning to swell the illusions of politics? And once the balance of protection was inclined toward them, how much protection and solicitude have they not swindled from voiceless and defenseless agriculture?

325. In such a contradictory system, nothing seems more repulsive than to scorn a profession without which no growth or prosperity would come to those favored and

protected by the government. Can there be any doubt that agriculture is indeed the base of industry, trade and navigation? Who but she produces the materials that industry transforms, that trade puts into circulation and that navigation exports? Who but she lends the arms that continuously serve and enrich other professions? How did the illusory notion arise that these professions could be fruitfully erected without agriculture's promotion, when they are entirely dependent upon it for their prosperity? Could this situation be anything but analogous to laying weak foundations before constructing a building?

326. Another origin of this evil lies in our mania for imitation. Perhaps the example set by the medieval republics that flourished, not through agriculture, but through the impulse received from their industry and navigation, along with the instances of a few empires of the ancient world and modern Europe, infected Spain with this harmful notion. But what folly is greater for a country such as ours than imitating countries forced by nature, which did not grant them a suitable territory, to base their subsistence on the feeble and contemptible foundations of trade, when in our rich and vast territory the most abundant, the most secure source of public and private wealth is agriculture?

327. Yes, Sire, industry in a state without agriculture will always be precarious: it will always depend on those countries that consume its products and from which it receives its raw materials. Its commerce will invariably follow its industry's fortunes, or it will be reduced to a *comercio de mera economía*; that is, the most uncertain, and in terms of public wealth, the least profitable of all. Both will be necessarily precarious, hinging on a thousand contingencies and revolutions. A war, an alliance, a trade treaty, the vicissitudes of caprice itself, of opinion and the changing customs of other peoples can bring its ruin, and, with it, that of the state. In this way, the glory of Tyre and the immense power of Carthage vanished like a dream, going up in smoke. In the same way, the world saw the disappearance of the great power and glory of Pisa, Florence, Genoa and Venice, and perhaps those of Holland and Genève will share the same fate; and their fall would confirm the truth that only a prosperous agriculture can form the permanent basis of a state's power and greatness.

328. The Society does not mention these things to persuade Your Highness that industry and commerce are unworthy of the government's protection. On the contrary, it acknowledges that in Europe's present state, no nation can be powerful without them; and without them, agriculture itself will be weak and impoverished. It merely seeks to persuade Your Highness that, since the state's subsistence ultimately depends upon it, the primary object of the government's care always should be agriculture. This is the most certain, most direct and shortest way to create powerful industry and prosperous trade. When agriculture provides an abundance of the raw materials required by the industrial arts, and the necessary number of hands that will transform them; and when goods are plentiful, and salaries can therefore decrease, industry will have the encouragement it requires to grow and succeed; and once industry flourishes, commerce will closely follow it, achieving an invincible competitiveness in all markets. Then, the mercantile professions need not

expect from the government anything other than the equal protection that all useful professions deserve. But protecting industry and trade with exclusive favors and graces; shielding them to the detriment of agriculture, is akin to traveling backward on a road, or following the longest, most winding, difficult, bumpy and treacherous road to reach a desired destination.

329. How has it happened that the government has so prodigiously dispensed such graces, discouraging the first and foremost, the most important and necessary, of all professions? How much has thus been squandered? How many sacrifices has agriculture been forced to endure in order to multiply the number of commercial establishments? Was it not enough to aggravate her condition, by making her shoulder taxes and services from which the nobility, the clergy and even classes of lesser rank, were exempted? Was it not enough to bear the burden of all the exemptions granted to industry and all of the prohibitions decreed in favor of trade? The most expensive and costly charges are fixed upon the poor farmers' backs to offset the exemptions granted to other arts and occupations. Military service, providing pack animals and lodging for the troops, the levies on bulls and sealed paper and many other civic burdens fall on the unfortunate husbandman, while a generous hand relieves the members of other classes and professions. Shepherds, carriers and colt and mare breeders have all been graced with these exemptions, as if these professions, the daughters or maidservants of agriculture, were more worthy of favor than their mother and lady. The employees of the royal treasury, customhouse officers, guards, those granted *estancos* [monopoly contracts for the sale] of tobacco, card games and gunpowder, salt-duty collectors, and other incredibly numerous employments also enjoy exemptions that escape the farmer. But there is more. The Ministers of the Inquisition, of the Crusades, of Brotherhoods and Confraternities and even the trustees of the mendicant orders have ripped from the government's hands these unfair and shameful exemptions, making a heavier weight fall on the backs of the most important and precious class of our state [*la más importante y preciosa clase del Estado*].

330. The Society does not claim such exemptions for farmers, even though, if they were ever fairly granted, nobody would be more deserving and worthy than those who support the state. But it knows that the defense of the state is a natural burden that all its members must share, and if the Society sought to unburden farmers, it would be disregarding this sacred and primordial obligation. Let all run gladly to trade their plows for muskets to defend their country and its cause if need be! But is it fair that even in the greatest conflicts, the villages and fields should be abandoned in order that the workshops, countinghouses and other havens of idleness remain filled?

331. To banish such opinions once and for all, the Society believes that Your Highness should promote the study of civil economy [*Economía Civil*], a science that teaches how to combine public welfare with individual interests, and how to set the power and strength of empires upon the solid foundation of their members' fortunes; a science that appraises agriculture, industry and commerce in relation to these two objectives,

and identifies the fair measure of protection that each should receive; and that, at the same time, enlightens [*esclarece*] legislation and politics, keeping at bay partial systems, chimerical projects, absurd opinions and the trivial and petty maxims that have so often perverted public authority, which is supposed to protect and edify, into an instrument of oppression and ruin.

2nd. On the role of agriculture's agents

332. The realm of opinion is not any less significant when it considers agriculture as a source of individual livelihoods. In this relationship, agriculture is regarded as the art of cultivating the land, and thus the first and most necessary of all of man's occupations. The Society will go to the root of the opinions that hinder and discourage agriculture; however, it cannot engage in the theoretical aspects of cultivation, for who would be capable of following the long sequence of errors and preoccupations keeping it in a deplorable state of imperfection.

333. Indeed, even at its crudest level, agriculture requires a considerable sum of knowledge. Let us consider how, after having seized his dominance over nature from the beasts, forcing some to live in hiding in the impenetrable wilderness, while subjecting others to obey the empire of his voice, so that with their help he cleared the forests and the undergrowth that covered the land, man learned how to rule over it and make it serve his needs. Let us consider the labors and operations he undertook to excite the land's fecundity; and the instruments and machines he invented to ease his own work; and how from the infinite variety of seeds that existed, he selected and perfected those best able to provide nourishment for himself and his livestock; and materials for his dress, his home, his shelter, his defense and even his desires and vanity.[53] Finally, let us consider the simplicity of these discoveries, and the marvelous ease with which they were acquired and executed, and how without teachers or apprenticeships they are passed from father to son, and transmitted to the remotest posterity. Considering all of this, who would not admire the portentous advances of the human spirit? Or, to put it differently, who would not laud the ineffable designs of God's providence in the conservation and multiplication of the human species?

---

53 The wheat that man eats, says the Count of Buffon, is produced thanks to the progress made in the first of the arts, for no wild wheat is to be found anywhere on the earth, and therefore it is a seed perfected through careful labor. It was, therefore, necessary to select this plant among thousands of others, to plant it and to harvest it many times to ensure that its multiplication was always proportional to its cultivation and nourishment. On the other hand, the unique and marvelous capacity to adapt to all of the world's climates, to resist even in its first year the coldness of winter, and to keep for a long period, without losing its alimentary qualities or its germinating capacity, prove that its discovery was the happiest of all discoveries made by man; but no matter how old it is, it was preceded by the art of agriculture. *Époques de la nature*, époque 7, vol. 2, pag. mihi 195. See also the observations made by Saint Pierre's lord on the alimentary harmonies of plants in his admirable work *Études de la nature* vol. 2, p. 469, ed. 1790.

334. Yet in the midst of these astonishing advancements, there is also evidence of man's sloth and his ingratitude toward the Creator's generosity. Vain and lazy even as he is needy and miserable, he scrutinizes the heavens trying to uncover the arcane mysteries of Providence while ignoring or scorning the gifts that with generous hands that very Providence filled his home and lay at his feet. It is enough to glance at agriculture, to which man was called from the very beginning, to understand that even in the wisest and most civilized countries, those where the arts have been most protected, the cultivation of the earth is still far from reaching the perfection that it could so easily attain. Is there a nation whose knowledge and wealth, whose luxuries and pleasures, cannot be shamed by testimonies of the unfortunate primitiveness in which this essential and primary occupation is held? Is there a nation where no fields lie abandoned, sterile or imperfectly cultivated? Where no fields are condemned to perpetual sterility due to the absence of irrigation, or proper drainage, or for want of clearing? Where instead of producing the fruit to which nature beckons them, lands are dedicated to useless productions that waste time and labor? Is there a nation that does not need to greatly improve the instruments of agriculture; the methods of cultivation; the ways labor and rural operations are employed? In sum, is there a nation where the first of all human arts is not the last in terms of advancement and care?

335. This, Sire, is our situation.[51] But if, forgetting for an instant what we have stated, we shifted our gaze to how much we still have to travel in this immense path, we would understand the cost of our lethargy, the degree of our agriculture's backwardness and the great need to remedy it. What is the cause of such a great evil? Notwithstanding the political obstacles already analyzed, the Society finds the moral order as that which, in its lack of instruction and knowledge, has had the most immediate influence on agriculture's state of imperfection. Let us hurry toward the remedy!

336. Complaints against this negligence and ignorance are as general as they are old. Centuries ago, the great Columella lamented how across Rome academies and

---

54 Speaking only of uncultivated lands, few nations have more than Spain, and we can see evidence of this sad truth throughout the Agrarian Law dossier. Let us recall the 15,527 *fanegas* of land sold in the past century to Doña Ana Bustillo y Quincoces in Jerez, which gave rise to bitter and protracted legal disputes that were quite contrary to public interest: the records of that lawsuit reveal that there were immense *baldíos* in that municipality. In Utrera at the beginning of this century, after Luis Curiel distributed a great part of his land, there were still more than 21,000 *fanegas* of *baldío* land. In Ciudad Rodrigo there are more than 110 deserted hamlets with 30,000 *fanegas* of uncultivated land. A similar number exists in the municipality of Salamanca, despite the efforts carried out by its population board (*junta de repoblación*). And what could the number be in Extremadura? See what Zabala says of its districts (*partidos*): that in Badajoz alone, the leagues of uncultivated land measure 26 leagues in length by over 12 in breadth, all fertile and arable, and this number does not take into account the brush that covers a third of the province. But there is more! Does not Catalonia, the wealthy and industrial Catalonia, have 288 deserted hamlets? These are indeed clear testimonies of the harmful influence of our laws and opinions. Who can look at this predicament without horror and without tears? This shameful neglect! Such poverty and depopulation in the midst of such fertile lands!

learning institutions had multiplied, and professors of all the arts, including the vilest and most frivolous, had increasingly more students, while agriculture alone lacked disciples and teachers. "Without such arts," he said, "and even without advocates, there were happy peoples in past times, and many are so still; but it is evident that without farmers, no nation could be happy, nor even exist."[55] With the same zeal, Herrera, that modern Columella, along with the renowned Lope de Deza and numerous other good patriots [*buenos patricios*] of the sixteenth century, called for the establishment of academies and professorships of agriculture. This clamor, renewed in various moments since that time, still resounds in the Agrarian Law dossier.

337. Applauding the zeal displayed by these venerable Spaniards, the Society would like to follow a safer and easier path to reach the aims that they proposed. It finds the notion of teaching farmers agricultural knowledge using theoretical lessons and academic dissertations rather futile and perhaps even somewhat absurd. It does not censure this idea, but it considers it ill-suited to the great end that is sought. Agriculture has scant need of disciples who have been trained and taught in classrooms, nor doctors to teach from their chairs or sitting around a table. It needs practical and patient men who know how to plow, sow, manure, reap and gather the crops; thresh, winnow and improve and preserve the harvests; and these things are far from the method used at schools, for they cannot be taught using the scientific apparatus of instruction.

338. Yet agriculture is an art, and there is no art whose theoretical principles are not derived from a science. In this sense, the theory of agriculture must be the most extensive and multifaceted, for agriculture, more than an art, is an admirable gathering of many sublime arts. Agriculture's perfection in a nation necessarily rests upon the degree to which that nation possesses the kinds of knowledge that embrace and encourage it. Indeed, who will be closer to improving the theoretical principles of cultivation, the nation that is acquainted with the sum of agriculture's theoretical principles or the nation that ignores them completely?

339. This line of reasoning inescapably leads us to a very sad and embarrassing truth. In what state of shameful neglect does our system of public education find itself! It appears as if we were fervently bent on both disregarding useful knowledge and multiplying the institutes dedicated to imparting useless instruction.

340. The Society, Sire, is far from repudiating the fair esteem that intellectual sciences [*ciencias intelectuales*] deserve, and further still from disparaging those whose object is the sublime mysteries. The science of religion, which teaches man the Creator's essence and attributes, and the science of morality, which teaches him to know himself and to walk down the path of virtue toward the ultimate end, will always be worthy of the highest regard among all the peoples blessed with the joy of knowing and respecting such sublime objects. But since all other sciences are meant to promote the temporal

---

55 "Nam sine ludioris artibus, atque etiam sine causidicis, olim satis felices fuere, futuraeque sunt urbes: at sine agricultoribus nec consistere mortales, nec ali posse, manifestum est." Columella in praef.

felicity of man, how is it that we have forgotten the one that is most indispensable to achieve this aim, and we have instead ardently promoted the most useless and even destructive kinds of knowledge?

341. This obsession with the intellectual sciences as the sole concern of public education is not as old as some may suppose.[56] Instruction in the liberal arts was the main object of our first schools; and even when these studies were reformed, the useful sciences; that is, the natural and exact sciences, owed much to the dedicated efforts of the government and the commitment of the learned. Every single one of our first institutes produced men renowned in the fields of physics and mathematics; and, what is more remarkable, all of them applied their principles to achieve ends that were beneficial for all. What a plethora of examples the Society could cite were that its present purpose! But it is enough to know that when Master Esquivel measured the surface of the Spanish empire with Reggio Montano triangles to write the most learned and complete geography[57] that any nation had ever known; and when the wise Valle and Mercado applied their discoveries and knowledge of physics to banish the maladies that afflicted the provinces; and when the indefatigable Laguna travelled to remote countries with Dioscorides in his hands, studying the botany and nature of the fields of Egypt and Greece, the celebrated Alfonso de Herrera,

---

56 See law 1st, title 31st, 2nd partida [*ley 1ª, título 31 de la partida II*].

57 Ambrosio de Morales speaks of this work in his treatise on Spanish antiquities. It is thanks to him that we know that Pedro Esquivel wrote it under Philip II, and that besides inventing new instruments to secure a better result for his operations, Esquivel used the triangle method created by Juan de Reggio Montano. Morales also stated that Esquivel fixed the standard of the Spanish foot and its relation to the Roman unit by means of the milestones he discovered in the *ancient military roads*. But the highest praise for Esquivel and his work is found in the testimony left by renowned historian and mathematician Don Felipe de Guevara, which is worth quoting at length. Speaking to Philip II, Guevara recalled how Marcus Agrippa's depiction of the orb was placed on the Octavian Portico in Rome by his father-in-law, Augustus, saying, "Following his example, Your Majesty could have mastered Esquivel's description of Spain that *he will soon bring forth*, painted wherever it can bring the most pleasure to Your Majesty, who commissioned it. For certainly, though there are many things that Your Majesty can boast of, which will perpetuate your name and immortalize your fame, no other human work done under Your Majesty's auspices compares to this magnificent accomplishment, and nothing would augment Your Majesty's glory as much as awing visitors with the reason, account and history of this notable country as it is therein described. *Your Majesty does not fear*, as other Princes might, having such things published. On the other hand, we can say without exaggeration that since the creation of the world, no other country has been surveyed with as much attention, diligence and truth as ours. All other such geographies, made by Ptolemy and others, were drawn up using reports written by local inhabitants, or surveys made by predecessors and contemporaries. *On the contrary, in the geography of Spain that Your Majesty has commissioned, each part of the land described has been seen or trod by its author, who inasmuch as his mathematical instruments allowed, ascertains with his own eyes and hands the truth of all he records*." See the cited speech by Morales and the Commentaries of Don Felipe Guevara. Esquivel's splendid work was given to Philip II upon Esquivel's death, but it no longer exists, or nothing is known of it. Indeed, it is truly difficult to determine whether there is more glory for us in having accomplished and possessed such a work or more shame in having forgotten its existence.

encouraged by the good Cardinal Cisneros, had already taught his compatriots all that the Greek and Latin agronomists and the physicists of the Middle Ages and his own period knew of the art of cultivating the land.[58]

342. But these important studies have perished, and those that replaced them provide us with no progress on the matter. Science ceased to be a means to search for the truth, and became a capricious means to gaze at life. Students multiplied, and, with them, the imperfection of studies. For, like insects bred in putrefaction, which only serve to extend it, scholastic and dogmatic scholars, casuists and bad professors in *intellectual schools* have enveloped the principles, and even the memory of the useful sciences, with their rot.

343. Deem it worthy, Your Highness, to restore the liberal arts and sciences to their former esteem; deign to promote them again, and agriculture will once more advance toward perfection. The exact sciences will improve its instruments and machines, and advance its economy and calculations; they will also open the door to the study of nature, and subsequently those branches of knowledge whose object is to understand this great mother [nature] will discover its powers and its wonderful treasures for agriculture's use. And Spaniards, enlightened by both, will finally understand the great loss incurred for failing to study the prodigious fecundity of the soil and the climate that Providence bestowed upon them. Natural history will reveal what is produced across the globe, providing our agriculture with new seeds, new fruits, new plants and herbs to cultivate and adapt, and new members of the animal kingdom to tame. Aided by these discoveries and knowledge, new ways of mixing, enriching and preparing the soil will be developed, along with new methods of

---

58   Although Herrera's treatise on agriculture is more a compilation than an original work, three circumstances recommend it above all other agricultural texts written during his period. First: the author's erudition, evidenced not only by the frequent references to all the agronomists known at that time (the Greeks Hesiod, Theophrastus, Aristotle, Dioscorides and Galen; the Romans Cato, Varro, Columella, Palladius, Pliny, Virgil and Macrobius; the Arabs Averroes, Avicenna and Abenzenef; and the moderns Crescentius, Bartholomew of England, Vincentin, etc.), but also by the long fragments that he cites and translates from these authors, and which he sometimes refutes; and especially by the confidence with which he references them, all of which shows that he indeed read them carefully, as we can gather from the following passage: "I do believe (he says in chapter 39 of book 4, speaking of eggplants) that the Moors brought them from afar, for I cannot recall any word or memory of them in any of the ancient writers' texts, whether Greek or Latin, or the moderns, or even in any medical writings other than those of the Moors; and this proves, I think, that they did not grow in cold or northern countries." Second: the long trips that he undertook to observe the rural customs of other nations, so that when he proposes some as models, it is after having witnessed them himself, particularly those from Dauphine and other French provinces; Lombardy and the Roman Campagna; Piedmont; and even Germany. And third: that even though his practical knowledge is somewhat circumscribed to the territory of Talavera, where he resided, he saw and observed the rural customs of the rest of Spain, and even those of the Arabs of Granada, whose flourishing cultivation he always describes whenever it is relevant. These sentences spoken to honor the first among our agronomists should be enough to commend the craft and merit of his excellent work.

breaking and cultivating it. Land clearings; drainage and irrigation systems; methods of conserving and improving harvests; the construction of granaries and vaults, mills, winepresses; in a word, the immense variety of arts, subordinate and auxiliary to agriculture, which are today carried out according to absurd and reprehensible practices, will be improved in light of that knowledge that is termed "useful" precisely because man can apply it to better fulfill his wants.

344. Despite evidence of the positive influence of this type of instruction, many still view it with contempt, convinced that since it is inaccessible to the rough and illiterate populace, it will merely become an armchair endeavor that will only serve to increase the vanity and entertainment of the learned. The Society does not deny that there is some truth in this allegation, for nothing harms the propagation of useful scientific knowledge more than the loftiness with which professors treat and expound them. Their jargon, their formulas and the general apparatus of their doctrines make them suspect of purposefully misrepresenting this type of instruction as if it were indeed an arcane and mysterious doctrine that could never be comprehended by the minds of the common folk [*comprensiones vulgares*].

345. And yet, despite all calumnies, the utility of the applied sciences cannot be denied. It is impossible for a nation to possess them in any degree without some of their light reaching the lowest classes of the people. Because the nectar of wisdom flows from one class to the other, so to speak, and being distilled and simplified in each step, when it inevitably reaches the simplest and roughest minds it is adapted to their understanding. Thus it is possible that, without penetrating the mysterious jargon of the chemist's analysis of marls and clays, or the naturalist's daring investigation into how and why they formed, the husbandman and the artisan understand their utility in the fertilization of the soil and in the scouring of wools. From all that science teaches of marl, they know that which is most useful.

346. And why would it not be possible to breach this barrier, this wall that pride has erected between those who work and those who study? Is there no means to bring the learned closer to the artisans? Is there no means to bring science itself closer to its primary and most worthy object? What actually explains this separation, this distance between these groups? Would placing instruction closer to interest not encourage a most beneficial association? Here, Sire, is a task worthy of Your Highness's paternal vigilance, and the Society will point out two simple methods to accomplish it.

3rd. Means of removing both [obstacles]

347. The first is to promulgate useful knowledge among the propertied class. The Society, God forbid, does not intend to discourage any one of the classes that compose the state from aspiring to the sciences, but what wrong is there in hoping that they are pursued mainly by those who are in a position to bring about more general prosperity? After all, if landowners were instructed, interest, combined perhaps with vanity,

would encourage them to conduct experiments and use new techniques in their lands, applying the knowledge acquired in their studies, including new methods that have proved successful in other countries. And upon their success, would not their advice and example lead their tenants to imitate them and partake in these improvements? It is generally believed that farmers are slaves to customary preoccupations and traditions, and they are indeed, for old customs cannot be overturned but by new lessons whose positive results are seen with their own eyes. However, are not farmers, because of these very reasons, more prone to the type of combinations that moves [*anima*] and strengthens interest? The pride of the learned even denies this quality to such peoples: however, the mere reflection upon the large amount of knowledge amassed by agriculture—even in the stupidest part of its agents—will reveal how much cultivation owes to the submissiveness of agricultural workers [*labradores*].

1st. The instruction of the propertied classes

348. The Society will not recommend the construction of seminaries and schools to instruct the propertied classes, for these would not only be difficult to establish and endow, but also useless. The Society, moreover, does not wish to separate sons from fathers to improve education, for this would weaken both paternal tenderness and filial respect. It does not wish to have the young removed from domestic vigilance and control and placed in the mercenary care of strangers [*mercenario cuidado de un extraño*]. The physical and moral education of children belongs to parents, and it would never be well taught by those who are not. However, the government should undertake youth's literary education [*educación literaria*], and if the instruments of useful knowledge were multiplied across the kingdom, seminaries would not be so necessary among us. The nation would be indebted to Your Highness for multiplying public instruction; and without having to send their children away from their home, parents could have them fulfill their vows to both nature and religion.

349. The Society does not propose to add this type of instruction to our universities either. As long as they continue to be what they are and what they have been until today; as long as they are dominated by the spirit of scholasticism, the experimental sciences will never take root in them. Different objects, a different character, different methods and a different spirit animate each of them, making them incompatible, a truth confirmed by long and unfortunate experience. Perhaps it is not impossible to unite intellectual and practical sciences, and perhaps one day Your Highness will devote his efforts to bringing this joyous alliance about, given, Sire, your sincere commitment to improving general instruction. But to reach that worthy calling, it will be necessary to transform the structure and content of our entire system of education, and the Society does not seek to destroy, but rather to build.

350. Therefore, what the Society proposes is the multiplication of institutions of useful instruction across all the cities and towns of certain import; that is, in those where

the propertied class is ample and wealthy. Since this is an object of general and public utility, there should be no resistance to endowing these academies with revenues from municipal endowments [*fondos concejiles*], both from the capital or from the district [*partido*] of each city or town. This endowment would be easier to arrange if the teachers' salaries came, as they do in other countries, from the students' tuition, so that the government would only take care of the expenses related to the buildings, instruments and machines, libraries and the like. Moreover, funds that are now spent in notoriously useless academies could be transferred to these instead. The numerous professorships of Latin, and outdated and absurd philosophy established across the country, go against the tenor and spirit of our wise laws, for they do nothing but lure youth to intellectual careers and away from the useful arts that nature and sound policies would prefer, stealing them from the productive classes to bury them in sterile pursuits. This profusion, again, serves only to generate a superabundance of chaplains, friars, physicians, lawyers, scribes and sextons, whereas we are in dire need of artisans, farmers, cart drivers and seamen. Would it not be best to suppress these professorships and reallocate the funds instead to endow institutions that promote useful and profitable instruction?

351. Do not fear, Your Highness, that the multiplication of these institutions will generate a superabundance of scholars, because even if they are open to all—as they very well should be—people do not embrace scholarly professions because studies are readily available, but because they appear to provide some benefit. The faculties of moral theology, law and medicine promise their graduates that they will easily find placement as academics, and this is why so many are attracted to them. The useful sciences, however, do not promise such prizes. Their excellence is indeed revealed in the fact that a superabundance of mathematicians and physicists would be beneficial, whereas that of other doctors, as politician Saavedra wisely remarked, serves only to increase the number of parasites that feed off the state and debase the scholarly professions.

352. To ensure that the proposed institutions are indeed dedicated to useful instruction, a corpus of treatises on mathematical and physical sciences—especially the latter— must be drawn up. These should both gather the knowledge and truths that can be usefully applied to improve the diverse practices and labors of civil and domestic life, and also discard or avoid the vain and treacherous objects of investigation that pride and intellectual levity have introduced into these sciences' jurisdiction. If Your Highness were to reward the writer of this important work with honor and a great prize, many would rise to the challenge, for Spain is not lacking in men who would vie for such an illustrious reward and for the glory of instructing the youth of the country.

2nd. The instruction of farmers

353. Another way to reconcile science and interest is to instruct farmers. It would be absurd to try to subject them to long studies; but providing them with the results of

others' studies, which is what we advocate, would not be absurd at all. The aim of such an undertaking is great indeed, but the means needed to achieve it are simple and easy. The object is to diminish the ignorance of those occupied in the cultivation of the soil, or rather, to multiply and perfect their means of comprehension. The Society merely wishes that they all should read, write and be proficient in arithmetic. What an immense universe this simple knowledge opens up for men's perceptions! It allows all individuals to enhance the faculties of their reason and their souls; it is beneficial for every parent to conduct the daily business of civil and domestic life; and it is important for every state to improve the spirit and the heart of its members. Such is the education that the Society desires, and it will be enough for farmers, as well as all laborers, not only to grasp the sublime truths of religion and morality more deeply, but also to comprehend the simple and palpable laws of physics that could improve their arts. With the means of his perception perfected, the results and the discoveries of the more complex sciences could be understood by the most rustic man if these were communicated simply and clearly, free of scientific jargon and complications.

354. Your Highness should therefore establish elementary schooling everywhere: let there be no place, no village or parish without such schooling; let there be no individual, however poor or helpless, who cannot receive this instruction freely and easily. If the nation did not owe this assistance to all its members as the most poignant act of its protection and zeal, it owes it to itself as the simplest means of increasing its power and its glory. Indeed, is this not the most shameful testimony of our neglect: that we have abandoned and forgotten such a general, necessary and advantageous branch of instruction, while we ardently promote partial, useless or even harmful studies?

355. Fortunately, literacy and arithmetic are not difficult to teach, and they can be imparted with the same ease with which they are attained. Their teaching does not require great scholars as instructors, nor expensive endowments to pay for their honorarium; they only demand good, patient and virtuous men who respect innocence and would be pleased to instruct them. Nevertheless, the Society regards this undertaking as so important that it should be carried out by ministers of the church. Far from being foreign to it, this function requires the charity and gentleness that characterize our clergy, and it concurs with the duty of enlightening the people, which is at the very heart of their profession. If adding this charge to parish priests already burdened with other duties seems untenable, the church, using part of the tithes that go to prelates, chapters, loans and simple benefits, could appoint and endow an ecclesiastic in every town and every congregation, however small, to teach under the supervision and direction of the parish priests and local judges. Could the zeal and commitment of our reverend prelates and civil magistrates find a more commendable object? And what of the great benefits this establishment would receive if the methods and books of instruction were improved? Why not incorporate dogma and the principles of religious and political morality into this elementary schooling? Oh! The moral perils and misguided steps that citizens would be spared if the ignorance of these sublime matters were banished from their minds! How it would please God if the many horrible acts of impiety that the simple folk commit out of ignorance were forever reduced by their knowledge of these truths!

356. Once the propertied classes became acquainted with the principles of the useful sciences, and the remaining classes are initiated in the means to share in the knowledge enjoyed by the former, great and advantageous benefits would accrue to agriculture and all of the useful arts. Nothing more would be necessary than that our learned scholars should abandon their research, the only results of which are a presumptuous and sterile wisdom, and dedicate themselves instead to useful discoveries, simplifying and accommodating the knowledge thus obtained to the understanding of all men, and thus banishing forever the absurd notions that hold back progress, especially that of agriculture.

3rd. The creation and use of technical manuals

357. Focusing on this object, the Society believes that the simplest means of communicating and propagating the most useful and relevant scientific findings among farmers would be through technical manuals or primers that, written in simple language and adjusted to laborers' comprehension, explained the best methods for preparing the soil and selecting and conserving seeds; for planting, sowing, weeding, threshing and winnowing grain; for storing and conserving crops; and for how to best reduce them to liquids or flour and so forth. They could simply and effectively describe the instruments and machines available for the diverse agricultural tasks and explain their use. In a word, they could point out clearly how to secure the profits, the resources, the savings, the benefits, the improvements and the advantages that might be enjoyed in this profession.

358. The Society does not wish for these manuals to be taught in schools, which should be dedicated entirely to literacy and arithmetic and the sublime truths. Neither does it want to force farmers to read them or follow their indications, for nothing that is done forcibly can bring any lasting benefit. It only wishes that someone would make the effort to persuade farmers of the advantages to be gained from studying these manuals; and the Society expects that once they realized such activity is in their best interest, landowners would undertake this function. After all, once their interest has been enlightened, proprietors will readily perceive the profitability of communicating and propagating useful agricultural knowledge.

359. And why should we not expect this same zeal from parish clergy? Let us hope that once extended the teaching of useful science, their same principles will be propagated among such precious and important class of the state [the clergy]. Let us hope that our priests will also become, in this regard, fathers and teachers of the people![59] Then the people will be truly blessed! Blessed, for their shepherds will have shown them the way to eternal felicity, but also opened their eyes to the true

---

59 This same desire was expressed by famed Linnaeus in his *De fandamento scientiae aeconomicae e physica, et sciencia naturali petendo*, in the following terms: "Qui ecclesiis praeficiuntur, si scientiarum istarum lumine ipsi gauderent, brevi completam patriae nostrae agnitionem, immo summum perfectionis fastigium sperandum haberemus." We are sure to find more on this important point in a dissertation written by a wise and zealous ecclesiastical scholar, honored by the Sociedad Bascongada [sic] with an award, which will soon be published.

sources of abundance; and taught them that abundance, which rewards virtuous and honest work, provides the only happiness that is to be had on earth! Parish priests will also be blessed when, destined to live in the solitude of the countryside, they can find through the useful sciences that sweet and wonderful solace that the contemplation of nature brings to those who live closest to it, and which, raising man's heart toward his Creator, opens it to the workings of virtue, which is indeed the first aim of their holy ministry!

360. But, Sire, above all, Your Highness can expect great enthusiasm from the Patriotic Societies on this point. Although they remain at an early stage of development, still lacking protection and support, what great progress would they have helped agriculture achieve already were farmers capable of understanding and using their knowledge? Since their creation, these Societies have worked incessantly and applied all of their zeal and their knowledge [*luces*] to improving the useful arts, particularly agriculture, which is the principal object of their foundation and their care. Although they are persecuted everywhere by sloth and ignorance, and they are disparaged and abused by preoccupation and envy, have they not carried out great and useful experiments? Have they not examined and communicated great truths? Their reports, their memoirs and their prize-winning dissertations are enough to prove that in the brief period in which they have existed, more and better works on how to secure national prosperity have been written and published than in the two centuries that preceded them. And if they have done so much without recourse to the useful sciences, without protection, without resources and even without favorable public opinion or support, how much more will they be able to do when the people everywhere are acquainted with the principles of the exact and natural sciences and are capable of understanding their doctrines, so that they can dedicate themselves to uniting knowledge with interest, which ought to be the primary aim of government?

361. The Societies by themselves, Sire, can spread the principles of the economic science [*las luces de la ciencia económica*] across the entire kingdom, and thus banish the fatal notions that the ignorance of these principles has engendered; and they alone will be capable, in time, of developing the manuals recommended above. The work of solitary, reclusive scholars does little to encourage the people's enlightenment: first, because they carry it out in the retirement of their chambers, isolated from the local problems as well as from the knowledge granted by observation and experience; and, second, because they are usually given to sweeping generalizations, and therefore their conclusions can often lead to misguided rather than to successful applications. The Societies are not afflicted by these problems. Established in every province, comprised of landowners, magistrates, scholars, farmers, manufacturers and artists, with their members hailing from various districts, towns and territories, they gather and concentrate all the lights [*luces*] that study and experience provide, and they enhance and perfect them by repeated experiments and continuous conferences and discussions. Would their contribution to the propagation of useful instruction among all classes not be great?

362. Here, Sire, are two easy and simple ways of improving public instruction, spreading useful knowledge across the kingdom, banishing the obstacles that mistaken opinions and ignorance place in agriculture's path to progress and enlightening its agents so that they improve cultivation. There is only one remaining issue to consider: the removal of the natural and physical obstacles that hinder cultivation. This third and last point of this Report we will attempt to elucidate as briefly as possible.

THIRD KIND

PHYSICAL OBSTACLES, OR THOSE DERIVED FROM NATURE

363. The work of every farmer is a constant struggle against nature, which when unattended produces nothing but weeds and brush, and must be labored on and cultivated in order to bear fruit; and, yet, nature sometimes presents obstacles so powerful that the exertions of one individual alone cannot overcome them, and the combined forces of many must be marshalled. The need to overcome this kind of impediment, which was perhaps what first awakened in men the idea of a shared or common interest, and therefore what induced them to live in groups or villages, is still one of the most basic objects and chief obligations of all political societies.

364. Nature undoubtedly owes its greatest improvements to this necessity. Wherever one turns, nature appears beautified and perfected by the hand of man. On every side, will you discover wilderness cleared; savage beasts vanquished; lakes drained; rivers channeled; the very seas curbed; everywhere across the earth, the land has been cultivated and filled with farmsteads and villages, and beautiful and magnificent cities; all of these monuments bear witness to the admirable and indefatigable spirit of human industry, and to the capacity of common interest to protect and facilitate that of individuals.

365. And, yet, as has been noted previously, no nation, not even the most opulent and the most refined, has paid this subject all the attention that it deserves. Though it is true that nations have more or less promoted agriculture, in each and every one there are still physical impediments to be removed, obstacles that impede prosperity. Indeed, perhaps the most unequivocal sign of a nation's progress toward civilization is the degree of attention that it has paid to overcome these obstacles. Holland, where the best towns and cities have been built upon lands reclaimed from the ocean, and where formerly sterile and ungrateful soil, crisscrossed by innumerable canals, has become a delightful and prolific garden, is a prime example of how human art and genius can perform upon nature. In the same way, nations that have been favored with a more benign climate and a more extensive and bountiful soil yet contain immense tracts of uncultivated land that is either swamped, or covered by bush and scrub, or abandoned and reduced to endless sterility, are striking and unfortunate examples of negligence and sloth.

366. But instead of classifying the nations of the world according to this odious comparison, the Society shall proceed to identify the physical obstacles that hinder the prosperity of our agriculture, bringing Your Highness's attention to this important object, which has been so wisely contemplated by our legislation.[60]

367. These obstacles are of two sorts: those that are directly opposed to the advancement of agriculture; and those that, blocking the circulation and consumption of its products, have the same effect. The Society shall address the first type only in passing, not because there are no longer ponds to drain, forests to uproot or lands to clear and bring under cultivation, but simply because these are present for all to see, and the provinces frequently have brought these obstacles to Your Highness's supreme attention. However, the Society will say a few things about the natural obstacles related to irrigation, because they are worthy of a deeper analysis.

1st. Neglect of irrigation

368. There are two reasons why public authority should particularly attend to irrigation: the intensity of its necessity and the severity of its difficulty. Its necessity derives from the fact that the Spanish climate in general is arid and dry, and, without irrigation, a vast part of our land either produces nothing at all, or else is converted to pasture. With the exception of the northern provinces located at the base of the Pyrenees, and the mountainous tracts that branch out from that alpine chain into the interior, there is practically no district where irrigation would not multiply threefold the soil's production; and since anything that tends to this increase must be considered essential, then undoubtedly irrigation should be regarded as an object of general utility.

369. But what renders irrigation even more worthy of Your Highness's zeal is the difficulties agricultural workers encounter when undertaking works of irrigation. Where rivers run through level fields; and it is enough to scratch the surface of the land in order to redirect their waters onto the farmsteads, as is the case with the banks of the Esla and Orbigo rivers, and in many of our valleys and meadows, there is no need to ask the government to intervene. In such instances, irrigation lies within the reach of individual work, and should therefore remain under its charge, for undoubtedly landowners and tenants, stimulated by their own interest, will procure it as long as legislation protects their efforts. For in this as in many other areas, the maxim is that the government's obligations begin where the power of the individuals ends.

370. But beyond these fortunate territories, irrigation cannot be procured without large and costly projects. Spanish topography is irregular and varied, and most of its rivers are deep, their currents rapid and abundant. This makes it necessary to fortify riverbanks; dig deep canals; and maintain their level by means of weirs, or by

---

60 See l. I tit. IX, and laws VI and VII, title XX, of the second *Partida*, which are admirable and worthy of a better century.

lowering the ground in some places and raising it in others, or bypassing mountains to conduct water to the thirsty lands awaiting it. This is the situation faced by
Andalusia, Extremadura and most of La Mancha, not to mention the kingdom of
Aragon; and since these colossal projects evidently cannot be undertaken by individuals, it is clearly the government's obligation to carry them out.

371. It must also be observed that according to a nation's general circumstances, this
obligation is more or less incumbent on the state. It is often the case that in extraordinarily wealthy countries, where commerce leads to the daily accumulation of
capital in the hands of a few individuals, private persons often undertake the construction of great and expensive endeavors, whether to improve their own possessions or [as an investment] to further increase their revenues from them that
compare favorably to those of their neighbors. In such instances, irrigation enterprises are undertaken as speculative investments, and the government has to do
nothing other than encourage and protect them. But in less wealthy countries; in
large countries where there are more investment opportunities than capital available to invest; and where there are a million more useful and less risky speculative
prospects for capital, as is our case, it is clear that no individual will embark upon
such great enterprises; and if the government did not undertake them, the country
would be deprived of their benefits altogether.

372. But although the government's zeal and capacity are necessary for the execution
of these enterprises, its wisdom is equally indispensable to render them beneficial.
Evidently, it is impossible to undertake them all at once: they must be undertaken in
succession. And since it is impossible for each and every one of them to be equally
necessary and equally advantageous, it is up to the government's discernment to
determine the order to be followed, beginning with some and postponing others.

373. Justice would dictate that the most necessary works be executed first, and only after
their completion should attention shift to those that are merely advantageous. Since
the object of the former is to remove obstacles in territories where unfavorable
natural endowments obstruct the subsistence and the growth of the population of
the state; whereas the object of the latter is to remove impediments to the growth
of wealth among those who are in more advantageous situations, it is evident that
social equity demands that public attention focus first on the former and then
on the latter. This warning is all the more necessary, insofar as the importunity
of claimants and the preferences of magistrates who adjudicate such works can
unduly influence the observance of equitable proceedings. For this same reason, the
Society will let itself be guided by this principle when it analyzes the second kind of
physical obstacles that hinder our agriculture.

374. When the natural obstacles that directly hinder a country's agriculture are removed,
attention must be turned toward those that indirectly obstruct its prosperity, and
which are those that hamper the free and easy circulation of its products. Because
if, as we have stated earlier, consumption is the true engine of agriculture, it follows
that nothing will result in its increase and progress as decisively as augmenting the
means and facilities of consumption.

2nd. Absence of proper communication

375. The importance of internal and external communications and means of transport in a country is so clearly and generally acknowledged that it seems unnecessary to elaborate upon it; yet it would not be superfluous to demonstrate that though they are necessary for the prosperity of all branches of public industry [*industria pública*], they are even more essential to agriculture's progress. First, the products of the earth are generally heavier and more voluminous than those of industry, and are therefore more expensive and difficult to transport. This is evidenced when comparing the value of agricultural and industrial goods of equal weight, for an *arroba* of the most valuable produce will sell for less than an equal load of the most ordinary manufactures. The reason is that the price of the former does not reflect more capital than that of the land itself, nor more work than that involved in the process of cultivation, whereas the price of the latter reflects both these inputs, plus the labor and expense employed in their fabrication.

376. A second reason is that agricultural products are generally perishable, so that their conservation is more difficult and expensive than those of industry. Many of them, such as fruits, vegetables, legumes etc., spoil if they are not quickly consumed, while the rest are nonetheless susceptible to risks and damage in their transportation as well as in their conservation. Finally, industry is movable, and agriculture is stable and immobile: a manufacturing enterprise can close in one place and reopen in another, while a cultivated field is locked in place. The former, in a word, fixes the markets that the latter must reach. Thus, we observe that industry, always attentive to consumers, follows them like a shadow, placing itself close to them and accommodating itself to their whims; whereas agriculture, tied to the earth and unable to follow consumers wherever they might be, languishes when markets are distant, or perishes entirely when there are none to speak of.

377. This amply demonstrates the need to improve our provinces' internal roads; the external roads that communicate them with each other; and the general ones that cross from the center to the outer boundaries of the kingdom and the sea ports through which our produce can be exported—a need that, however, has more often been recognized than met.

Overland transportation

378. However, we should not suppose that to remove this obstacle to circulation, it is enough to facilitate the circulation of our agricultural commodities, for transportation must be eased to the highest degree possible. Opening up a bridle path so that the products from a given province or district can circulate is often not an adequate solution, for conveyance using beasts of burden is the most expensive of all, and regardless of how close a market is, the cost of transporting the goods might raise their price so much that they would be unsalable or unprofitable; therefore, roads are clearly indispensable.

379. Facts confirm this conclusion. For instance, the highest consumption of Castilian wine from the fertile territories of Rueda, la Nava and la Seca, takes place in Asturias. Since there is no roadway between these two points, the wine is transported using pack animals at an ordinary cost of 80 *reales* per load, so that wines that in their place of origin had very low prices are sold at approximately 36 to 38 reals per *arroba* in the market where they are consumed. The difference increases even more with the *millones* tax, which brings the final price to 44 to 46 reals per arroba. [The consequences of transportation costs on prices] shows us that, despite the preference among consumers in cold and wet provinces for the dry wines of Castile, Catalan wines that are transported easily and inexpensively to Asturias, may substitute Castilian wines; and it would not be surprising that eventually the consumption of Catalan wine would eventually ruin Castilian vineyards.

380. There is more: wheat purchased in León is sold in the Asturian capital and ports at 20 to 24 *reales* per *fanega* more than its original price, because even though the distance between these two points is a mere 20 leagues, the average cost of conveyance is of 5 to 6 *reales* per *arroba*. Evidently, [Asturias] would derive great benefit from a proper road, but, more importantly, without it, [León] cannot prosper at all, for its surplus produce is sold only in the former's markets or exported through its ports.

381. This also leads to the conclusion that when the distance between a district and the places where consumption takes place is so vast that transportation on carriages is still costly enough to make their products unsalable, reason and justice demand that a route of communication be opened by water, whether by rendering the most appropriate of its rivers navigable, or by opening a canal, because the state must provide all of its members with the means that they need to procure their subsistence, wherever they are located.

382. Our population's present distribution gives more credence to this maxim, insofar as the great centers of consumption are dispersed, having barely any contact with one another or with the agricultural provinces. The court is situated in the middle [of Spain], while Seville, Cádiz, Málaga, Valencia, Barcelona and the rest of the most populous cities occupy the extremities, extending the radius of circulation over an immense circumference that makes transportation expensive, slow and difficult. Under such circumstances, the regular means of transportation are inadequate to secure our agriculture's prosperity, and it is necessary to aspire to those that can link all of the territories and districts with the utmost ease and efficiency, and bring them closer, so to speak, to the furthest nodes of consumption. This will encourage agriculture even in the remotest corners of the kingdom, providing the means to promote their felicity, and distributing abundance everywhere, so that eventually the country's population and wealth will be more evenly dispersed across the land, correcting today's horrible concentrations in the center and the extremities.

383. But since it is impossible to undertake all these works at once, nothing is more important, as we already observed, than establishing an order for their execution, and it does not take much thought to realize that such an order will be determined by the very

nature of things [*la naturaleza misma de las cosas*]. The Society will make key observations regarding this point below.

384. First: one should never lose sight of the fact that necessary works are preferable to purely useful ones, for not only are the former always inherently useful, but their necessity involves a more evident utility; and, as has already been observed, the need to secure subsistence is more deserving of the government's efforts than the desire to secure prosperity.

385. Second: attention should first go to roads and trails, for although navigation canals offer greater advantages to transport, these can only be realized if general circulation in the districts has already been facilitated by better roads, for only then will canals produce the benefit that is expected of them. Canals are more costly than roads, and sound economics [*la buena economía*] demands that the funds destined to these enterprises, which are not infinite, be allocated first and foremost to those that, costing less, provide broader and more general benefits.

386. This rule, however, admits an exception in favor of canals that could facilitate both navigation and irrigation, for if there is evidence that a province or territory absolutely needs such a canal to subsist, such an undertaking should receive priority, despite its costliness.

387. This maxim appears to have been forgotten during the reign of Charles I and his august son, for when Spain's dire want of roads and trails was leading to the decadence and ruin of cultivation in many provinces, they promoted navigation of rivers and by means of canals.[61] The Acequia Imperial, which makes the Guadalquivir and Tagus rivers navigable, and the Jarama and Manzanares canals, as well as similar works, all date from this period, the expense of which, better employed, would have secured a more general prosperity.

388. Third: regarding roads, those located in the interior of each province merit greater attention than those leading from it, because the latter facilitate the export of their surplus production, but the former are necessary to facilitate the creation of such surplus.

389. We also seemed to have forgotten this maxim when, during the preceding reign, and thanks to the royal decree of 10 June 1761, we embarked upon the improvement of our roads with great zeal. This decree ordered to take up first those roads that

---

61 A letter written to Phillip II from Portugal on 22 May 1585 by Juan Bautista Antonelli reveals that during such times, the zealous author found it plausible to offer to make the interior of Spain navigable in its entirety. However, circumstances were not ripe for the kingdom to undertake this project, despite the evident benefits it promised; and yet, notwithstanding that proper economy dictated that improvements upon the kingdom's transportation should begin with the opening of roads, how different would its agriculture, industry and commerce be today if the government had adopted that renowned engineer's maxims, and fortified itself with the necessary discipline to carry it out? See Antonelli's letter in the works of Don Benito Bails, whose analyses offer the nation hope that someday canals will be constructed and its rivers will be made navigable. *Elementos de mathematicas*. Tomo 9, part. 2.

linked the court to the extremities; then those that linked the provinces with one another; and, finally, the internal roads within each province, without taking into consideration that need and utility recommended the absolutely opposite order: it was more essential to increase cultivation itself in the interior of each province, and, therefore, across the entire kingdom, than to establish the means to make it more profitable, for these vast plans to improve communications would be futile as long as unhappy tenants and farmers were unable to go from one village or town to another, or from market to market, without exhausting their patience and the strength of their pack animals; and at the risk of losing the fruits of their toil and the hopes of their very subsistence in the mud.

390. Fourth: a just and proper order also demands that not too many roads be built at once, in case there are not enough funds to finish them; since it is uncontestable that the efforts to connect two points produce utility only when they are carried to completion, it is clear that it is better to finish one road than to start many and complete none of them, for 20 leagues of a single finished road provide more benefit than hundreds of other roads left unfinished.

391. This principle went unheeded in the observation of the just cited 1761 decree, for the great roads of Andalusia, Valencia, Catalonia and Galicia were all begun at once, and work on the roads of Old Castile, Asturias, Murcia and Extremadura followed soon after. But since the funds allotted to these enterprises proved insufficient, 30 years have elapsed and not one of these roads has been completed.

392. In a matter such as this, good examples are sometimes pernicious. The Romans undertook the construction of all of the great roads of their empire at once, and what is even more admirable, they finished all of them, taking them from the Plaza de Antonino in Rome to the interior of England on the one hand, and to Jerusalem on the other; and these roads are so broad, so solid and magnificent that their remains still fill us with just admiration. Many modern nations sought to imitate them, but lacking the same means, and unwilling to adopt them, they caused their people affliction without providing the promised benefits.

393. However, this rule admits a reasonable exception: those roads that the provinces themselves undertake with their own means. This poses no inconvenience, provided that they follow the maxim of improving or opening up the interior roads first, before undertaking those that lead from it.

395. The Society will cite an example to lend more clarity and credence to its doctrine. In the middle of this century, the fertile territory of Castile desperately needed to improve its connections with the rest of Spain: the commerce that it once dominated was overtaken by Andalusia, and, therefore, Castile's industry had been ruined, and its great cities, which consumed its agricultural products, were also ruined and lay practically deserted. Where could this unhappy province send its surplus? To New Castile? The Guadarrama port was inaccessible to carts! To the coastal provinces of the east and south, shipped through the Cantabrian Sea? Those parts of the Pyrenees that extend from Fuenterrabia to Cape Finisterre blocked the way! In such

dire circumstances, the court in Madrid decided to build a road to Guadarrama, and wisely so, for this not only satisfied a more urgent want, but also provided the widest possible benefit by linking the country's two greatest centers of consumption and agriculture.

396. And yet, this remedy was not sufficient. In years of abundance, Castile produces enough grain not only to supply the capital, but also to export the surplus to other provinces, and even to foreign markets. Hence, roads to Santander, Biscay and Guipuzcoa were opened, providing Castilian goods with access to the sea, and enhancing the province's cultivation.

397. And it may be difficult to believe, but this was also insufficient to make the province prosperous! Overland conveyance is so expensive that even if the original prices were the same, the foreign grain that reaches Santander by sea can be sold for less than the Castilian grain that comes by land.[62] Although in the markets of Palencia, a *fanega* of wheat cost 6 *reales* in 1757, its price in Santander, the closest point outside Castile, reached 22 *reales*. Did the grain of Campos, which was more distant, suffer a similar fate? This alone justifies the construction of the canal of Castile, if the significant advantages it will bring to irrigation were not justification enough.

398. It is anticipated that this canal will extend across the territory of Campos and through most of the kingdom of León, and it is surely the greatest and most glorious enterprise that can be undertaken by the nation. Let us imagine that this canal is actually built, touching the foothills of the Guadarrama on one side, and Reynosa and León on the other. Let us also imagine that a road connects this latter point to the Asturian Sea, and continues on to the fertile fields of El Bierzo, La Bañeza, Campos, Zamora, Toro and Salamanca; and, right before our eyes, the effects of an active and more general circulation will be made clear through the improved and increased cultivation and population growth that would grace the land, opening up all the sources of wealth in the country's two largest and most fertile territories, which today are the least populated and the most deprived.

[Transportation] by water

399. And what would happen if the multiple branches of the Duero were to be extended, prolonging the river's flow even farther inland? What if the Eresma was succored in its passage across the mountains to meet the Jarama and Manzanares Rivers, to carry, as it did in another time, our goods to the port of Lisbon?[63] What if

---

62 It would be unbelievable, were it not an undeniable fact, that the wheat of Beauce and Orleanais, more than 100 leagues away by sea, arrives in Cadiz sooner and at [sic] 100 percent less expense than those of Palencia, which is only 40 leagues from Santander. See note XXIII of the many excellent notes in the eulogy to the Count of Gausa published by the Society.

63 For the history of navigation in the Tagus, see the letters of Jesuit thinker Andres Buriel, published by Don Antonio Valladares, especially the one written to Don Carlos de Simon Pontero on 13 September 1785, p. 180.

the Guadarrama, linked to the Tagus, provided another port for La Mancha and Extremadura and then continued south to the source of the Guadalquivir, and in Córdoba met the ships that could then again continue on to Seville? What if the Ebro, touching the Alfaques on one part, and Laredo on the other, carried to the eastern provinces the products of the north, and linked our Cantabrian Sea with the Mediterranean?[64] What if the roads, canals and navigable rivers of the interior, linked by all their arteries in an immense circulation, filled the many and happy provinces with abundance and prosperity? Without letting itself be dazzled by its hopes for such a glorious future, the Society will now examine the last of the physical obstacles that it has identified, and which, if removed, would make its hopes a reality.

3rd. Lack of commercial seaports

400. Among the natural advantages that nations may enjoy, the most desirable one under Europe's present circumstances is undoubtedly proximity to the sea. Europe, united by sea to the most remote continents, and, at this time, with its industry called to furnish an enormous quantity of goods, extends its reaches and hopes to partake in all the Earth's products. And if one pays attention to the advanced state of the art of navigation today, it appears that only ignorance and sloth can deprive peoples across the world from so many, and such precious, goods.

401. But such an advantage is usually offset by great difficulties. On the one hand, the sea's fury permanently threatens the populations that live, or would live, on its shores; and, on the other, nature seems to have destined precipices and inclement beaches to restrain this wild element or to highlight its danger so that communications often end up being challenging or impossible. But who does not see that these very difficulties offer a stimulus to men's exertions? Called at times to provide for their own security, and at other times to extend the sphere of their interest, men find themselves urged to overcome powerful obstacles. This, Sire, is why the progress of nations in almost every instance has derived from such an advantage; and knowing how to use it, no nation will fail to find in its proximity to the sea the origins of plenty and prosperity.

402. In this as in many other respects, Spain has been favored by nature. The country not only enjoys an advantageous climate and fertile soil; most of its territory is also bathed by the sea. Located between the two greatest bights of the world, and situated, so to speak, at the door through which the waters of the [Atlantic] Ocean meet

---

64 In his *Historia de España*, bk. 10, ch. 15, Mariana notes the following: "to repress them requires a fleet, and so the King (Don Alfonso de Aragon) ordered the construction of many boats and vessels in Zaragoza: and it is well known that under Vespasian's imperial rule and that of his sons, the banks of the Ebro were repaired and straightened and channeled, and the river was navigated up to a town called Bario, located not far from the present city of Logroño, 65 leagues from the sea, which afforded great advantages to trade and commerce."

those of the Mediterranean, Spain seems particularly endowed to be connected with every part of the globe. And if to this we added its vast and fertile colonies of East and West, which were procured precisely by its seafaring advantage, we cannot deny that Spain seems destined by providence to found a great and glorious empire.

403. How is it, then, that being so fortunately and happily situated, we have neglected one of the most necessary means to reach this end? How can we have so appallingly neglected our ports and harbors, without which the great advantage of our access to the sea is vain and futile? There is barely one of them that has been transformed from the original state nature gave it, and though it is true that she provided us with singularly excellent and strategic harbors, many more cry out for improvements that only mankind's ingenuity can provide! How many maritime provinces find that their industries are deprived of the benefits of navigation, and all of the goods that depend on it, for want of a proper seaport? And how not to see in this situation one of the chief obstacles thwarting the prosperity of our agriculture?

404. The Society need not remind anyone that if such an object [accessibility to seaports] is so necessary to industry, it is more so to agriculture. The Society has already said that industry naturally follows consumers and meets their needs, whereas agriculture cannot seek herself for advantages, but must wait for them still.

405. On the other hand, though all provinces can be industrial, not all can be agricultural: and since some enjoy in abundance the [agricultural] produce that others lack, it is necessary for the surplus of the first to succor the second. This is the only way for the surplus of all to feed that robust and lively commerce that is a key ambition of all governments.

406. Therefore, if we aspire to generate such trade, it is necessary to improve and increase the number of our seaports, so that, facilitating and encouraging the exportation of our precious fruits, we give national agriculture the final impulse that it needs. Providing the country with a proper system of internal circulation would generate overall abundance, leading to a reduction in the cost of living for all classes of society, and therefore to an increase in both population and industries; this would further augment the fruits of the earth and labor, and domestic trade would be encouraged and revived. Then, the very superabundance of produce and manufactures that would invariably result would beckon us to provide outlets for external commerce, without which it could not generate great benefits.

407. This subject could furnish material for extensive reflection, but the Society will content itself with submitting to Your Highness's wise deliberation only two of the most vital: first, that it is absolutely necessary to combine external with internal routes, as well as the works of canals and roads, with those of seaports. This principle has not always been observed among us: it is not unusual to find a good port without any communication to the interior, or exceptional roads or means of transport unconnected to any port. The port of Vigo, for example, which is probably Spain's best, and has the added advantage of adjoining a foreign kingdom, has no proper road linking it to the interior. And although Old Castile has had a road

to the sea for 40 years, it is only now that the port of Santander is being improved. Moreover, no cart roads link the fertile kingdom of León with the Principality of Asturias, which has around 30 tolerable to second-rate ports. Thus, though certain public works have been undertaken, the advantages of circulation are squandered when they are not properly directed and coordinated.,

408. Second: that after facilitating exports by multiplying and improving our seaports, attention should be directed toward the promotion of national navigation, removing all the burdens that plague it. Indeed, bad fiscal legislation, municipal rights, merchant guilds, license requirements, the police and an ill-defined mercantile jurisprudence; in sum, anything and everything that obstructs the growth of our merchant marine by augmenting the difficulties of its expeditions, driving up freight charges, and annulling both the advantages of our location and the effects of laws and incentives designed to favor it, destroys external trade.

409. Such, Sire, are the means to encourage our agriculture, or more specifically, to remove the obstacles that nature places on its path to prosperity. We are aware that executing this is challenging, to say the least, and it is not entirely dependent upon Your Highness's zeal. To overcome the political obstacles, it is enough for Your Highness to speak and repeal. Those related to public opinion will yield naturally to proper and useful teaching, the way light dispels darkness; but struggling against nature, bending her to one's will, requires great and powerful efforts that entail vast costs and significant means that are not always available. We will now say a few things about these means.

Means of removing physical obstacles

410. When you consider, on the one hand, the immense expense of the enterprises that we have described; and, on the other, that a single one of these, a port, for instance, or a canal, or a road, usually costs more than the entire budget destined to the yearly maintenance of all existing elements of its kind, the despair with which most governments approach these efforts is understandable. And since these funds ultimately come from individuals' wealth, it seems that the only available option is to deprive many future generations of the felicity that such works would provide so as not to make the present generation unhappy; or to oppress one generation for the welfare of those that follow.

411. However, we must acknowledge that if nations had dedicated the resources that they have employed in other less important matters to this essential object, all of them, even the poorest and most unfortunate, would have flourished. For it is not insufficient public revenues that thwart nations' progress in mastering nature, but the unfair preference given to objects that are less directly relevant to the general welfare, and, in fact, are sometimes inimical to it.

412. To demonstrate this proposition, it is enough to consider that the greatest part of public revenues is often spent on war, and though no expenditures may be more

just or necessary than those dedicated to national security and defense, history has shown that for every war waged with this object in mind, there are countless others pursued either for territorial expansion, or to increase commerce, or merely to satisfy national pride. What country would not be graced with ports, canals and roads, and therefore, plenty and prosperity, if, adopting a peaceful system, it had invested the resources misspent in projects of vanity and destruction in these undertakings instead?[65]

413. But putting the frenzy of war aside, what nation would not have flourished if instead of granting piecemeal and indirect incentives and succors to commerce, industry and agriculture, which are most often not only useless, but downright harmful, it had employed these funds in the improvements of which we speak? By Jove, is there any object whose benefits are comparable in extension, usefulness or duration, to those brought about by such works? At this point, one must confess that Spain, perhaps more generous than any other nation, has also been the most unfortunate in its selection of means to promote general welfare.

414. This general and entrenched delusion also includes a love of splendid but useless works, so that we can unequivocally state that no nation would lack the seaports, roads and canals demanded by the welfare of its people if it had only employed in the construction of these undertakings the means wasted on works that provide merely comfort or beauty. Prompted by another mania that the love for the fine arts has spread across Europe, every nation aspires to represent its splendor through the magnificence of what are termed public works; and thus their royal courts, their capitals and even their smaller cities and towns have been filled with grandiose edifices, so that while they begrudge the resources to construct works of public utility, they prodigally lavish them on ostentatious monuments; and, what is worse, they glorify themselves in this.

415. The Society, Sire, is far from censuring the taste for the fine arts, which it shares, or the befitting protection afforded to them by the government; and it is even further from denying architecture the appreciation that it merits as the most important and necessary of all arts. Finally, it does not pretend that a single rule be applied to the public works erected in a court or capital city as well as in a common village. But it cannot lose sight of the fact that the true measure of a nation's decorum, and more importantly, its power and political representation, which are the bases of its splendor, are ultimately derived from its members' welfare. And there is nothing more shameful than the contrast between a nation's great cities, adorned with magnificent arches, squares, doorways, theaters, promenades and other ostentatious monuments, and the barrenness and desolation of its countryside, which languishes for the want of ports, canals and roads, and lies fallow and desolate while its inhabitants go about naked and dirty.

---

65 "Quid enim tam populare quam pax? Qua non modo ii quibus natura sensum dedit, sed etiam tecta, atque agri mihi laeturi." Cic. De Leg. Agr.

416. The most significant conclusions to be drawn from this are that the improvements that we have described must constitute the largest expenditure to the public treasury; and that no system will satisfy a people's needs as well as its desires better than one that can distinguish between the latter and the former, and treat them accordingly. For when funds are invested in other, less useful enterprises, they are lost to the common good, while those invested in improvements are like capital that, put to good use, increases its benefit every day, and, at the same time, encourages the rapid growth of individual fortunes and public revenues, providing the means to attend to the secondary but commendable necessities of comfort, ornament and even vanity common to all peoples.

1st. Improvements with respect to the kingdom as a whole

417. The Society also maintains that, just as specific shares are calculated and allotted for the support of the royal household, the army, the armada, the courts of law and public offices in the distribution of public revenues, a specific public fund for improvements should be created to carry out the works just mentioned. And since the nation will be closer to achieving prosperity the greater this fund is, no economy will be more sacred or laudable than the one that encourages this fund's growth, with the savings generated by the deferment of the other objects of public spending. Finally, the Society considers that if these policies directed at economizing [*esta economía*] do not generate sufficient revenue, it will be necessary to devise a general tax or contribution to fund an endowment for improvement, which will be gladly accepted insofar as its product is destined to enterprises that will increase the general welfare and happiness. And why should the Society not hope that Your Highness's zeal will set in motion Your Majesty's will to employ a resource that is always at hand, subject only to his supreme authority, and one that is as dear to his pious heart as it is necessary to carry out these important works? Why not, as has been done at other times, employ our troops to construct roads and canals when the nation is at peace? If the soldiers of Alexander, Sulla and Caesar, the greatest enemies of mankind, carried out useful labors in times of peace, can we not expect that a just, peaceful and virtuous king, who loves his people, would use his armies to work for its felicity, filling with blessed and useful toil their idle periods, which would otherwise be devoted to vice and dissipation, corrupting valor and offending public morality? What splendid works could we not complete with such powerful aid! Oh, would the wealth and strength of the state grow indeed!

418. Regarding the creation of a public endowment for improvements: first, it should only be used for the construction and maintenance of works of general public utility; that is, the great general roads that go from the kingdom's center to its frontiers; trading seaports; the great canals; or to secure navigation in the country's main rivers; in sum, works that are destined to facilitate our products' general circulation and exportation. It should not be employed in defraying undertakings that are only partially useful insofar as, however great their benefits, they are mostly of a private

or a geographically limited scope. Second: resources should be invested following a certain order: according to necessity and utility, following the principles that the Society has already established.

2nd. Improvements with respect to the provinces in particular

419. But this method would deprive many provinces of works not only useful and ben- eficial, but also urgently necessary for their inhabitants' well-being. Therefore, provincial endowments for improvements should be devised to defray the costs of these undertakings left out of the general system of improvements. The Society believes that resources for these provincial endowments should be appropriated from the sales of *baldíos*, if Your Highness adopts the resolution to sell them; or from their rents, if Your Highness prefers emphyteusis. After all, it is undeniable that the people of the territories where *baldíos* are located have a preferential claim over these lands and whatever benefits they produce. If, however, some provinces cannot obtain enough resources from these assets, they can complete their endow- ments with a provincial contribution that, again, will be well received and gladly paid if it is established following considerations of equality, and if it is dependably and faithfully invested in the proper objects.

420. There are two ways to guarantee equality, that most essential element of justice. First, by having all residents contribute, without exception, as established in the Alphonsine legislation and the Cortes of Guadalajara, and as dictated by equity and reason; for nothing can justify the exemption of a class or individual from contributing to works of public utility that will benefit them as much as their fellow citizens; and, second, by having all contribute proportionally to their capacity to do so, because one cannot and should not expect the poor to pay as much as the wealthy; and though the advantages generated will reach every class, it is evident that those individuals enjoying greater fortunes will derive greater utility from such works, and should therefore pay accordingly.

421. Perhaps these two conditions are met by the duty on salt; for salt consumption is practically universal, but it is also proportional to each individual's economic capacity. This duty has the advantage of being practically imperceptible, for it is levied gradually and in small amounts, without any vexations or conflict- generating procedures complicating its collection; and it is raised practically without expense, for even in those provinces where collectors take a percent of the product, this does not exceed 6 percent. Perhaps the best arrangement is to let each province keep the revenues generated by this duty so that they carry out the aforesaid works, trusting their zeal and capacity to do so well. Nothing would ensure a better investment in terms of economy and scrupulousness, for after all, these works would primarily benefit the province and its residents, so that those most interested in their prompt and proper execution are the provinces themselves. On the other hand, such undertakings require great and constant

care, which means that if the government were responsible for them, they would either burden the ministry in terms of attention and expense, or they would be neglected or improperly cared for by those with little or no stake in their proper functioning.

422. The Society, Sire, cannot refrain from this reflection, which it considers to be of the utmost importance. We frequently and with good reason lament the lack of zeal and public spirit among us; but the source of this evil is the profound mistrust with which individuals' zeal and integrity are held. A few examples of misappropriation have unreasonably generated this general wariness, which is as unfair as it is harmful. Municipalities are not allowed to invest a single coin of the council rents that they collect; provincial governments have no say in the works and projects carried out or planned in their districts: their roads, their bridges, their public works are always carried out under mysterious orders brought by unknown and independent commissioners. What is done to stimulate the zeal and commitment of municipal and provincial officeholders and citizens? How can we expect them to be moved by their public spirit when the present system severs the relations of affection, interest and decorum that reason and politics themselves should establish between the whole and its parts, between the community and its members? Trust these enterprises to individuals of the provinces, and, if it were possible, to individuals chosen by them: trust municipal and provincial authorities with the distribution and use of the funds that they have contributed, and the direction of the works in which they are the most interested parties; form provincial juntas constituted by property owners, members of the clergy, members of the economic societies, and Your Highness will see how public zeal and enthusiasm will soon be reborn in the hearts of those provinces where it seemed to have been banished by suspicion and mistrust, and flourish even more in those where these deleterious influences have yet to enter.

423. This provincial endowment should undertake those improvements that secure general benefits for the province, such as provincial trading ports; the roads that connect these with the interior; the roads that connect the province with the general roads; those that connect it with other provinces; the navigation of their rivers; and the opening of canals; in sum, all of those works whose utility is somewhat limited to the province, as opposed to spread throughout the kingdom or circumscribed to a specific locale.

3rd. Improvements with respect to municipalities

424. Enterprises that, however, benefit only specific districts must be paid for by each local council and the endowments for improvement will be made up of the *propios* of each council, or of new resources [*arbitrios*] to be paid by the inhabitants of its jurisdiction, according to principles of generality, equality and proportionality.

425. This municipal endowment for improvements could be increased with the product of the sale of council lands; or from their lease, if they were to be ceded in emphyteusis, by borrowing on the quit rents the value of the required capital. The Society

has shown that the distribution or privatization of these lands is necessary; and that its just execution is based on the fact that the communities themselves possess the absolute property rights over these lands.

426. With this fund, a council would be responsible for opening, improving and maintaining the roads and paths that connect it with the provincial and general roads, as well as with the main market or consumption points of each district; it would also pay for irrigation ditches or dikes; vicinal bridges; the wharves or docks of their fishing ports; in sum, all of the works under its jurisdiction that would bring general benefits to the population, excepting those that would only benefit specific individuals.

427. However, the particular circumstances of some provinces complicate this question and demand further consideration. Where the rural population is dispersed, such as in Guipúzcoa, Asturias and Galicia, where households are scattered widely, there is naturally a greater need for common paths and roads, such as those that lead to the church, the market, the woods, the river, the fountain. Usually, the local citizens [*vecinos*] themselves undertake these works, although custom dictates various means of doing so. In Asturias, for example, one day of every week is dedicated to these works, the so-called *sostaferia* or *sestaferia* [sixth day], perhaps because in ancient days it used to be Friday. The residents of the parish gather to repair their roads together. This is certainly a beneficial institution, except for the following abuses, which can and do occur, perverting the custom's beneficial character: 1st. That those who own property in the parish but do not reside there, and the ecclesiastics who do reside in the parish, exempt themselves from participating, even though reason dictates that both should at the very least send their servants, because the benefits derived from this work are received by all; 2nd. That if a farmhand who owns a cart or carriage, works for the same amount of time as one who does not, the inequality in their contribution is 200 to 100, for the salary of a cart driver is of 11 *reales* while that of a laborer is 3 ½ *reales*; 3rd. That since all of the residents of a given municipal district gather at one point, which can be two leagues away from some households while being quite close to others, an instance of even greater inequality than the previous situation occurs, for if those who live the furthest away happen not to have carriages, they would need to walk three to four hours at night to be able to meet with their neighbors by dawn, and another three or four hours to return home, thus contributing the equivalent of two workdays; 4th. Finally, that powerful individuals sometimes make use of this customary work on private roads; that is, those that lead to particular households or fields; and other times, villagers are made to work on provincial or general roads, something that is not only unreasonable but inhumane.

428. This last issue merits Your Highness's close attention. The Society has stated previously that the great national or general works that will improve communication between the provinces and abroad will be useless as long as the roads and paths across the kingdom's interior are not improved. And now it states that if it were impossible to build or improve them all at once, work should begin on the smaller

ones and gradually proceed to the largest. This order would produce a great and powerful benefit worthy of Your Highness's consideration: the proper distribution of our rural population. It would not be enough to allow land enclosures if, at the same time, circulation and transport cannot secure the sale and consumption of the products obtained. But once both enclosures and good local roads are in place, should we not expect that tenants and farmers will be induced by their own interest to move into the fields? Who can doubt that smallholders and farmers will not follow in their footsteps, and cultivate and improve their lands as well? And who doubts that, cultivated and improved, a beautiful countryside will also attract the large and wealthy landowners, at the very least during the delicious warm seasons when nature beckons to them with the irresistible charm of its tranquillity and splendor? And, finally, trades and crafts capable of satisfying the wants of this newly invigorated and increased rural population would come in the wake of all, an industry that, small but essential to civilization and felicity, is today concentrated in towns and cities. After all, is it not the lack of proper communications and the scarcity and high prices of everything else that keeps our fields depopulated?

429. Of course, other causes contribute to perpetuate this evil, but the same remedy will eventually prevail over each and every one of them. Undoubtedly, our towns' public order regulations, with their excessively harsh and indiscreet measures, constitute another of these causes. Let the licentiousness of the large cities be policed with severity; let the city people's spectacles and diversions be closely controlled! This seems fair and necessary; and, moreover, Your Highness's zeal could discern and eradicate any abuses that arise from close policing. But extending such precautions to the remotest villages and fields that dot the countryside is certainly strange and pernicious. The furor of imitation [*furor de imitar*] has led municipal councils to adopt rules and policies that are only suited to a great city. There is no *alcalde* who does not decree a curfew, or ban festivals and charivaris; or set up an inquisitorial vigilance over the residents, constantly pursuing not only those who pilfer or blaspheme, which is reasonable, but also those who sing and dance, so that the poor peasant, tired of sweating and toiling every day of the week, cannot, come Saturday night, change into his Sunday best and give a hearty bellow, singing or dancing ballads in the village hall. He is monitored by the authorities during his feasts and merrymaking, in his assemblies and repasts, wherever he is and wherever he goes, so that he sighs for the honest and innocent pleasures that made his soul free, and that are now denied him. Is there any other reason for the melancholy, the unkemptness and the sort of unsociable, surly character that our peasants display?

430. But, Sire, when our laborers move from the towns to the countryside, and adopt the simplicity and innocence of its atmosphere; and come to know no pleasure greater than the village festivals and *romerías*, its dances and picnics, gathering to enjoy these innocent pastimes peacefully and freely, the way they are enjoyed in Guipúzcoa, Galicia and Asturias; frankness and joy will infuse their character, and they will know true happiness. Then, they will no longer miss town or city life, and the magistrates' only concern will be to protect and admire their rustic customs.

And smallholders will not shun living among the laboring peasants and participating in their mirth; and the nobility and the powerful will sometimes come to witness this rural felicity, admiring its candor and its purity, and perhaps they will sigh in remembrance of this delight when they return to the tumultuous pleasures of city life. Then, the population of our kingdom will no longer lie interred in the ample cemeteries of the regional capitals. Distributed across small cities, towns large and small, rural villages, hamlets, and across the fields themselves, the population will carry with it industry and trade, so that wealth will also be more widely and equally distributed, and plenty and prosperity will reign everywhere.

CONCLUSION

431. Such are, Sire, the obstacles that nature, opinion and the law place on agriculture's path to perfection, and such are the means that the Society recommends for their removal, so that individual interest is stimulated and agriculture attains the greatest possible prosperity. Without question, Your Highness will need unwavering perseverance and valor to repeal detrimental legislation, to eliminate the many harmful opinions and to embark on the myriad necessary improvements detailed here, combating the vices and errors that plague us. But such is the nature of grave ills: they can only be cured by great and powerful remedies.

432. Furthermore, the remedies proposed by the Society demand an even more vigorous effort, insofar as they must be undertaken simultaneously, lest greater evils beset us. The sale of common lands could place an enormous portion of land in mortmain without a law against entailment to prevent it. Without a special restrictive law ordering the dissolution of the small *mayorazgos*, ecclesiastical mortmain would devour that immense portion of property that civilian entailment has so far preserved from that abyss. What good would enclosures do if the system of partial protection and herding privileges continued, undermining farmers' interests? What would be the use of irrigation ditches or canals if enclosures were not authorized? The construction of ports must be accompanied by that of roads; but roads would only be useful if produce were encouraged and allowed to circulate freely; and free circulation of products necessitates a system of taxes and duties compatible with property rights and liberty of cultivation. All of this, Sire, is related to both nature and politics, and a single incongruous law, a single erring decision, could ruin the whole nation; just as a single spark in the bowels of the earth produces the horrendous convulsions and tremors that can break up and upset an immense portion of its surface.

433. Indeed, the depth and magnitude of the evil, the urgency of the remedy and the inevitable need for success demand not only great and vigorous exertions, but also Your Highness's wisdom. For it is nothing less than the key source of both public and private wealth; the means to raise the nation to the highest degree of splendor and power; and the path through which the people, entrusted to Your Highness's vigilance and protection, will reach the utmost happiness. Located in the center of

civilized Europe; occupying an extensive and fertile territory; blessed with a climate that is favorable to the most varied and precious harvests; enclosed by the two greatest seas of the globe, and, through them, in possession of the wealthiest and largest colonies, all that we require to achieve prosperity is a single wave of Your Highness's powerful hand to remove the obstacles that block our path, so that we may enjoy the goods and comforts that seem preordained by providence. It is, Sire, nothing less than the most sublime end, pursued not with chimerical fancies but by means of fair laws. It is more about repealing and correcting those we have than about promoting and enacting new ones; it is about restoring the property of both land and work to its legitimate rights and reestablishing the proper place of justice and reason over error and outdated preoccupations. And this worthy triumph, Sire, will augment the glory of our Sovereign's paternal love for the people who revere and obey him, and will immortalize the patriotism and virtue that animates Your Highness's peaceful character. Let other nations seek glory in ruin and desolation; in the subversion of the social order with brutal methods that prostitute truth, trample justice and oppress innocence in the name of reform; while Your Highness, guided by a profoundly religious wisdom, is concerned only with discovering the proper limits that eternal reason has placed between the humble rule of the loving monarch who protects the people, and the contemptuous rule of the tyrant who oppresses them.

434. Therefore, Sire, abrogate with one stroke the barbarous laws that condemn to perpetual barrenness the vast lands held in common; and those laws that make private property prey to greed and sloth; and those that, preferring sheep to men, have afforded more protection to the wool that they wear than to the grain that they eat; and those that tie private property in the eternal hands of a few institutions and powerful families, driving up the price of private property and its products, and driving away the capital and industry of the nation; and those that tie up the sales of produce and fruit, for they have the same effect; and those that, directly taxing the consumption of agricultural goods, multiply in and of themselves the lethal impacts of all the rest. Instill in the propertied classes the useful knowledge upon which the prosperity of all great states is based, Your Highness, and perfect the instruments of education that would enlighten the laboring classes sufficiently to permit them to profit from scholarly investigations. Finally, Your Highness, confront nature and make her do your bidding, so to speak, transforming her into a vehicle for individual interest, or, at the very least, preventing her from blocking it. This is how Your Highness will be able to crown the grand enterprise that has so long occupied your attention; this is how Your Highness will fulfill that dear and precious trust that the nation has always placed upon your zeal and wisdom. And this is how, in sum, after profound meditation, after reducing this matter to a simple yet luminous principle and after having presented with the faith that befits our institution all of the great and noble truths that it embraces, the Society is honored by the glory of having collaborated with Your Highness in the reestablishment of agriculture, and, consequently, the general prosperity of the state and its members.

ON THE NEED TO COMBINE THE STUDY OF HISTORY AND ANTIQUITIES WITH THE STUDY OF LAW*

Madrid, 4 February 1780

"*Et illud in primis statuo frastra tentare plurimos inter perfectos, consummatosque jurisconsultos numerari, nisi una simul historiarum periti sint, et antiquitatis colligant memoriam.*"

JANUAR. IN REP J. C.

Gentlemen:

Today, standing here before you to acknowledge the distinction with which this illustrious Academy has honored me, is the most joyous and laudable of my life. The embarrassment of seeing myself adorned with a title that I did not deserve would diminish my pleasure of receiving it, if I did not recognize that when you granted me the right to sit among you, you are not honoring what I am today, but what I wish to become, rewarding my desire with a sort of anticipatory distinction. And to stimulate even further my love of wisdom, you award me the prize beforehand, even though it should only be given after wisdom has been attained.

Incorporated, then, into this assembly, the wellspring of erudition and learned criticism [*crítica*] in Spain; sitting among the wise, whose knowledge of history is enhanced by that of the useful sciences; part of this circle of select men who, fleeing idleness and dissipation, come to worship truth in its sanctuary while ignorance and preoccupations [*preocupaciones*] overpower the masses, I am beginning to regard myself as a different man, and, enthused by a powerful spirit of emulation, I wish to follow in your footsteps and imitate your zeal, because I am convinced that only by accompanying you in your vigils and labors might I justly aspire to share in your reputation and true glory.

Nothing satisfies me more than the hope of acquiring from your company and conversation a small portion of your learning; of enriching with it the limited patrimony of my own ideas; and thus making myself worthy both of standing beside you, and of my own profession. Because, gentlemen, if the science of history is, as I believe, entirely necessary for jurisprudence, where else but among you could I attain the knowledge that I confess to lack, and without which I cannot duly discharge my duties as magistrate?

---

* Oration given by the author upon his induction into the Royal Academy of History, [entitled] "Sobre la Necesidad de Unir al Estudio de la Legislación, el de Nuestra Historia y Antigüedades."

Alas, confessing my ignorance of history does not take an extraordinary toll on my self-regard. I make this confession with the simple candor that characterizes both me and this place. After all, can I be blamed for not having undertaken a serious and profound study of history? In the first years of my education, I had no choice but to follow the route and methods set out by our preceptors, and, thus, according to the common method and curriculum of our schools, I turned to philosophy. I began my studies of jurisprudence without any preparation other than a barbaric logic and a sterile and confused metaphysics, and these I thought gave me the master key to penetrate the sanctuary of the sciences. My tutors regarded other studies as useless, including that of history; they spent their time analyzing Roman law, but considered it unnecessary to read the annals of that republic. And so, even the example of my masters contributed to distance me from the study of a subject that in time would prove indispensable.

After I finished studying Roman civil law, I turned to the laws of Spain, those laws that I would one day have to implement. The difficulties that I encountered in trying to grasp their spirit [*penetrar su espíritu*] made me seek to understand their origin, and this desire naturally guided me to history. But I then found myself suddenly elevated to the judiciary, enveloped in the tasks and duties of criminal justice. Young, inexpert and ill-taught, I was barely capable of understanding the extensive obligations that fell upon me. From that point on, I could only see before me the laws that I was meant to enforce, the risks of doing so badly and the absolute necessity of penetrating their spirit in order to enforce them well. It was then that I finally understood the true nature of the problem, for I found that legal codes were written in an enigmatic language whose mysteries could not be deciphered without the science of history. This was a useful, albeit belated, awakening from delusion that did more to reveal the risks I took than to free me from their peril.

Allow me, then, gentlemen, to take from this rude awakening inspiration for my speech; allow me to communicate some of the reflections that such an experience suggested, and that made me understand that the study of history is altogether indispensable to the jurist. This argument is not irrelevant to my present obligation, nor to your institution, and I undertake it not only to prove my commitment, but out of a desire to occupy myself in objects that truly deserve attention. I wish that I could make my words deserving of your wisdom!

History, in Cicero's phrase, is the best witness of times past, our guide in daily life, and brings us tidings of antiquity. There is no profession to which men can devote their talents that would not benefit from its study. The statesman, the military man, the ecclesiastic can learn great lessons from history to better fulfill his obligations. Even the private man, whose only place in the public order is that of a simple citizen, can learn his rights and his obligations from her. And, finally, every member of political society can gain from history useful and salutary teachings to help him remain constantly on the path of virtue and away from vice.

But among all the professions, that of the magistrate is the one that would most profit from the study of history. The magistrate must, in his profession, govern men. But to govern them, he must know them, and to know them, he must study them. What better way to study men than to study history, which represents men in all stations of life: in subordination or independence; given to virtue, or lost to vice; raised up by prosperity, or overcome by misfortune? On the other hand, what other study is as relevant as history for the science of jurisprudence? I truly believe that this science cannot be considered complete if it does not include other branches of knowledge. A jurist must learn grammar to speak properly, rhetoric to move and persuade [his listener], logic to reason, critical thinking to discern, metaphysics to analyze, ethics to evaluate human actions, mathematics to calculate and proceed in order from one fact to another; but only history can teach him to know men, and therefore to govern them according to the dictates of reason and the precepts of the law.

Cicero himself, whose vast talent comprised all of the aforementioned studies, used to say that those who ignored history were like children, no doubt because the sphere of their knowledge occupied such a brief span of time. He added that a man's life was but an atom, if it was not expanded with the knowledge of times past. Alas! What would Cicero say if those ignorant about the past were those who studied the law? The great scholar Aurelio de Januario has insightfully asked, how is it possible that a man who lives in perpetual puerility, according to Cicero's argument, can be an accomplished jurist? Men who do not know of the revolutions and occurrences of past times? Indeed, the wisest jurists—Gravina, Heineccius, d'Aguesseau and all the proponents of the historical methods—have recommended this study, because it is in the history of each people that the best commentary on its laws can be found. And this is why Januario himself ridiculed all those jurists who, slaves to their own obsession, dared to proclaim that the study of Roman law was all the learning that scholars needed to acquire, all the knowledge that could adorn the spirit and rectify the heart of man.

So far we have used general arguments to show that the study of history must be united with that of the law; but the most conclusive evidence is to be found in the intimate and unique links that exist between each country's history and its legislation. Let us, then, go from the general to the particular; and, to avoid infinite and useless musings over strange laws, let us center our reflections on Spanish law. We shall seek the bonds that tie our laws to the history of our nation, and thus demonstrate that those who strive to know the former must inevitably understand the latter. Having proven this, we should not believe that we have uncovered a hidden, unknown truth; this is instead an admonishment of those who, aware of this maxim, fail to practice or follow it.

We, gentlemen, are today governed by laws that were written in our monarchy's remotest past, and even by laws that preceded its foundation. The most authoritative code used by our tribunals is a collection of ancient and modern laws in which the most recent additions are confusedly nestled alongside those written in the most distant antiquity, for it reformulates and renovates various collections written in the Middle Ages [siglos medios]. But the primitive authority of the laws that did not make it into the collection is also valid, for they are to be consulted when there are no relevant recent judgments. Thus, good jurists must continually delve into our ancient and modern codes, studying in the immense accumulation of our country's laws the civil system that the nation has followed in the last three centuries, if they want to understand Spanish law.

Evidently, describing each of these codes would be an arduous task; and an analysis of each of their laws even more tedious. But the object that we have set out obliges us to at least look at the most important of these, however briefly, to find the sources of the rights that underlie them, and discover the relationships between these rights and the constitution and customs of its contemporary society. This simple revision will reveal the need to make the study of history part of the legal discipline more than the most strongly argued reasoning. Let us, then, commence with the primitive source of our law, and discover the ancient spring from which the laws that govern us came forth, laws written under the domination of the Goths from the fifth to the eighth century and which are still obeyed by Spaniards of the eighteenth century.

The Goths, a ferocious and bellicose people that the north wind expelled from its bosom, became successively enemies, allies, subjects and destroyers of the Roman empire. Unhappy with the scarce fortune that the lords of the world, in their decadence, could bequeath to them, they sought their own fortune, one that they owed solely to their own efforts and victories. With this aim they invaded various provinces of the empire, and while some of their tribes occupied other parts of Europe, the Visigoths overran Spain and part of Gaul, and founded here one of the most brilliant monarchies of that time. Their rule brought their laws and their customs, and though relations with the Romans had led them to adopt their religion and partake of their culture, they did not entirely renounce the natural ferocity of their character, nor their inclination toward indepen-dence and warfare. Valor was their most prized virtue, and liberty their idol.

The politics of the first princes who dominated Spain sought to reconcile the inter-ests of the conquering people with those of the conquered. The former was given two-thirds of the seized lands, and allowed to live according to their customary, unwritten rights; and the latter were allowed to retain the remaining third of the lands and the use of Roman laws. Curcio compiled the Gothic laws [*costumbres góticas*] and Alaric II had Roman laws gathered and published in a code.[1] Spain, thus, lived divided, such that though there was a single dominating force, the condition of the subjects varied. Not only did they differ in the laws that they obeyed and the rights they consequently enjoyed, but also in the protection and shelter that such laws granted, and even in their names, for the victors were called Goths and the vanquished Romans.

Visigothic domination was thus constructed upon a precarious dual system until the princes began to fear the inconveniences that it produced and the risks to which it exposed them. Believing that the distinctions between victors and vanquished were as dangerous for the rulers as they were odious for the ruled, the princes sought to make the two peoples into one by eliminating these distinctions. First, they gave them the one and the best belief to unite their spirits, separated as they had been between the true religion, idolatry and Arianism; they also allowed intermarriage, to mix the two peoples in their very families; they banished the name Romani, so that all would thenceforth be called Goths; and, finally, all subjects were governed by the same laws, making their political

---

1   E. N.: Jovellanos, in other texts, referred to this same compilation of *costumbres góticas* by Eurico. ("La muerte de Munuza (Pelayo). Notas para aclarar algunos pasajes de esta obra." 1769, *Obras Completas*, 1, 362–67).

condition equal. Thus, by making government uniform, the princes consolidated their authority and secured their domination.

After this initial period, a unified people was indeed formed, and even those two great wills that always arise, separated less by conflicting interests and more by the conflict between those who held them, were forced to concur, united and in accordance with the proper conduct of public business. Indeed, frequent assemblies, that were both Cortes and councils, decided matters concerning to the governance of church and state. In these assemblies, presided over by the prince, palace officials, great lords of the court, bishops and prelates debated and examined what evils should be remedied and dictated laws to address them. Such laws truly expressed the general will, insofar as they were passed by the most important representatives of the church and the state, an admirable union that gave Spain security and repose in a period of confusion and civil discord, when many of those who aspired to rule or to counsel juvenile or imbecilic kings, endangered the state with their edicts and ambitious pretensions. The ultimate remedy was thus found in the Cortes, which could attract some of these men into their fold; or intimidate, estrange or restrain others; and could strictly enforce a law's observance, or temper its rigors, all to conciliate the contending parties and secure, through constant exercises of firm prudence, the kingdom's inner peace and tranquility, which were unattainable using any other means.

But the laws passed in these august assemblies concerned, for the most part, matters related to public right and the kingdom's higher politics. The dealings and business of individuals were decided by the Gothic customary norms that Curcio had compiled, or by the laws of their successors, gathered and published in the times of Leovigild and added to the Codex Euricianus; or by the Roman laws that the clergy and the Spaniards had obeyed, some of which were gathered in Egica's compilation. In sum, Visigothic conciliar laws simply complemented this assortment. Chindasuinth, Recceswinth and Wamba successively added laws to Leovigild's compilation, until Egica, who seemed selected by fate to perform this glorious task, formed the admirable code that we know today as the *Fuero de los jueces*.

When one considers the diverse sources of the laws that are gathered in this precious collection; when one examines the system of civil government that it informed; and, finally, when one wonders at the causes and the hidden relations between the *Fuero*'s decrees and the genius, the customs and the ideas of the people for whom its laws were written, one cannot help but ask, who would dare sustain that it is not necessary to study history to penetrate the spirit and the essence of these laws?

Indeed, their first source is constituted by the unwritten consuetudinary rights brought to Spain by the Goths. But who could know what these were without knowing the ancient history of these peoples? How they governed themselves when they lived on the other banks of the Rhine; their religion; their culture; their customs and usage? And such a study would be incomplete if it did not add to the analysis of the northern codes the analysis of the historians who have written about those peoples. Caesar and Tacitus, says Montesquieu, were so taken by the laws of the northern peoples, that, when reading their books, one will constantly encounter the northern codes, and when reading those codes, one will see Tacitus and Caesar everywhere.

And why would things be any different regarding the institutions established in Spain by the predecessors of Reccared I, the second source of Visigoth law? Who would understand the spirit of these laws without first understanding how Gothic domination came to pass in Spain; what shape Goths gave to their government; the political, civil and military hierarchies of their society; the rights and obligations of the Goths and of the Spanish; or the degree to which the character of the former was influenced by the constitution that they adopted, the climate in which they lived, the religion that they professed and the new ideas, practices and customs that they learned from the latter? Let there be no doubts, says Montesquieu again, that these barbarians kept the inclinations, uses and customs that they brought from their own country to the lands that they conquered for quite some time, because a nation cannot alter its way of life overnight. And yet, who doubts that a nation that moves to a distant climate, under a different government, in new and unknown regions, would not slowly change its ways?

I regard Roman law as the third source of the Visigothic laws; and I will not tire in insisting that in order to truly understand the laws of that famous republic, it is necessary to study its history. Others have happily carried out the relevant analyses, and maybe someday I will make this the object of another speech presented for your consideration.

What I cannot refrain from exploring further at this point are the conciliar decrees passed during the reign of Reccared I, which form the fourth and chief source of Visigothic legislation. Why not state it clearly? These decrees altered the constitution of the State and gave it a new shape, produced in part by the clergy's new predominance. Let us see if we can discover the causes of a revolution that was previously experienced by Rome under the Catholic emperors, and which is inscribed for all to see in the various laws contained in the Codes of Theodosius and Justinian. God hold my tongue were I to besmirch the saintly intentions of those venerable prelates without whose counsel everything, even the church itself, would have foundered in those times among laymen for whom there was no virtue beyond valor, no activity beyond fighting and no science beyond victory and destruction. No, gentlemen, I sincerely applaud the zeal that guided them, and if I dare go into the origin of the laws that they dictated, it is only to know more about them, not to censure them.

A martial, superstitious and ignorant people necessarily has simple yet tough and ferocious customs. To know happiness, it needs instruction and cultivation. The princes entrusted these duties to the clergy as the only depositaries of learning and virtue in those days. Ecclesiastics were therefore granted the authority necessary to carry out the task of reforming the people. History shows them attending the law-generating councils since the seventh century. There they dealt not only with ecclesiastical discipline, but also with the political rules related to the conduct of the people, magistrates and public ministers; the great and low lords of the court; and even the monarchs themselves. Palace officers, treasury prefects, judges and high magistrates had to answer to the Council regarding much of their activity. And even outside the Council, bishops exercised a type of superintendence over the civil administration, to the degree that those decisions made by secular magistrates that were considered unfair, were elevated to the bishops. In this way, the most significant elements of temporal power were increasingly subordinated to ecclesiastical power, and the influence of bishops in public affairs grew indefinitely, so that in the end the laws themselves authorized that which, viewed from the vantage point of the present century, strikes us as astonishing and even prodigious.

In any case, who could understand these laws without the helping hand of history? And how, without history, could one form a complete and intelligible notion of their spirit and character? If law professors do not study them with history's assistance, how many wrong and fatal principles will they deduct from them? This is why I have considered it necessary to discern the relations between history and the laws written in those times. But another, more urgent reason compels me. In the subsequent period of our legislation's history, princes were determined to renew laws, and despite the changes that our constitution suffered due to the multiple revolutions of that period, we shall see how respect for these [Gothic] laws and their origin has been preserved up to the present time.

In effect, the years that followed the Arab invasion witnessed a rebirth of Visigothic legislation, and with it, the ancient constitution, which only lost its shape very gradually. To comprehend this alteration, I must examine the historical events that produced it, however briefly, discovering in them the nature and character of the new constitution and of the new laws that Spain would obey for centuries.

While the Goths and the Spanish, united as one nation and one people, enjoyed the protection of the aforementioned laws, the eternal wisdom that presides over the fate of all empires chose Roderick to be the last king of the Goths. The eighth century saw in its first years the hints and fulfillment of this revolution. Attracted perhaps by the Jews, who had been excessively beleaguered by the conciliar legislation; or perhaps called by Wittiza's children, who, unable to suffer others on their father's throne, decided to conspire against Roderick, the Arabs who inhabited Mauritania suddenly invaded Spain, and inundated practically all of its provinces, like an impetuous torrent that destroys any obstacle opposing its fury. Everything disappeared then under the heavy boot of the new conquering people: nation, state, religion, laws, customs, everything would have disappeared entirely, if that same Providence that sent this calamity did not keep in the mountains of Asturias a refuge for the remnants of the old Gothic empire.

These remnants, gathered under the protection of heaven and the conduct of the invincible Don Pelagius, not only stopped the irruption of the Arabs in that province, but helped establish a new empire, destined to repair the loss of the old, and to carry its glory and splendor forward. In effect, Don Pelagius, whose heroic and virtuous deeds were rewarded by heaven with high and mighty benefits, laid the foundation of a new kingdom in Asturias. He occupied its throne for 20 years, and during that time he was able to secure the fate of that small nation, so that it would never again fall under the Saracens' chains. Pelagius's son-in-law, Don Alfonso the Catholic, and his grandson, Don Fruela, added most of Galicia and Biscay to the new kingdom of Asturias, and even parts of Portugal and Castile. Don Alfonso the Chaste, Pelagius's great-grandson, victoriously carried the kingdom's banner across the Tagus River, and during a reign that lasted nearly half a century, and in which the glory of his arms shone as brightly as the glory of his wisdom in government, he managed to restore the ancient constitution to its primitive splendor.

Indeed, this had been the main object of his predecessors. But it seems Providence brought Don Alfonso II to the throne so that he would finally realize it. After this period, we see the consolidation of a government that is quite similar to the Visigothic constitution: the tasks and offices of the court and the palace, and the ceremonial proceedings and etiquette, are determined by the orders of the old court; the civil hierarchy is established according to that of the Goths; and the reconquered lands are divided into counties, with a count entrusted with the defense and jurisdiction of his district.

Those assemblies that functioned simultaneously as Cortes and councils were revived, and in them, lords and prelates managed the affairs of the state and the church. Finally, the Gothic laws, from then on called *Fuero de los jueces*, were reinstated and public and private affairs were governed according to them, when circumstances permitted such governance.

From then on, every new place added to the Crown of León was placed under the Gothic laws that until recent times still governed many areas under the Castilian Crown. And this is a clear and undeniable testimony of the respect these laws have garnered among.

In any case, what has been said so far demonstrates that the first kings of Asturias seriously considered reestablishing the Visigothic constitution. But this was untenable: a constitution perfected in the space of two centuries and whose object was the conservation of a large empire, peace, and the unification of two peoples, was not a proper fit for the new polity, which was a small and weak state, surrounded by powerful enemies, lacking strength and resources, whose main objects were increasing the population and defending itself.

Castilians realized this truth when, having shaken off the yoke that oppressed them, and faced with the strength of the Moors of León, each count was acknowledged as an independent sovereign so as not to compromise the liberty of the whole. And although this phenomenon was a natural consequence of the period's circumstances, it irrevocably altered the old system of government. Thus we see the slow but steady consolidation of another constitution, one visibly different from its predecessor, whose origin also merits our consideration, given the influence that it exerted upon the laws that were born from it. If only my pen were gifted with that happy energy capable of conveying the most complicated ideas with one stroke, so that I could describe to you the essence of this constitution and the progressive stages it went through since its inception, thus sparing you the trouble of a long oration!

The kings of Asturias, who began taking the occupied towns back from the Saracen, soon realized that their retention was more more difficult than their conquest. Don Alfonso the Catholic expanded his domain so rapidly that he was forced to abandon some of his conquests, lest he risk losing all of them. Eventually, garrisons were established in some towns; capitulations were signed in others in front of their residents and the Moors; and the rest were abandoned to the faithfulness of the few Spaniards who had been saved from destruction by the victors' interest.

But when victory had reaffirmed the foundations of the throne of León; when Spaniards and foreigners from across the land came to live under its protection, and to share in the fatigue and recompenses of the new conquests, did they consider distributing the reconquered lands and setting up new towns in them? The lords and masters of the court, the noblemen, knights, foreigners and volunteers who rallied round the kings in the battlefield obtained lands and places from them, charged only with the obligation to settle them and, when the time came, to join with their new neighbors in the state's defense. The princes, whose liberality and largesse found abundant land to continue these gifts, were loved by all. Their piety and religious zeal led them to extend their munificence to churches and monasteries. From this remote time derive many of the great fortunes that we admire today in various monasteries. So that in the end, the kings rewarded those who followed them in victory [*los compañeros de sus victorias*] with towns and estates, reserved many for themselves, and left the rest [of their subjects] to live free of obligations or services, or free to choose the lord or protector that pleased them.

It was also during this time that certain feudal obligations arose. Princes' distribution or *repartimiento* of land was more than a gift: it amounted to payment for the services rendered unto them by their vassals. An army composed of free men demanded, as a just recompense, a portion of the land over which they had spilled their blood and sweat. The counts of Castile were even more hard pressed to follow this maxim, for they had founded their own independence upon it. This is why we see it uniformly followed from the remotest times, and why Castilian noblemen were the first to secure the privileges, liberties and franchises that the new constitution granted to their class.

It would take too long to look into the entirety of these royal *mercedes* [grants], both in terms of their essence and in terms of the duration of the grant. Early ones were granted for life, or restricted one way or another; but soon they were absolute and perpetual. The lords not only possessed the land, but they also possessed the jurisdiction, the tribute, the services and the rest of the rights that came with the distributed lands and their inhabitants. It appears that the princes were forced to share their sovereignty with those who helped them extend it. Moreover, the lords, and the churches and monasteries, also subdivided their property, and distributing it in smaller portions, retained vassals to assist them in both common and private wars. Sometimes these vassals became lords themselves, distributing their land among others, in exchange for assistance in war. Such were the circumstances in those days when the right of possession was linked to martial obligations. Therein lies the origin of that multitude of classes, each subordinated to another, and all of them to the monarch; and the origin the different manors [*señoríos*], *realengos, solariegos, abadengos, behetrías*; in sum, the differences in status—between *ricoshombres* (first among the nobles), hidalgos, *infanzones*, lords, *deviseros*, vassals, subvassals and many others—which link the right of possession with the obligation to serve and take up arms; a relation that could only be discerned by studying history together with law.

The law always followed behind the progress of this system of population and defense, and it was always in accordance with this constitution. Let us leave aside the laws that were obeyed in the Kingdom of León, which had deviated less from the Visigothic constitution, and let us focus on the legislation of Castile. This can be found in a code the origin of which was lost in the darkness of the first years of the restoration. In it, the obligations and rights of the higher classes were specified along with the charges and duties of the inferior ones; it included a collection of feats, juridical customs, *fueros* and good practices that were nothing other than the consuetudinary rights that Castilians had followed when their constitution was in the process of consolidation. In the code, in sum, are the fundamental principles of this constitution, and the legislation upon which it rested. It is probably unnecessary for me to say that I am speaking of Castile's *Fuero Viejo*, a treasure that remained hidden practically until our own time, regarded with disdain by preoccupied and finicky jurists, but whose study should concern all men who love their homeland, for it is the main source of a constitution, or form of government, that still exists, albeit altered by the vicissitudes of time and changes in custom and circumstance.

I wish that I had the time to address these origins in greater detail, and explain the character of the laws contained in this code, which are as venerable for their wisdom as for their antiquity. Let those who ignore them call them barbaric and uncouth, for they are incapable of penetrating their essence; but I will always admire the remarkable fit between them and their constitution. The private wars waged by lords; the duels, truces and the assurances of private individuals; the legal combats; the pecuniary aspect of personal offenses; the trials by fire and water; the solemn formulas to adopt or abandon nobility [*hidalguía*], demonstrate legitimacy of birth, testify to a wedding, judge rape and abduction, and a thousand other elements that seem absurd and monstrous to those who are but pilgrims in the foreign country of the past, what are they if not clear and simple rules to settle conflicts between the members of a militaristic society, a society of illiterate, earnest and generous people? And honestly, gentlemen, what do laws need in order to be wise, if they are useful? Was the greatness of the laws given by Zoroaster, Solon, Lycurgus or Numa to be found anywhere but in their capacity to accommodate the people for whom they were written?

But what is even more relevant to my purpose is that the spirit of these old laws can only be discerned in the light of history. Without it, the jurist who embarks upon their study will merely wander in the dark of an unknown country full of obstacles. I would love nothing more than to illuminate these difficulties and enigmas, to reveal a truth as valuable as it is important; but the generality of my object does not allow me such liberties. That is why I will only address one of these obstacles upon which only history can shed light—perhaps the most important of all.

That difficulty is the very language in which our old laws were written: that venerable language which vulgar jurists consider boorish and uncouth, but which is in fact full of profound wisdom and mysteries that can only be discerned by those who, illuminated by history, penetrate the arcane uses of the past. The words and phrases that fill the code have practically been banished from our dictionaries, and since our jurists have preferred to study foreign laws, written in a foreign language, our old legal language has been forgotten. Its meanings are either entirely lost, or completely disfigured; lexicographers have not explained them; I dare add that they have not even understood them. Is this not the most daunting difficulty faced by the jurists who must study these laws? And is there any other way to overcome it, if the study of history and antiquity do not open to these students the sources of etymology?

Gentlemen, do not think that understanding this primitive language constitutes an eccentricity: it is, in fact, an absolute necessity. Without this knowledge, we cannot appreciate the true essence of the property of the lands, the extension of the royal eminent domain, nor that of the different types of private domains: *realengos, solariegos, abadengos* and *behetrías*. Without it, we cannot discern the political and military hierarchy of the kingdom, nor who constituted it, who were its *ricoshombres*, *infanzones*, hidalgos, lords, *devi-seros*, vassals, knights, *atemaderos*, peons, villagers and *vecinos mañeros*. Without it, we cannot comprehend the civil hierarchy nor the duties and faculties of its members: the royal councilors, counts, *adelantados*, *merino* judges, mayors [*alcaldes*], sheriffs [*alguaciles*], *sayones* and other such persons. Who without it could understand the words *solar* [lot], *feudo* [fief], *honor*, *tierra* [land], *condado* [county], *alfoz*, *merindad*, *sacada*, *coto*, *concejo*, *villa* [*village*], *lugar* [place] and others, which signal the essence of properties, or the limits of their jurisdictions? What about *mañería*, *infurción*, *conducho*, *yantar*, *abunda*, *martiniega*, *marzadga* and the rest of the terms that distinguish one tribute from another? And what can we say of *amistad* [amity], *fieldad* [fidelity], *fe* [faith], *desafío* [challenge], *riepto* [dare], *tregua* (truce), *paz* [peace], *aseguranza* [assurance], *omecillo* [homicide], *desprez* [contempt], *caloña* [calumny], *coto*, *entregas* [restitutions], *enmiendas* [amends] and the other terms related to civil jurisprudence and criminal law? Who, without history, could understand the infinite appellations, verbs, phrases and idioms of that language, whose meanings have been lost or transformed by the culture of our century? But let us go back to our codes, and take up a little more hurriedly the history of our old legislation.

Following the path laid out by history, we must turn to regard particular codes whose authority was no less respected in the old days than the *Fuero viejo*. They contain part of the legislation that complemented the law back then, and were born, so to speak, in the same cradle. I am talking about the *fueros* and charters [*cartas-pueblas*] given to villages and cities that our kings brought under their rule through military conquest. The number of this kind of codes would correspond to the number of capitals recovered or founded after the restoration, if time and neglect had not consumed some and forgotten others. In those days, everybody wanted to live according to laws of their own, and this maxim was so strictly followed that often a single town had more than one *fuero*. In Toledo, the conqueror Don Alfonso VII gave the Castilians who carried out the conquest a *foro*—he gave another to the residents who had lived under Saracen domination, the Mozarabs; and yet another to the foreigners, generally referred to as Franks, who had joined his army to assist in the conquest. Besides this, each particular class also had its own *foro*; which meant that each individual lived under the protection of laws that were particular to him, and that were interpreted by judges of his same class.

But what is more relevant and noteworthy is that thanks to these *foros*, towns' local government was slowly perfected. Municipalities (*ayuntamientos*) were authorized from the onset to handle affairs related to the public's well-being. Councils operated like small republics, and their government could call itself democratic, both because the town's senators were chosen by the people; and because the rights of all classes were represented by one or more council members. These political bodies also received lands in *repartimiento*, some to be used by the residents and others to serve as the community's patrimony. With the rents obtained from these lands, which councils could use at their discretion, public needs were attended, both of the people and of the state. We have seen these councils play an important role since ancient times, participating with their banners in war, with their vote in the Cortes and with their influence in the resolution of communal conflicts and in the state's aid.

But this system of government, in which the various parts that formed our nation were organized independently from one another, would have made our constitution weak and faltering if the Cortes, established since the most primitive times, had not taken onto itself the elements that affected the general interest. In the beginning, as we have shown, the Cortes were also like councils, and the king, the great nobles, the prelates and the lords dealt with the affairs of church and state. But after the nation began to grow in population and provinces; after the distinctions between the three estates (nobility, the church and the people) began to increase; and the representation and influence that each exercised in society was increasingly established, the Cortes dealt only with the civil and political government of the realm. Everybody knows how important these assemblies were in the procurement and preservation of peace within the kingdom; in keeping classes in their proper interdependence; and in limiting the excesses of power and ambition of the greater nobles. They embodied the general will of the nation through the representatives of each stratum; they sought to remedy public ills, discovering their causes; and they devised the means to end the evils that disobedience or neglect of the laws introduced in public administration.

But, gentlemen, may I reflect on the vices and defects of this constitution? What misfortune renders men timid, unwilling to reveal their opinions on government matters? Is the holy name of truth not enough to place them above any kind of censure? Why should they silence a valuable truth, regardless of whether they find it disagreeable? It is precisely those who find it disagreeable who, in their own self-interest, shamelessly try to keep the truth hidden from those who would most benefit from knowing it. I am speaking to this assembly [*congreso*] of wise men endowed with as much good faith as enlightenment, who will not find novelty in what I say, nor will it sound extraordinary. My voice is directed toward their ears, to inspire in these men ideas that are less worthy of their gravity, than of the speaker's modesty.

Let us say it clearly: if we acknowledge that the old legislation of which we speak is worthy of our praise because of the absolute coincidence [*absoluta conformidad*] that existed between it and its contemporary constitution, it is also necessary to confess that this constitution contained certain vices that conspired against it; and that these vices were, somehow, sanctioned by the law. The power of the lords was too great, and there was not enough authority vested in the first among them, the monarch, to moderate this power. All of the state's strength was in their hands: each could raise his own private army, made up of his vassals, friends and relatives; the grand masters [*maestres*] of each military order had the most illustrious and numerous parts of the militia in their retinues; prelates, as property owners, also held a portion of the nation's laboring hands living and working in their lands; and even municipal councils went to war with numerous men fighting under their banners. It is true that all of this strength was subordinated to the prince, whom all vassals were obligated to follow; but in reality, the assistance given by vassals was always precarious, dependent on each lord's will or caprice. Even when they gave it without resistance, the monarch had to provide sustenance during warfare. The nobles had the privilege of fighting for the prince only if he paid them. The public treasury was therefore impoverished; tributes were few and limited, for resources were hard to obtain, dependent on the Cortes's mediation. What was, then, the role of the prince in this constitution, if not that of a commander subordinated to his vassals' caprice?

I realize that this dependence was reciprocal in some aspects, and that the nobles had to support and obey the monarch because he could crush those who did not, and because only he could provide the great rewards that they coveted; but the nation was often divided into parties, and the prince's side was stronger only when the largest property owners sided with him. The constitution did not provide the prince with the means to curb these excesses; it was necessary to find them in the art of politics and his own guile. And nothing was more successful than keeping the lords divided in order to weaken them; and since self-interest was the universal motive, astute princes manipulated this expertly to win over some and to punish others, rewarding the first group with what they took from their rivals. The state thus found itself faltering, the nation buried under the weight of the most terrible anarchy, with the arms that should have been turned against the common enemy, pointed at each other in internecine wars.

But, above all, what I search for most intently in this constitution is a free people. But I cannot find one. Between subordinate princes and independent lords, what could the people be but a herd of slaves, destined to satisfy the ambition of their masters? A people compelled to maintain the prince with the sweat of their brow was separated from him to feed the lords' greed; placed under the protection of the lords, the people were forced to rise up against the prince whom they should protect. Nothing could free from its fate a people that did not grasp the meaning of freedom. Indeed, freedom was so unfamiliar to the last of the classes that even those free towns, called *behetrías*, believed that they could not survive if they did not have a lord. To escape the ambition that threatened to oppress them at every turn, they searched for protectors but found only tyrants; and since they had the right to break with their owners, they did so, only to find themselves entangled in more chains, like those miserable souls of whom Aristotle speaks, who voluntarily sold their liberty to secure a wretched subsistence.

The only element [in society] that could enable the constitution to overcome the obstacles that it produced were the Cortes. But in the Cortes the power of the first classes was also preponderant: the nobility and the clergy were equally interested in maintaining their own independence and the people's oppression; the councils that were supposed to represent the latter were also influenced by these same interests, so that the fate of the lowest plebeians stirred them little. And so, a constitution in which the state was formed by many strong and powerful members; in which the ties between nationals were few and weak and the principles of division many and active; a constitution, in sum, in which the lords could do anything, the prince could do little, and the people could do nothing, was without any doubt, weak and imperfect, dangerous and hesitant.

Legislation closely followed the constitution, and though one must acknowledge that the law was wise and noble in comparison, it is also true that it could not but share in the constitution's vices and defects. Among the most notorious was the absence of uniformity. General laws barely existed. All lived according to their own laws, and were judged by their own judges: *hidalgos* had their particular *fuero*; each council had its own; and even within the same village, as we already noted, each class of residents had its laws and judges. This naturally made the civil government uncertain and fragmented; so that the part of Spain that was free from the Saracen yoke, was more like a confederated state composed of various small republics than a nation composed of provinces and towns.

Such was the state of things when in the thirteenth century the desire to reduce legislation to a uniform system prompted the monarchs to compose a general codex. Two great princes worked on this project, Don Ferdinand III and Don Alfonso X [respectively], the holiest and wisest kings who ruled the land in those days. The first barely went beyond designing the code, but his indomitable constancy and support for literary projects encouraged his son to undertake the formation of the *Partidas*, the wisest, most complete and most orderly code that those crude times could produce.

The Wise King [Alfonso X] knew that it was necessary to prepare the nation to accept this benefit and, with this purpose in mind, he created the *Fuero de las leyes* and gave it to some villages and cities. In 1255, he declared it to be the *fuero general* of Burgos, and also gave it as such to the councils of Castile. Thus he tried to accustom them to accept and live under common, uniform legislation, before introducing the treasure of his *Partidas* everywhere.

The nobles of Castile, who understood that the acceptance of these codes was a direct threat to their authority, tried to stop the king. They began to express their resentment openly, without concealment, complaining that the *Partidas* violated their own ancient laws, and imposed laws that were new and foreign to them. They demanded the restitution of their *fueros*. They informed Don Alfonso that he must respect their *fueros* as his father and grandfather had respected them. The Wise King would have ignored these complaints, motivated as they were by self-interest, to stop the preponderance of the lords once and for all, if the need to secure their friendship did not force his hand. After 17 years, the *hidalgos* had Castile's *fuero viejo* reinstated in the courts, thanks to an ordinance decreed on 1272.

It then took a century of tentative actions and foiled pretensions for the *Partidas* to prevail: they were published in Alcalá in 1348. Yet even then the authority of municipal *fueros* was upheld, so that the *Partidas* were received more like a supplement, that completed partial or antiquated laws, than as a new corpus of law that swept the others away. But the passage of time, the tenacious efforts of some, the tolerance of others and the hidden and small causes that always and invariably influence public affairs, finally led to the general acceptance and respect of the Alfonsine codes.

This marked the beginning of a new epoch in the history of Spain's legislation, and it is easy to grasp that the *Partidas* led to its alteration, or, should I say, its corruption. For it seems to me that nothing contributed as much as the *Partidas* to reviving a taste for Roman law among us. The jurists who helped Don Alfonso with this compilation, and who were undoubtedly from the Bologna school, included not only the text of the Roman laws, but even the opinions on them pronounced by Italian jurists, so that the *Partidas* could not be understood without consulting those sources. The study of Roman jurisprudence was thus soon consecrated as the most esteemed, and those who professed it became a separate and distinguished class in the public's eyes. The interpretation of the *Code* and the *Digest* was not its main object; it was practically its only object. Everything was judged according to Roman jurisprudence, and the Bolognese jurists' opinions were increasingly accepted as laws unto themselves, so that a system of law that was not only different from our own, but often quite contrary to it, was introduced among us with fatal consequences.

But what is even more noteworthy is that the *Partidas* were also the conduit through which canon law was introduced, with all of the maxims and principles of Italian canonists. A perusal of the first *Partida* is proof enough. And we see here that a nation, one that could create its own pure and complete ecclesiastical code with the decisions of its own councils, indiscriminately embraced the *Decretum Gratiani* and the Gregorian decrees, with all the false and apocryphal verdicts introduced in them by the malicious impostor Isidoro, the good faith of the compilers and the Bolognese jurists' adulation. These increasingly became part of our national legislation, which embraced these foreign maxims and turned them into laws. And, in time, they not only dominated our schools, but also our tribunals, and the most enlightened of our jurists and the wisest of our magistrates were unable to banish them forever to the other side of the Alps, where they were born.

Allow me to inquire at this point: could our jurists, unaided by history, comprehend this disruption in our legal thought caused by the Alfonsine codes? Could they, without history's aid, know the sources of the various laws contained in these codes? Could they penetrate their spirit, understand their strength, calculate their effects and deduce whether they are useful or detrimental? But I do not wish to tire you with the reflections that the narration of these events excites in me. Who among you has not harbored these same reflections when reading our nation's history?

On the other hand, as the *Partidas* altered our legislation, they also uplifted the nation. Despite the differences between them and the constitution that they legislated, we must acknowledge that they introduced principles of equity and natural justice in Spain, tempering the crudeness of earlier legislation along with the roughness of old customs and ideas. On every page of this precious code, one finds wise moral and political dictates that suggest that its enlightened authors belonged to a more cultivated period. The words of the ancient philosophers and, moreover, of the holy fathers, which are frequently cited in the *Partidas*, guided the nation to the study of profane and ecclesiastical antiquity and inspired the maxims of humanity and justice that shone so brightly in the governments of antiquity. The ferocity and rudeness of the soul inspired by feudal slavery, the spirit of chivalry and the ignorance of those first centuries, were thus gradually softened by the *Partidas*. Since then, men were more highly esteemed, and their liberty was more precious. The nation, which congregated more frequently in the Cortes, imbued with brighter and better ideas, demanded and obtained useful rules from the kings to safeguard liberty. Finally, the idea that the people were the foundation of all authority, that without them there was neither nobility nor sovereignty, awakened the love [*amor*] for the masses; and this love, albeit born from self-interest, slowly led to the extension of liberty, which in turn caused all the benefits that it ordinarily produces.

Simultaneously, the liberty of the plebeians in the larger towns expanded under the protection of the government and municipal privileges. The lords resided in their castles and forts, exercising a ruinous and oppressive domain over their vassals and tenants, while the townspeople, gathered in villages and *lugares*, enjoyed the beginnings of a fruitful peace. The natural consequence was that part of the rural population moved to the towns. Slowly, the population in the cities increased, and industry and commerce grew together with them. The arts of peace were cultivated, and the increase in their products also led to an increase of those who cultivated them under the protection of municipal councils. If these men, whose subsistence no longer depended on their lords' begrudging largesse, were also free from military service, they could remain quietly within the city walls while war altered everything outside of them, uprooting farmers from their fields and forcing them to exchange their plows for muskets. Spain thus became a wise and warlike nation, industrious, commercial and opulent; and it also began its rise to that that summit of glory and splendor that no other empire founded on the ruins of Rome would ever attain.

Various factors converged to accelerate this happy revolution: the Moors were expelled from Spain; the Crowns of Aragon and Navarre were united with that of Castile; the military orders were subordinated to the royal dignity of the monarch; a wealthy and vast empire across the sea was discovered and conquered. Royal power and authority grew to levels that had never been reached before. And before this colossus, the prerogatives that divided national sovereignty vanished, and nobles and grandees became nothing more than distinguished vassals. Finally, the great, profound and systemic genius of Cardinal Cisneros finished tempering the power of the great lords, strengthening sovereignty so that it would be a perpetual foil for seigniorial prepotency, if the ambition of ministers did not sometimes turn it into an instrument of oppression and tyranny.

In any case, we must regard this period as that which gave our legislation its final shape. Since all of the branches of administration multiplied in size and complexity, it was necessary to increase the number and scope of our legislation accordingly. All of the laws, pragmatic sanctions, orders and rules related to the arts, agriculture, industry, commerce and navigation; all those laws that defined the operations of municipal governments; all those that set up the civil hierarchy and fixed the authority of the courts, judges and magistrates that constituted it; in sum, all those laws that completed our civil and economic system, owe their origin to this period, and were a consequence of the auspicious revolution that we have described.

The multitude of new laws, and the differences between them and the old codes evidenced the necessity of a new compilation. The immortal Isabella, the princess who was born to elevate Spain to its greatest glory, began such a compilation; but death prevented her from completing this great project, granting her only the opportunity of endorsing its execution strongly in her will. Don Charles I warmly promoted it, spurred on by the Cortes, and he had the legal genius of *doctores* Pedro López de Alcocer and Escudero dedicate themselves to this compilation, but they could not finish it either. Finally, Philip II, for whom Providence seemed to have reserved this glory, had the compilation completed by López de Arrieta and Bartolomé de Atienza, publishing it through the Pragmatic Sanction of 14 March 1567 as the *Nueva Recopilación* that we know today.

But, gentlemen, allow me to inquire: is there a man so blessed by heaven with intelligence and talent that he could analyze this code, where the laws of all of the preceding periods of Spain's constitution are confusedly ordered? I confess that this enterprise is beyond my own capacity. Only a man who dominated all historical knowledge and all legal doctrine, a man, therefore, who was both a consummate jurist and a perfect historian, only he would be capable of undertaking and completing this task.

But for the time being, who dares to interpret these laws without first understanding the history of the times in which they were produced? All Spanish jurists should come to this assembly, especially those who consider the study of history a superfluous and useless enterprise: I beseech them to tell me, is it possible to grasp the spirit of the laws compiled in the *Nueva Recopilación* merely by reading them? You, ministers, magistrates and judges, entrusted by the king with the arduous and distinguished task of executing these laws, tell me: do you consider yourselves capable of truly understanding them without knowledge of their history? I tremble at the prospect of what you might answer. If you tell me that indeed your demanding and important positions require that you combine legal doctrine with a thorough knowledge of history, why then is history barely studied at all by those men in our profession? And if you say that studying history is useless, what can we expect from minds tyrannized by absurd preoccupations that, ignorant of the past, are incapable of turning their eyes away from the beautiful simulacrum that they take for truth?

Let us admit, then, in good faith, that without history there cannot be a proper knowledge of our constitution, and our laws. Let us also admit that without this learning magistrates cannot take pride in asserting their mastery over national law. Since, indeed, what is the obligation of a vassal [the Magistrate] who is entrusted by his king with the important matter of being the depository of laws? Is it enough to know the principles of private right, so as to bring the disputes and conflicts arising between individuals to a close? And if he is called to defend the prerogatives of sovereignty; the privileges of the clergy and the nobles; the rights of the people, how can he do so if he does not understand national public law? Without this knowledge, how will he know where the limits of royal and ecclesiastical power lie; what are the duties of the clergy and the nobles; what are the charges and obligations of the towns? How will he know the hierarchy that the government is based on, the authority of its political bodies and that of each of its members? How will he understand where sovereignty resides, where legislative power lies, where it is executed and modified, and under what terms? How, in sum, can he calculate the degree of political liberty that our constitution grants citizens, and how inviolable are their property rights? How often in the exercise of criminal jurisprudence has this political liberty been ignored and annulled! How often have property rights been trampled in the exercise of judicial prerogatives! And in the imposition of tributes, in their amount and type and in the means of collecting them, both the political liberty of citizens and their property rights have been violated too often! And if the study of history can free us from these ills, how can those men whose shameful sloth keeps them from it not quake in their boots?

I confess, gentlemen, that perhaps what we have said of our jurists is too serious an accusation: their profession forces them to study an immense number of old and new laws without whose knowledge they would be exposed to continuous errors. If we also demand from them that they dedicate themselves to the study of history, how many volumes would they be forced to read! I am not ashamed to state it: the nation lacks a history. The perusal of our chronicles, annals, histories, compendia and memoirs provides us with a mere semblance of an idea of what our past was like. They are fraught with descriptions of wars, battles, commotions, famines, plagues, desolations, prophecies, wonders and superstitions; in sum, of everything that is useless, absurd and deleterious to the country. But where is there a civil history that explains the origins, progress and transformations of our constitution, our political and civil hierarchies, our legislation, our customs, our glories and our miseries? Is it possible for a nation that harbors the most complete collection of ancient monuments, a nation where criticism has reestablished the empire of truth and banished even the most authoritative fables, a nation that has this Academy at its center, full of deep and wise intellects, to lack such an important and indispensable work? Allow me, gentlemen, to be the organ of the public's desire: those who cultivate the sciences, and those who esteem their country, and those who love truth, we all expect this valuable benefit from you, and, in particular, those whose ministerial obligations impose upon them the need to understand laws that are incomprehensible without the aid of history.

These are, gentlemen, the reflections that after much effort and thought I have been able to contemplate in the midst of the many affairs that demand my time and attention. When I conceived of this oration, I did not foresee that I would embark on a project that went well beyond my ability and instruction, as well as beyond the leisure that my daily employment permits. Perhaps if I had been able to work more slowly, following more serious and thorough research, I would have been able to present my ideas in a less dry and more organized fashion. But working tirelessly and precipitously, distracted by multiple inopportune tasks and constantly roused by the desire to come here and express my gratitude, what could I write that was worthy of the gravity of the subject matter and the attention of my audience? And yet, what an opportune occasion for this illustrious body to practice the indulgence that they have already shown me! I humbly beg you, and your wise members, to forgive an involuntary delay on my part and my inevitable defects; and, certain of my burning desire to support the noble ends of your valuable institution to the best of my ability, to accept my sincere and heartfelt gratitude, which will last as long as my life.

EULOGY IN PRAISE OF CHARLES III*

Madrid, 8 November 1788

"It is the duty of kings to honor and love the teachers of the great arts by whose counsel kingdoms are upheld and often improved."

R. D. Alfonso el Sabio, l. 3, tít. 10, Partida 2

Advertencia

Since this text was written as a eulogy that demonstrated how much had been done to promote useful instruction in Spain during the reign of the good king Charles III, who now rests in peace, other events related to his reign were described briefly, and the reflections that such a vast subject required were also abridged. The very nature of the piece demanded concision, but some people have suggested that several of the topics that the text mentions hurriedly deserve elaboration in a series of notes.

Though the author generally concurs with this view, he believes that he cannot, and should not, follow it, for two especially powerful reasons. First, that those readers who chose this text among the many written to honor Charles III, some of which contain a greater number of details and lengthier descriptions, do not seem to need the commentary to understand it; and, second, that having been asked by the Royal Society of Madrid to present this eulogy, and thus been so generously honored, the author cannot regard the text as his own, nor add anything that did not receive the Society's accolades. The eulogy appears here, therefore, exactly as it was read to that illustrious body on Saturday, 8 November of last year; with the author conceding, in deference to the Society, to both publish a text that was incapable of fulfilling the great object that was his aim, and to do so without altering it, and thus renouncing the improvement that a meditated and thorough revision might have brought about.

But if the public, which tends to dispense with circumstantial merits when judging works directed to its utility, were to embrace this one, the author reserves the right to revise it and publish it again. Then he would strive to include notes that clarify those

---

* Delivered to the Royal Economic Society of Madrid, [entitled] "Elogio de Carlos Tercero. Leído a la Real Sociedad de Madrid por el socio D. Gaspar Melchor de Jove Llanos, en la Junta plena del sábado 8 de noviembre de 1788 con asistencia de las Señoras asociadas."

points related to the literary history of political economy, which are, to his mind, in greater need of elaboration, and more worthy of it, too.

Gentlemen:

This eulogy in praise of Charles III, pronounced in this abode of patriotism, should not be an exercise in adulation, but a tribute of recognition. If antiquity timidly invented panegyrics for the sovereigns, not to celebrate those who professed virtue but to silence those who persecuted it, we have perfected that exercise by turning it into praise for those good princes whose virtues have been devoted to the well-being of the men whom they governed.[1] Therefore, while eloquence, instigated by fear, is intoned in some places to sanctify oppressors, here it freely and selflessly commends the beneficial virtues that are the basis of its happiness and solace.

Such is, gentlemen, the obligation that our institute [*instituto*] imposes upon us; and my lips, devoted for such a long time to the service of truth and justice, will not betray their vocation by praising Charles III. Considering him as a father to his vassals, I will extol those laws and actions that make him even more worthy of that glorious title; so that this eulogy, as modest as his virtue and as simple as his character, shall sound to your ears like those hymns through which the ancient peoples innocently worshipped the Divine, all the more pleasant because they were sincere and because they were sung out of pure gratitude.

Alas, if a Sovereign never feels the joy of benevolence in his breast; nor hears true blessings of acknowledgment from his people's lips, what good is that vain and sterile glory that he so zealously seeks to satisfy his ambition and his nation's pride? It is easy to find in Spain's annals the pompous titles in which this deadly splendor is embodied. Its flags have been flown to the furthest reaches of the globe, so that its empire is measured by the extension of the world itself; its ships have gone from the Mediterranean to the Pacific, and were the first to navigate the earth, circumscribing the limits of human ambition; its great scholars have defended the church; its laws have enlightened all of Europe; its artists can compete with the most celebrated artists of antiquity. Spain could amass examples of heroism and patriotism, valor and constancy, prudence and wisdom. But what good did all these signs of glory do to bring happiness to the country?

If men have organized themselves in societies, if they have acknowledged a sovereign above them and sacrificed their most precious rights to him, they have undoubtedly done so to secure those goods that their very nature pushed them to possess. Oh, princes! You were placed by the Omnipotent to attract abundance and prosperity to your nations. That is your first obligation. Guard yourselves from what may distract you from its fulfillment; close your ears to the saccharine suggestions of flattery and the charms of your own vanity; and do not let yourselves be dazzled by the splendor that surrounds you, nor by the authority that is deposited in your hands. While despondent peoples raise their arms to you, posterity looks at you from afar, observing your conduct, writing down your actions in its memoirs, and reserves your names for praise, oblivion or the execration of future men.

---

1   Mr. Thomas, Essai sur les Éloges.

It seems that this philosophical precept resonated in the heart of Charles III when he came from Naples to Madrid, brought by Providence to occupy his parents' throne. A long practice in the art of rule [in Naples] showed him that a sovereign's greatest glory is that which is based upon his subjects' love; and this love is never more sincere, more enduring, more splendid, than when it is inspired by gratitude. This lesson, so often repeated in the administration of a kingdom that he had conquered himself, would not be any less true in the one that he received like a gift from heaven.

The list of policies and actions with which this benign sovereign won our love and gratitude has already been the object of more eloquent speeches. I will but recall them briefly here. With the creation of new agricultural colonies [*colonias agrícolas*], the distribution of common lands, the reduction of livestock's privileges, the abolition of the *tasa* and the free circulation of grain, he improved agriculture. But there was also the proliferation of trade schools, the reform of guild policies, the multiplication of industrial establishments and the generous profusion of graces and licenses for crafts to benefit industry; the severing of national commerce's old chains, the opening of new export points, peace in the Mediterranean, the regular correspondence and freedom of communication and commerce with our ultramarine colonies. In order to perfect municipal government, the people's representation was reestablished, and so was the sacredness of parental authority in the home for the perfection of domestic governance; the objects of public beneficence were directed away from willful sloth, and a thousand places where charity is bestowed to alleviate the indigence of those who struggle were opened; and, above all, patriotic societies such as this one were founded across towns and cities, paragons of political affairs, where all matters related to the common good were zealously discussed. What broad and glorious reason to laud Charles III and secure for him the title of father of his vassals!

But let us not fool ourselves: the worn and commonplace path of reform would only have brought Charles III passing glory if his zeal had not led him to pursue the means to truly perpetuate the good that he sought. His wisdom discerned that even the most well-considered laws are not sufficient to bring prosperity to a nation, and much less to secure it. He knew that the utility produced by the best and wisest laws is but ephemeral, rewarding their creators with but a sad and belated disappointment. Exposed to the inevitable torrent of contradictions that assails them; flawed by the very novelty of their nature; hard to perfect gradually due to the discouragement caused by the slowness of the process; and harder to conceive as a coherent unity that successfully addresses the mass of circumstances that may blunt or enhance their ill or good effects: Charles III foresaw that reforms would do nothing to favor the nation if he did not prepare it first to receive them, if he did not infuse it with the spirit upon which the success and stability of all reforms depend.

You, gentlemen, who have collaborated with so much zeal to realize his paternal designs, you know very well what our nation lacked. Useful sciences; economic principles; a general spirit of enlightenment: that is what Spain will eternally owe to the reign of Charles III.

If you doubt that the happiness of a state lies in this, turn your eyes to those sad times when Spain lived under the spell of superstition and ignorance. What a horrible and pitiable spectacle! Religion, sent from heaven to enlighten and console man, was distorted by interest so that it saddened and abandoned him; anarchy reigned instead of order; the head of the state was either a tyrant or a victim of the nobles; the people were like flocks, existing only to satisfy their lords' greed; intelligence overwhelmed by public duties and opulence freed from assuming any; indeed, allowed to increase their weight; the laws openly resisted or insolently trampled; justice scorned; the restraints of custom broken; and all of the objects of public good and order disheveled and confused. Where did that spirit reside then, the spirit to which all nations owe their prosperity?

It took Spain centuries to climb out from that abyss, but, by the dawn of the sixteenth century, sovereignty [*la soberanía*] had finally recovered its authority; the nobility had seen its privileges reduced; the people had secured its representation; the courts ensured that the laws and justice were respected; and agriculture, industry and commerce were prospering, encouraged by protection and order. What human power could have been capable of deposing Spain from the apex of power that it had reached, if the spirit of true enlightenment had taught it to secure that which it had so rapidly attained?

Spain did not disdain the arts and sciences. No: instead it aspired to attain fame through them. But alas! How useful were the truths that it gathered through its scholars' zeal? What good did ecclesiastical studies do, after scholasticism hoarded the attention that was owed to morality and dogma? What good came from jurisprudence, with its adamant intent on multiplying legislation on the one hand, and, on the other, submitting all of it to the interpretation of jurists? What good came from the natural sciences, known only for the ridiculous abuse that astrology and chemistry subjected them to? What good, finally, was mathematics, cultivated solely in a speculative fashion, and never used or applied to benefit man? And if utility is the best means to measure value, what is the true worth of those great names that are cited at every step to flatter our sloth and our pride?

Among all these studies, there seemed to have been no place for civil economy [*economía civil*], the science of government, whose principles have not yet been corrupted by interest, unlike those of politics; and whose progress makes it entirely accordant with the philosophy of our present era. Public misery would one day awaken patriotism and conduct it to inquire into the causes and remedies of the many evils that beset the land, but that time was still far off. So while the abandonment of our fields, the ruin of our factories and the degradation of commerce caused worry, foreign wars, the pomp of the court, the greed of the ministry and the public treasury's need engendered hordes of miserable *arbitristas* whose art of draining the people of their money was equivalent to a physician's bleeding of his patients, and precipitated the disappearance, in the span of two reigns, of what had been attained over generations.

It was then that the specter of misery, flying over fallow fields, over deserted workshops and over destitute towns, spread horror across the land. It was then that patriotism inflamed the breasts of the most generous Spaniards, who meditated so much upon the public evils, and clamored so vigorously for their reform that, for the first time, the notion of a science that taught how to govern men and secure their happiness was contemplated. It was then, at last, from the very bosom of ignorance and disorder, that the study of civil economy was born.

But what sum of truth and knowledge could our economic science then contain? Should we even honor it with that name? Hesitant in its principles, absurd in its consequences, mistaken in its calculations and so bedazzled in the examination of problems as well as in its selection of the remedies that would put an end to them, it failed to prescribe consistent rules for good government. Each economist abstracted his own peculiar system; each derived it from a different source, without any concurrence in their elements; each one devised a different path to reach his own ends. Deza, a lover of agriculture, recommended teaching, assistance and exemptions for farmers and rural workers; Leruela, who favored livestock, thought that the enormous privileges of the *Mesta* should be extended; Criales discovered the sad influence of entailed estates and screamed for the circulation of land and its products; Pérez de Herrera saw laziness and sloth everywhere, and wanted to fill the sea with forced labor and the provinces with hospices; Navarrete, dazzled by the authority of the *Consejo*, saw Spain's happiness banished along with the families it expelled; and Moncada saw misery entering with the foreigners who flooded the land. Cevallos believed poverty was caused by the introduction of foreign manufactures; Osorio blamed the metals that came from America; and Mata their departure from the continent. There was no evil, no vice, no abuse that did not have its own censor. The wealth of the ecclesiastical class and the poverty and excessive growth of the religious stratum; *asiento* privileges, *sisas, juros,* sumptuary laws; everything was examined, calculated and even condemned, but nothing was remedied. Effects were mistaken for causes; nobody ascertained the true origin of the nation's plight; nobody tried to apply a remedy to the core of the matter. And while Germany, Flanders and Italy buried Spain's men, gobbled its treasures and consumed the substance and resources of its state, the nation suffered in the arms of the medics [*empíricos*]who were entrusted with its recovery.

Such was the sad situation of our nation, abetted by ill-conceived studies, when the Habsburg dynasty passed in the seventeenth century. Heaven had reserved the restoration of the country's splendor and strength for the Bourbon dynasty. At the beginning of the eighteenth century, the first Bourbon crossed the Pyrenees; and, in the midst of a war as just as it was cruel, he turned his eyes to the people who were so valiantly fighting for his rights to the throne. Philip [V], realizing that they could not be happy if they remained uneducated, established schools and libraries, founded seminaries, protected literature and the arts and, during a reign lasting almost half a century, taught them to appreciate the value of enlightenment.

In an even shorter reign that was even more prosperous and peaceful, Ferdinand [VI] followed in his father's footsteps: he created the merchant marine; fomented industry; favored internal trade and circulation; rewarded and mentored the arts, protecting those with talent; and in order to encourage the proliferation of useful knowledge, he sent outstanding young scholars across Europe to collect this precious commodity, and welcomed foreign artists and scholars to Spain, purchasing their genius with pensions and awards. Thus, he prepared the path that was gloriously pursued by Charles III.

This pious sovereign was bent on banishing darkness from his domains, and his first acts aimed to remove the obstacles that could hinder the progress of light. This was his primary concern. Ignorance was still entrenched among us, but Charles III finally defeated it. The truth was on his side, and, at the first sight of it, darkness indeed vanished.

For centuries, Aristotelian philosophy had tyrannized the republic of letters; and, though most of Europe scorned it by the time of Charles III's accession, our schools were still in its thrall. Of little use in its purest state, because it rewards speculation at the expense of experience, and disfigured by the Arabs, to whom Europe owed the reintroduction of this fatal gift, it was corrupted beyond salvation by the ignorant efforts of its commentators.

Its devotees, sectarian by nature, made it even more obscure with their subtle minutiae, invented to buttress the empire of each sect; and while interest ignited their internecine wars, the Aristotelian doctrine served as a shield for their general preoccupations. Charles dissipated, destroyed and annihilated these parties with a single blow, and, by allowing the liberty of philosophizing to enter our classrooms, he attracted the wealth of philosophical knowledge that we observe today in the spirit of our youth, which is restoring the empire of reason in our schools. You rarely hear among us those barbaric voices, those sententious speeches, that vain and portentous reasoning in which the peripatetic gloried, delighting its believers. In sum, even the texts of Thomism, Scotism and Suarezian scholasticism, so celebrated before, have fled from our schools along with their mouthpieces [*corifeos*], Froilan, González and Losada. Thus, posterity justly allowed some names to be famous, disputed by praise and scorn, before banishing them to oblivion.

Theology, free from the Aristotelian yoke, abandoned scholasticism, which was its primary concern, and returned to the study of dogma and controversy. Charles, fomenting criticism, encouraged theology to seek the knowledge of its purest sources—the Holy Scripture, the Councils, the Church Fathers, the history and discipline of the Church— and thus restored the science of religion to its ancient decorum.

The teaching of ethics and of natural and public rights established by Charles III is improving the science of jurisprudence, which also had been led astray in the labyrinths of discretion and opinion by the scholastics among us. Charles stimulated the study of its origins, affixing its principles, placing natural right over all other teaching, making the voice of our legislators heard for the first time in our classrooms. Now Spanish jurisprudence is beginning to follow the glorious paths of equity and justice.

But Charles was not content with guiding his subjects toward the high truths that are the objects of these studies. Although their significant influence on faith as well as on custom and citizens' tranquillity makes them worthy of his attention, he knows that there are other, less sublime truths that nonetheless are more necessary to secure the people's prosperity. The inquiry into these truths is what will perpetually distinguish the reign of Charles III in the history of Spain.

Man, condemned by Providence to work, is born ignorant and weak. Without enlightenment, without strength, he does not know where to put his arms to work, where to direct his desires. It was necessary for many centuries to pass, for observations to be gathered into a sum of knowledge useful to work, and it was to these simple truths that the world owed the first population growth [*multiplicación de sus habitantes*].

However, the Creator placed a great counterweight to the weakness of man's constitution in his spirit. His capacity to simultaneously comprehend the extension of the earth, the depth of the seas, the height and immensity of the heavens; his capacity to penetrate the most hidden mysteries of nature by devoting himself to its observation; his capacity to subject the universe to his dominion by merely studying it, gathering, combining and ordering his ideas. Tired of losing himself in the darkness of the metaphysical inquests that had for so long occupied his reason and rendered it sterile, he is returning to himself, contemplating nature, tending to the sciences that have nature as its object, and enhancing his very being by exploring the vigor of his spirit and threading together his will and his felicity.

Desirous of carrying out this regeneration in his kingdom, Charles began to promote the teaching of the exact sciences, without whose assistance the investigation of natural truths could not proceed. Madrid, Seville, Salamanca and Alcalá have seen the rebirth of their schools of mathematics; and reestablished in Barcelona, Valencia, Zaragoza, Santiago and almost all other universities [estudios generales]. The strength of scientific demonstration banishes the platitudes of syllogism. The study of physics, supported by experimentation and calculus, is perfected, and so are the sciences in their jurisdiction: chemistry, mineralogy, metallurgy, natural history, botany. And while the observant naturalist investigates and discovers the first laws of the bodies, and penetrates all their properties and virtues, the politician studies the relations in which the Creator's wisdom placed them, so as to ensure the multiplication and happiness of humankind.

Yet another science was still needed to apply all of this knowledge in a useful manner, one that would disseminate its findings effectively to increase their utility by bringing them to bear on the objects of public welfare. In a word, to apply them as true and constant principles to the governance of the people. This is the true science of the state, the science of the public magistrate. Charles turned his eyes to it, and civil economy would henceforth flourish in his domain.

This science owed much to the zealous protection that Charles's heroic father had granted to the illustrious citizens who devoted themselves to it. As the Marquis of Santa Cruz, during his stay in Turin, reduced the vast knowledge that he had attained through profound observations and travel to a series of precious maxims, Don Jeronimo Uztáriz condensed in a treatise published in Madrid the insights that he had acquired through long hours of study and meditation. And, soon after, Zabala would devote his energies to studying the state of our provinces and examining all of the branches of the royal treasury while Ulloa evaluated the measurements and reasoning of those who preceded him in this precious field.

These economists [economistas] were superior to those of the previous century: there is more unity and firmness in their principles, and they better grasped the origin of our decadence. However, the unfortunate habit of regarding economic phenomena through particular systems was still present among them. Each one of them aspired to a particular reform. Proposing the reform of the royal navy, Navia [the Marquis of Santa Cruz] pushed for the creation of a merchant marine that would open the seas to the riches of an extensive and wealthy trade. Condemning the alcabala, internal customs and external or maritime tariffs, Uztáriz designed a commercial plan that was as comprehensive as judiciously organized. Zabala openly stated and demonstrated that the prosperity of agriculture and industry, necessary bases for any commerce, were incompatible with the system of provincial taxes, which was oppressive in its object, ruinous in its method and costly in its execution, and he believed the remedy is the *única contribución*. And after applying calculus and experience to the objects of the public economy and the systems that would lead to its improvement, aspiring to remedy the more general evils instead of singling one out, Ulloa's recommendations nonetheless amounted to a series of partial reforms.

Still further worthy analyses resulted from the study of political economy under Ferdinand's patronage. The doctrine of the illustrious José González, improved by Zabala, resuscitated by Loinaz and modified and adopted by the celebrated Ensenada, would have at least brought unity to the tax system, if the incompetence of its executors had not derailed it. But all of the effort that went into this project was not a waste, for the plague of the *asientos* was finally eliminated, along with the shameful practice of making vast and sudden fortunes off the people's sweat in the shadow of the government's indolence.

In the meantime, a wise Irishman, a happily adopted son of this land, enriched it with new economic knowledge. At Ferdinand's command, D. Bernardo Ward, instructed in the useful sciences and in Spain's political circumstances, traveled across Europe, visiting its major provinces. He stopped in France, in England, and in Holland, the core of the world's opulence; he examined their agriculture, their industry, their commerce, their economic government; and he organized his observations, applied them to Spain and wrote his renowned *Proyecto Económico*. Yet before he could see this precious gift published, death took him from us and buried in a sepulcher a great mind that was so widely cultivated.

Providence reserved for Charles III the glory of using the rays of light that these citizens had deposited in their work. The pleasure of disseminating their ideas throughout the kingdom, and the glory of encouraging in his vassals the desire to study [political] economy was reserved to him. Yes, good King, therein is the greatest glory with which posterity will adorn your name. The realm of science is open only to a few citizens [*ciudadanos*], those who would dedicate themselves to silently investigate the mysteries of nature and communicate them to the nation. Yours is the task of gathering their oracles; yours the role of communicating the light of their investigations; yours the burden of applying it to benefit your subjects. The economic science belongs exclusively to you and those entrusted with your authority. The ministers who surround your throne, constituted as organs of your supreme will; the high magistrates who must impel the public to follow it, and elevate their rights and needs to your attention; those who preside over the internal government across the kingdom; those who guard your provinces; those who have immediate power over your vassals: they should all study it, know it or be overthrown by the classes destined to work and to obey. Your decrees must emanate from its principles, and its executors must respect them. See here the source of prosperity, or the collapse of the vast empires that Providence put in your hands. Every evil that assails them, every vice, every abuse, is derived from contradicting of one of these principles. Error, negligence, a false economic calculation, can overwhelm the provinces with confusion and the people with tears, keeping them from attaining happiness. You, lord, have promoted this important study: chastise those whose actions should be guided by its lights, but who scorn it instead.

Almost immediately after Charles ascended to the throne, the spirit of reform and inquiry touched every aspect of public economy. Government activity awakened the curiosity of the citizens. The study of this science was reborn in Spain at a time when it was already philosophy's primary concern in Europe. Spain read its most renowned writers, examined their principles, analyzed their work: there was talk, there was debate, there was writing, and the nation was graced by economists.[2]

Meanwhile, a sudden convulsion overtook the government. What days of confusion and ignominy! But a superior genius born to be Spain's salvation arrived, and after the initial shock, serenity was restored and the government recovered its zeal; activity was revived, shaking and rumbling even more than before. Its ardor imbued the first senate of the kingdom [*el primer senado del reino*] and inflamed its members. Timidity, indecision, reverence for past errors, the horror of new truths and the whole retinue of petty preoccupations evaporated or were silenced, and the movement of justice was enhanced and propagated further. No memorial, no appeal, no record was presented that was not known and generalized. Matters of great import and general interest were explored and decided according to the truest economic principles. The magistrates, enlightened by them, reduced all their decrees to an orderly and unitary system in a fashion that was previously unknown. Agriculture, population, industry, commerce, education: everything was examined, everything was improved according to these principles, and in the agitated debates over such important matters, light was poured forth, illuminating all of the political bodies of the kingdom, spilling over every class and preparing the way for a general reform.

Oh! What great, what incredible progress would have been achieved, if preoccupation had not distracted our zeal then, and directed it to the defense of less precious objects! The nation, not yet capable of discerning which objects were more closely connected with its interests, expectantly turned to the fiery disputes that the sectarian spirit of the parties augmented each day. It was necessary to call their attention back to these principles, show them the light that was being eclipsed, so that its munificent rays could shine upon us once more.

And that is when an illustrious magistrate [*insigne magistrado*] with a vast knowledge of the nation's constitution, history and law, and an equally compelling comprehension of the country's domestic affairs, and of the political relations of the Monarchy [with other

---

2 I cannot refrain from mentioning a work that, taken alone, is sufficient to substantiate my claim. Its title is *Discurso sobre la Economía Política*, Madrid, 1769, in one volume in *octavo*, printed at the Casa de Ibarra. This writing, as excellent as it is hardly known, was published under the name of don Antonio Muñoz, but its true author is one of the men of letters who is most representative of our time, and with whose name I would have illustrated this part of my discourse if I were to lack due respect toward him. Notwithstanding this, I will not cease advising the lovers of economic studies [*estudios económicos*] to read this work day and night, because it is one of those books that in a few chapters condenses the great treasures of [economic] doctrine. E. N.: According to Llombart, Antonio Muñoz was actually Enrique Ramos (1738–1801). See Vicent Llombart, "Economía Política y Reforma en la Europa Mediterránea del siglo XVIII: una perspectiva española," in Pedro Schwartz Girón ed., *Variaciones sobre la historia del pensamiento económico mediterráneo* (Almería: Cajamar, 2006), 102.

states], stood in the middle of the senate, that body that he had often described as the first representative of the people.[3] His voice, holding their attention, drew for them the most perfect political institution that a free and fortunate people would accept and support with admirable examples of enlightenment and patriotism. The senate adopted this plan, Charles protected it and authorized it with his sanction and the economic societies were born.

These bodies were received expectantly, their operations watched by all, and many rushed to join them. Members of the clergy, attracted by their object and their beneficial and pious ministry, which was analogous with its own; magistrates, who for the moment were deprived of their authority; nobles, their privileges increasingly abridged; literati; merchants and artists, joined, not out of their own self-interest, but filled instead with a desire to seek the common good. All met and acknowledged one another as citizens [*se reconocen ciudadanos*], their membership in a common association taking precedence over their class; and all prepared to work for their brothers' benefit. Zeal and wisdom join forces, patriotism is greatly stirred and the nation watches, spellbound, how the hearts of all its children are turned toward it as one for the first time.

It was time to speak to the nation, to enlighten it and to put the principles of its happiness into action. The spirit behind the marvelous intellectual ferment that animated so many was called to perform this mighty service. Charles protected it, the senate encouraged it, the country regarded it expectantly and, moved by these powerful stimuli, prepared to undertake the arduous task at hand. It spoke to the people, it showed them their true interests, it exhorted them, it instructed and educated them, and opened their eyes to the sources of prosperity.

You, gentlemen, witnessed the ardor that inflamed our august founder's zeal in those memorable days in which he called our society into being. His was the first voice heard in our assemblies; the first who paid Charles the tribute of gratitude owed for this benefit, and whose anniversary we commemorate today; the first who animated it, who guided our zeal; the first, in sum, who showed us the way to perfect the knowledge of those good matters into which we inquired.

The old economists, although inconstant, had deposited in their work a copious number of precious facts, calculations and reasoning that were indispensable in order to know the nation's civil state and the effects of its political errors. All that was needed was a wise and laborious hand that would winnow the true principles from all this detail and bring them to light. The indefatigable magistrate read and extracted these works, published those that were as yet unpublished, dug out the forgotten ones, commented on all of them, rectified misjudgments and corrected their authors' conclusions. And, improved with new and admirable observations, he presented them to his compatriots. All hastened to enjoy this rich treasure; economic knowledge [*luces económicas*] circulated, propagated and grew in the societies; and an enlightened and enthusiastic patriotism infused the foundations of its greatest patrimony.

---

3   E. N.: Probably he was referring to Pedro Rodríguez de Campomanes.

Oh! If envy did not pardon the justice that I have done this wise collaborator of Charles III's designs, those of you who witnessed this memorable era; whose hands always carry his words, whose hearts are imprinted with his maxims, and these very walls where his voice has often resonated, can bear witness to his merit and my impartiality.

But you, good Charles, you deserve the greater part of this glory and our gratitude. Without your protection, without your generosity, without the ardent love that you professed to your people, these precious seeds would have perished. Falling upon sterile ground, the weeds of discord and ignorance would have suffocated them if they ever sprouted. You protected the tender plants that germinated by enforcing love and respect for them; therefore, their fruit, enlightenment and truth, the most certain assurance of your people's happiness, is your harvest.

Yes, Spaniards: see here the greatest of all the precious benefits that Charles III bestowed upon you. He sowed the nation with the seeds of light that will enlighten you, and he cleared the path of wisdom that the nation should follow. The vigilant minister's inspirations, who charged with public instruction, knows how to promote the arts and sciences with such noble and constant eagerness [*afán*] that, at last, gained the reestablishment of the empire of truth. In no other period has its circulation been so free, its defenders so firm, its rights so steadfastly sustained. There are barely any obstacles in its path, and while the bulwarks raised against error are strengthened, the holy language of truth is spoken in our assemblies, read in our writings and happily imprinted in our hearts. Its light is gathered from all the angles of the earth, it grows, it spreads and very soon it will inundate our horizon. Yes, flying above the immensity of the future my enraptured spirit sees there the fulfillment of this happy prediction. It sees the truth sitting above Charles's throne: wisdom and patriotism stand beside it; innumerable generations revere it and bow to it; the people, beatified by its influence, pay it sincere and pure homage; and to compensate for the centuries of oblivion with which they offended it, they offer it hymns of joy and share with it the gifts of abundance that truth itself secured for them.

Oh, friends of the fatherland [*amigos de la patria*], entrusted with the greatest part of this happy revolution, while Charles's munificent hand raised the magnificent monument to wisdom, while the sons of Minerva, consecrated to it, break the bosom of nature to reveal its most intimate mysteries and open an unending mine of useful truths for the industrious towns and villages, you must cultivate day and night the art of applying this light to the nation's well-being and prosperity. Make the splendor of truth inundate the throne room and flow into every palace and high council, until it penetrates even the most distant and humblest homes. This shall be your end, this your desire and your only ambition. And if you want to make Charles a gift worthy of his piety and his name, collaborate with him in his glorious enterprise of enlightening the nation to bring it true felicity.

And you, the noble and precious feminine part of this patriotic body, you can also partake in this rapturous glory, if you dedicate yourselves to the sublime task with which nature and religion have entrusted you. Every day the *patria* judges the citizens whom you have raised, seeing whether they are fit to carry forth the hope of its splendor. Maybe they wish to serve [the *patria*] in the church, or as magistrates, or in the army; but if you have not made them worthy of these high offices they will be ignominiously rejected.

Unfortunately, men have appropriated to ourselves the exclusive right to teach our young, and education has been reduced to formulas. But if you have left the care of enlightening their spirit to us, at least exercise the right to form their hearts. Oh, what is enlightenment good for, what are talents worth, what good is the whole apparatus of wisdom, without good and righteous hearts? Yes, illustrious companions, yes, I assure you, and the voice of a defender of the rights of your sex should not sound suspicious to you. I repeat: it is up to you to form the hearts of the nation's citizens. Inspire in them the tender affections upon which humanity's welfare and joy are founded. Inspire sensibility in them, a kind virtue that you have received from nature, but that man only attains through long reflection and study. Make them simple, hardworking, compassionate, kind; but, above all, make them lovers of truth, of liberty and of their *patria*. Predispose them to receive the enlightenment that Charles wishes his peoples to achieve [*Disponedlos así para recibir la ilustración que Carlos quiere vincular en sus pueblos*], and prepare them to be the reward and compensation of your ambitions, the glory of their families, the worthy imitators of your zeal and the benefactors [*bienhechores*] of the nation.

INAUGURAL ADDRESS TO THE ROYAL ASTURIAN INSTITUTE*

Gijón (Asturias), 7 January 1794

Quid verum, quid utile.

Gentlemen:

It has been 12 years since that day when, speaking to our Patriotic Society concerning the means to encourage the prosperity of Asturias, I had the honor of suggesting to its zealous members that no measure would be as effective and beneficial, nor as worthy of their consideration, as establishing an institute for the study of the useful sciences in this land. Some of those who are here now were witnesses to the ardor with which I sought to persuade my audience of this valuable truth, even when we believed we were far from the happy circumstances in which we find ourselves today, when this study is even more necessary than ever. Who would have told us then that scarcely any time would pass before we would see that dream realized in the midst of the bright future promised by a good king's protection under the influence of a committed minister? And who would have told me that I would return from afar to inaugurate this valuable establishment in my fatherland (*patria*), so close to the walls that witnessed my birth, among my childhood companions and surrounded by so many distinguished personages? For this, my beloved compatriots, is the mission with which I have been entrusted; this is the object of the present solemn occasion. Ready yourselves to receive the good that I bring you; prepare to celebrate it, not with vain demonstrations of joy, but with pure sentiments of love and gratitude toward the monarch who provides it. After employing all of my zeal in its procurement, what is left for me to do but to sketch for you the benefits that it shall bring and the obligations that it entails? This is what I will endeavor to do now, if you will give me your attention.

Yes, gentlemen, today we acquire a great debt, because the value of that with which our good king has made us wealthy is immense. Is there anything nobler or more precious than knowledge on this earth? And this is what Charles IV intends to establish here, among you. You will not have to abandon your homeland; you will not have to wander in pilgrimage, searching for it, like Pythagoras, in faraway lands. This institute of learning that we now inaugurate is a monument that our monarch's liberal hand raises for science,

---

*   "Oración Inaugural de la Apertura del Real Instituto Asturiano de Náutica y Mineralogía."

so that it is perpetually cultivated and honored within its walls. Here it will always receive nourishment and shelter, and the bearers of its doctrines will shed its light and treasures with constancy and care.

Is there a gift more worthy of your acknowledgment? Undoubtedly, among all the things that a just monarch can give his people, none is as great, as beneficial, as enlightenment [*ilustración*]. If you want to estimate its true value, think of the evils that it has banished from the earth, and turn your eyes for an instant to those unhappy peoples who are still subjugated to primitive ignorance. The land does not produce for them anything but thorns and briers. Poor, they wander the earth, competing with the wild beasts for the soil they tread, for the caves in which they live and even for the rude nourishment on which they depend. No arts assist them to fulfill their needs, let alone to satisfy their desires! Condemned to suffer the constant stimulus of privation and want, what hopes, what solace might bring peace and tranquility to their spirit? Is there a sadder spectacle than to see man enslaved by nature, when he was created to be its lord?

And this is why the instruction of the people was the first object of legislation among the wise men of antiquity. From Confucius to Zoroaster, and from Solon to Numa Pompilius, the great object of public institutions was to cultivate man's spirit and form his heart. Read their laws and you will find more ideas concerning education than those concerning communal regulations. All were directed to enhance men's souls; and if some addressed the physical faculties of the body, hoping to strengthen it and make it accustomed to fatigue and agility, it was only to cultivate among citizens those two great virtues upon which all states depend: valor, the primary support of public security; and love of work, the primary source of individual felicity. Such was the ancient, simple and sublime character of wisdom. Private and public morality was its only object. And this learning alone enlightened many celebrated men; it merited the dedication and vigils of legislators and philosophers; through it, the ancient republics were reinforced and ennobled; it exalted citizens' souls; and it engendered those great virtues that we still admire today and that will be eternal witnesses to the excellence of their knowledge.

God would be pleased, beloved compatriots, if on this day, dedicated to truth and public welfare, I had no other learning to propose to you! God would be pleased if the security of the state and the fortune of its members were still entirely dependent on this kind of wisdom! God would be infinitely pleased if in the present time of corrupt ideas and customs, we could still recover that simple and happy innocence! And, truly, the wisdom that reigned in antiquity would be the first, the only object of my exhortations, if it were indeed enough to guarantee all of this. In fact, fearful of corrupting it or banishing it from our soil, I would point to the august building that is our neighbor and give a very different speech, saying, "Turn your eyes to those high rocks to our south, and see in them the inaccessible wall that nature has placed there to separate us from the rest of the earth. Keep your eyes on the tempestuous Cantabrian Sea, and see in its stormy waves that crash against the foundations of our homes, the terrible limit that she has placed on your ambition. Across these barriers you will not find anything but monsters and dangers. Keep from trespassing them in search of a happiness that Providence placed closer to us. Regard them as boundaries that divide the people, to reduce the sphere of their work and of their desires so that they may focus on their families and those ties that bind them closer, bringing them happiness. Do not aspire to any other felicity; do not aspire to any other knowledge: to be happy, try simply to be virtuous."

But alas! Who could recall that simple age that passed like lightning, never to appear again upon the surface of the earth? Ambition banished it forever; ambition, which raised its throne over that of virtue, disrupting everything, corrupting everything, all, even the objects of knowledge that seemed as immutable as knowledge itself. It set off a wild frenzy that filled men's hearts everywhere, making them seek glory in death and desolation. Since then, force has triumphed over virtue and ignorance over wisdom. Thus wise Greece, ennobled with the sanctity of Cimon and Socrates, perished at the crude hands of Mummius; and prudent Rome, magnified more by the virtues of Regulus and Cato than their bloody conquests, ceded to the furor of the incipient and barbaric people that reestablished the empire of ignorance.

Alas! Let us turn our gaze away from this period that was as sinister to humanity as it was shameful to knowledge. What does the history of ten centuries show us but violence and injustice, war and destruction, horror and calamity? Oh, centuries of ignorance and superstition! Centuries of ruin and ambition and infamy and tears for mankind [*el género humano*]! Wisdom will always remember you with execration, and humanity will perpetually cry over your memory.

When this period finally ended, legislators again realized that the fortune of the states was inseparable from that of their peoples, and that to make the people happy, they had to be enlightened first. Then, the love of knowledge was born again, and the law, reconciled with wisdom, hurried to multiply the institutes of public learning.

And what were the objects of learning in this happy revolution? What could they be, when our sanctuaries had to be purged from the filth that tainted dogma, morality and the venerable discipline of the church? When the ferocious notions that feudal arrogance had introduced in the temple of justice had to be banished? When the greed of the powerful classes perched on the backs of the weak, oppressing them and violating their rights, had to be combated? When the foundation of sovereignty itself had to be reaffirmed, refraining with one hand the eruptions of power while using the other to shelter the defenseless people with its protective shield? These offices demanded new and various kinds of knowledge, and to reach them it was necessary to perfect the arts of discourse and reason, which had also been corrupted by ignorance. This is why the humanities, dialectics, theology and jurisprudence were the first objects of study when the love of letters was reborn in our country.

In that general impulse that swept across all the nations of Europe, none cultivated these arts as gloriously or as enthusiastically as ingenious Spain. Oh! If only this glory could satisfy our zeal! If in this wisdom alone were found the joy and security of a people, what nation would be stronger or happier than ours?

But while we were dazzled by this splendor, trusting our own greatness and dedicating all our waking hours to the sciences of the intellect, other nations, more concerned with their prosperity and faced with new political concerns, promoted the study of nature. They realized that the strength of a state was no longer derived from virtue or courage, but from the number and wealth of its members. They realized that a state's security depended upon that deadly art invented by ambition, as well as in the ingenious discipline and horrible weapons that it had cruelly perfected and multiplied. They realized, in sum, that this lethal power could not be purchased with anything but gold; that if the people had no wealth, they could not be free or happy; and that once this idol had made its appearance on the earth, it was necessary to acquire a wisdom that could teach how to placate it.

And, by Jove, could the legislators, threatened by ambition's ferocious designs at every turn, resist this cult? Fearing these designs was a matter of prudence; but preparing against them was a sacrifice owed to the people's peace and security. In the midst of this general convulsion, what could the most just government do but accommodate this terrible need and through its satisfaction garner tranquillity and happiness for its subjects? And if government's authority depends on the increase of private fortunes, what should the most just government do but seek the increase of private fortunes, to reinforce security and make itself respected?

Asturians, see here the object of the new studies that our good king calls us to begin today: promoting useful knowledge that can perfect the lucrative arts; producing or discovering new objects to which honest labor can dedicate itself; providing new material for commerce and navigation; and thus increasing the population, attaining abundance and securing the strength of the state and the felicity of its members by erecting them together upon the same foundation. This is the benefit that it can provide, and this should be the object of our vigils.

To reach these great ends, your king calls you to study nature, and invites you to look for those useful truths encoded within her. Such is the purpose of this new Institute. It will not clutter your spirit with vain opinions or fill it with sterile truths. It will not compel you to devote your time to metaphysical investigations or wander in those unknown regions where wisdom was lost for too long. What could the temerity of man find there? From Zeno to Spinoza, from Thales to Malebranche, what did ontology discover but monsters and chimeras, or doubts and illusions? Oh! Can man truly understand that which is beyond nature without revelation, that divine light that descends from heaven to enlighten and strengthen our dark and feeble reason? Could he have discovered those holy truths that ennoble his being and constitute the sweetest consolation in his suffering on his own?

If there is a study that can indeed raise us to the understanding of these truths, it is the study of nature, the study of the admirable order upon which all natural things rest, which reveals in every detail the workings of the wise and omnipotent hand that laid it out. It beckons us to know all creatures, and indicates the great ends for which we were placed among them. Run, then, beloved compatriots, to cultivate this innocent and beneficial study. While a part of our youth learns the principles of dogma and public and private morals in the general schools, desirous to practice the ministries of religion and justice, run to us, come with us to study nature. Regard this great book that Providence has opened before every man so that he could continually read and learn from it; look in this immense volume for those pages to which the finger of truth has not yet touched; increase the patrimony of knowledge, which is still small, but infinite in its worth; and let this be the object of your work, the culmination of your ambition and your glory.

I do not fear, beloved compatriots, that you will disdain this knowledge: I know that you are endowed with a clear and penetrating reason, a spirit that is capable of soaring to the highest peaks of science. Therefore, instead of motivating you to be diligent, my words must inspire you to be modest as you embark upon this new path toward wisdom. They need not excite you to run down it, but to consider and avoid the dangers and pitfalls that surround it, the dark and intricate sidetracks where you could lose yourselves. Truth and utility, which are the aims of this Institute, are also the aims of my exhortations. Happy shall I be if the zeal that informs my words inspires that sobriety, that constancy, without which no object as sublime as this can be reached!

There is no doubt that man was born to study nature. He was the only creature gifted with a spirit capable of comprehending its immensity and penetrating its laws; and he alone can recognize its order and feel its beauty. He alone among all creatures. Or is there, by Jove, any other capable of embracing the system of union and harmony that links every entity, from the bright squadrons of stars that wander above the immensity of the sky, to the smallest atom of matter that sleeps in the heart of a mountain? Can another creature discern in this harmony, in this order, the all-knowing hand of the Creator? Or can it, absorbed in the contemplation of so many wonders, rise up to his throne singing the most ardent hymns of gratitude and praise? See here, beloved compatriots, the Institute's calling; see here the ultimate object of your studies.

But these precious gifts that God gave man so that he would know nature, and knowing it, possess it, can be transformed by pride into instruments of oppression and ruin. Indeed, the truth that they contain ultimately holds the key to sovereignty, so to speak. If man were to dominate nature following simply his will or his passions, would he be born as weak and naked, as timid and unarmed, as he is introduced to this world? Undoubtedly, Providence would have given him more vigor and agility than those given to other creatures; and a strength superior to that of the elements; and it would not have surrounded him with dangers, nor subjected him to so much necessity and misery. Let us acknowledge then, that since reason is the only superior endowment given to man, and that it is through reason that we dominate nature, it is also with and by reason that we must exercise this domination.

Let us begin, then, by perfecting reason, whose excellence is not so much in its vigor, but in its capacity to acquire it; not so much in its perfection, but in its perfectibility. Weak and obscure when it is abandoned to its natural indolence, it is fortified and expanded when its faculties are exercised, until it soars above nature and contemplates the most sublime and distant truths.

But throughout this process, imagination can deceive reason, while passion can lead it astray at every turn. What precautions! What support is not necessary to remain constant on the path to truth, so as not to lose oneself on the innumerable paths of error! Let us, then, look for their support and try to perfect our reason before we call at the doors of wisdom.

We must first cultivate the gift of language. Let us foster this admirable instrument of perfection and communication given to man so that he can analyze and order his thoughts, bringing them forth from the secluded corners of the soul and impressing them upon the souls of his peers; extending them across the earth, and transmitting them from generation to generation for all posterity. Through it, all truths and all goods can be made common. Oh! Why have ambition and frenetic passions, multiplying this instrument, rendered it useless? Why have they turned language differences into walls that are more insurmountable than the mountains and the seas? Why have they divided man into peoples and nations? Why have they condemned the great family of mankind to perpetual discord? Alas, let us, acknowledging this powerful impulse, try to diminish it. Let us study the languages of the more cultured nations: those that hold the wealth of ancient and modern wisdom within them, and those spoken by Newton and Priestley, Buffon and Lavoisier, translating the great monuments of human reason for our compatriots.

And, by Jove, will you repudiate the art of design as unworthy of its fame? If luxury has enslaved it to the pleasures of the imagination, wisdom, aided by reason and our needs, will ennoble its vocation. Nature belongs to its jurisdiction: capable of imitating it, or capable, so to speak, of improving it, of creating it again, it will serve the demonstrative sciences as a faithful depository of their truths; and it will serve as the primary guide in the operations of the natural sciences and the useful arts. It is understood by all men in all nations, and it can express the productions of all climates and all times. Cultivate it, and the strokes drawn by your hands will be able to present the rich productions of our soil before the eyes of the Malabars and the Samoyed, the wise Englishmen and the industrious Chinese.

And do not settle for these aids alone. The exercise of your reason needs additional and firmer support. Look for the first, the safest, in those sciences that pay homage to demonstrated truths: the sciences that man invented and elevated to the highest peak. They are the greatest and most powerful instrument of human reason. They are the precursors of truth, its inseparable companions. There is nothing ambiguous or doubtful in their jurisdiction, nothing that has not been demonstrated or proven true. Skepticism is prostrate before them, and error flees in shame from their confines. With such wings, your spirit can safely soar from the simplest principles found in nature to the highest truths of its vastness. None perfect our being so much; none ennoble it more. Is there, by Jove, a greater, more worthy sight than that of man's weak spirit borne to the greatest heights by these sciences, so that he can weigh the immensity of the oceans; and discover the size, distance and movement of the planets, measuring their light and the splendid orbits that they follow, subjecting infinity itself to his calculations?

But beware of abusing this precious instrument, my compatriots: beware of applying it to objects that are not worthy of its excellence and your vocation. Let us never forget that it was given to us to improve our existence and to concur with the well-being of mankind; and that if we are called to know nature, it is not to satisfy our pride, but to relieve our misery. Would it not be a foolish temerity for man to throw himself into the immensity of the heavens, without first knowing the land that shelters him and feeds him?

And see here an advantage with which our age can certainly attain glory. Yes, we have few names that can compare with the brightness of Euclid and Archimedes, who were the world's teachers and are still its guides in the study of abstract truths. But what good did the presumptuous world of antiquity gain from them? Constructed on and within nature, antiquity barely took the time to observe it; and while it investigated bodies' abstract properties, it remained crudely ignorant of their essences and destinies, as if the precious gifts that dotted the earth were unworthy of its contemplation; as if that which is not consecrated to the well-being and relief of mortals can be called wisdom.

Let us conclude from this, that after perfecting our organ of thought, we must apply its powers to the knowledge of that which surrounds us. We must not be satisfied with discovering bodies' properties as separate entities in and of themselves, but we should be also eager to know the inseparable aspects of those bodies. This is the aim of physics, one of the exact sciences: guiding the human spirit in observation, bringing it out of the dark regions where it is still lost, and forcing it, so to speak, to follow the slow footsteps of experience, and to enter into the palace of nature, however timidly at first.

With such powerful support, what progress has been reached by the natural sciences! What portentous advancement after man linked observation and reason, subjecting the latter to experience and calculation, and growing accustomed to keeping these by his side! The ancient philosophers cultivated these sciences, it is true, but, mistrusting their senses, they gave themselves entirely to reason, and physics was for them naught but a speculative science, eternally concerned with the abstract properties of matter. Aristotle's great genius, that so ennobled the human spirit, ultimately tyrannized it; and his prodigious comprehension, which has amazed the wisest of men, subjugated all wisdom and its holders to his authority. How many centuries have not gone by in which the mere invocation of his name was enough to prove physics' dogmas, as well as those of dialectics and ontology? If Descartes and Newton, shaking off this yoke, had not submitted Aristotle's doctrine to the criteria of experience, how far would our reason still be from nature's threshold!?

Let us continue on, my beloved compatriots, and let us follow in the footsteps of these illustrious geniuses, born to know and to honor nature. Let us study it like they did, uniting reason and experience, and treating observation as the perpetual companion of both. But we should beware of having it as our only guide, trusting ourselves entirely to it. If the ancient philosophers, fearing the fallibility of their senses, trusted only their reason, forfeiting the assistance of experience, they erred on the side of vanity. But how many of those who now like to philosophize, mistrusting their reason, pretend to enslave truth to the tyranny of the senses? What absurd systems, what daring and mad hypothesis has this mania, this new frenzy, produced in the field of physics! But can man be so unaware of his own being? Can he ignore that this spark of celestial light was given to him to assist his fallible and weak senses? Can he forget that his spirit is tied to matter, so that, trapped within it, it conceives ideas through sensations, and it cannot perceive anything without feeling, nor think without having felt? Let us eschew these fatal and insane extremes. Let us respect this bond with which Omnipotence, ennobling our being, wanted to set us apart from all other creatures; this admirable bond that ties us to them while at the same time uplifting us to contemplate His magnificent works, and beckons us to know His holy and auspicious designs. Thus prepared, pursue these new studies that the country demands of you. Search for wisdom in this our new temple, regardless of your profession or your aspirations. Will you take to sea, braving the terrible ocean that roars before us? Wisdom will raise upon its abyss a safe and firm abode, and show you to steer it to the ends of the earth. She will place in your hands the keys to the winds, teaching you to read the route that you must follow in the heavens and on the waves, teaching you to triumph over danger and storms. While the sun illuminates the climates beneath your feet, wisdom will show you the guiding star above your heads; and when the dark removes it from your sight, wisdom will place in your hands a fragile but powerful insubent that will continually point to the poles around which the world rotates. Thus, you will traverse the vast seas, taking the peaceful merchant to the furthest regions of the earth where he will find the reward for your sweat. And if the desire of fame and glory fills your hearts, you will rise to the immortal glory that today adorns the names of Columbus and Magellan, Cook and Malaspina.

But if you are more timid, or less ambitious, and you prefer a more immediate and secure happiness, study nature, and she will share her treasures with you. Study the numerous republics of bodies that wander above our heads and lie beneath your feet [*las numerosas repúblicas de entes que vagan sobre vuestras cabezas y que yacen bajo vuestros pies*], and which are still, or move, around us. Investigate their essence and their properties; and, what is even worthier, investigate the uses that the beneficial hand of the Creator destined them for. Nature, pleased at being the only object of your studies and contemplation, will open her prolific womb and spread the riches of her cornucopia before you, for none will be turned away from her presence without improvement or wealth.

Oh, beloved compatriots! My soul is filled with joy as it contemplates your dedication to this innocent, this pleasant, this advantageous field of studies, so necessary to enrich and enhance your spirit! The marvelous scenes that physics will reveal to your reason, as it presents the rich collection of bodies that fill the universe, and as it decodes the laws that direct their movement and reproduction! When it shows you to distinguish between the fluids that bring us light and heat and fire and sound; and between those admirable and subtle substances that fill and penetrate all entities, and among which nature swims! What new and pleasant perspectives will be opened to you when chemistry, removing the veil of mystery that envelops the essence and properties of bodies, reduces them to their simplest components and reveals the mystery of those intimate relations of love or aversion by which bodies are attracted or repelled, those affinities that make them move toward one another or shun each other, and that conserve them in the long sequence of creation with such portentous harmony! Then you will find yourselves surrounded by movement and life, everything animated and everything placed in an invariable and all-knowing order; everything, finally, directed and created by a wise and munificent hand, for the good and solace of mankind.

May God forbid, beloved compatriots, that you lose sight of this great signature imprinted in all of nature's works, and which constitutes the final aim of all learning. May God forbid that you use it in sterile questions that can only feed insubstantial and presumptuous curiosities. Mistrust that terrible passion, more dangerous the more it flatters the human spirit. And if some of you find yourselves tempted to follow its voice, know that the truth hides from those who seek it with impudent pride; that it rejoices in frustrating their attempts, and that while it feeds their presumption with ghosts and vain appearances, it only presents itself as clear and brilliant as it descended from the heavens, to those who search for it with sobriety and honest intentions. This is how you should study nature; this is how you should look inside her for those truths that are characterized by goodness and usefulness. In sum, truth and utility, which form the two-sided insignia of this Institute, should be the constant and only aims toward which you work.

Could you deny this token of gratitude to the pious monarch who so kindly solicits it, and who, to excite your zeal, distinguishes you with such protection and beneficence? See how he struggles with nature to remove the obstacles that it has placed on our road to felicity, and how he forces it instead to aid us in its attainment; how he improves our ports; how he opens up roads for us; how he employs the activity and rare talent of the wise engineer that we see before us to make our rivers navigable; how, in sum, he seeks abundance and prosperity for all of us. And if this powerful stimulus is not enough, if you still need another, more private example of patriotism and public love, turn your eyes to the kind and honest minister who with such constancy promotes your well-being. Oh, how he strives to bring to light the treasures that lie ignored in our own territory! How he protects its property, promotes its circulation, animates its exports with graces and licenses! How, in sum, he calls you to study nature so that you yourselves may know the goods and resources that surround you and that you have disdained until now!

But alas! In the midst of these sweet hopes, a sad suspicion seeks to pierce my heart with mistrust, disturbing its constancy and its zeal! Without a doubt, this misgiving is caused by the terrible alliance that sloth and ignorance have forged everywhere. "Who (I almost hear them whispering), who will come to gather these precious doctrines? All men are classified in society: each profession, each stratum has a given destiny and a given role; each one has his occupations and his pleasures, and their pattern of fatigue and rest are determined for them. Who would sacrifice them to application and learning? Scientific truths can only be attained after exhausting study and wakeful nights, and the poor have time only to survive, while the rich want only to enjoy life. So who, then, will come here to look for these truths, apply them and communicate them to his brothers?"

Asturians, those are my fears; that is the pitfall into which many useful institutions have fallen. Will we be equally unfortunate? What am I saying? Will we be so indolent and lazy that we will not push our spirit to embrace the success that lies before us? Who cannot profit from studying nature? Is there, by Jove, a class of men that would not be aided by the important truths that it can teach?

Come to receive them, all of you, generous descendants of the great Pelagius, come! The country beckons you to this Institute; the people who support you need your guidance and your lights! If their poverty does not move you, be moved at the very least by your own interest and the decorum of your class. You are no longer the only bulwarks of national security, the only defenders of its rights, the only interpreters of its will, as you once were. Your pennants, your privileges, are no longer grounded on these firm roles. Only true patriotism, virtue, an enlightened virtue, can justify and conserve them. Come, instruct the people, assist it and reward with your lights and counsel the sweat that falls from its brow and waters your lands; that innocent and precious sweat to which you owe your splendor and your very existence.

Come, too, ministers of the sanctuary! Do not disdain this innocent study that promises to perfect your wisdom. Oh! A sad necessity powerfully beckons you to it! Impiety hopes to corrupt it: come and sanctify it, and help it keep its purity. A sect of ferocious and blasphemous men, seeking weapons in nature, is rising up like the titans against heaven. Come, study the varied and magnificent collection of beings, the constant order, the ineffable harmonies that unite them, the prodigious abundance of goods and joys spilled around you, and see how they preach and demonstrate to man the omnipotence, the wisdom, the goodness, of their maker. Come, study, and combat incredulity with the same weapons of its wielders: confound it, corner it, scare it away; the people who honor you and put food on your tables need you to protect their beliefs, which are their deepest solace; and while you teach them the doctrines of eternal truths, you will help them attain that scarce portion of happiness granted to them in this earth.

And you, laborious people, whose welfare keeps me up so many nights; you, who are less commendable in my eyes for your forgotten rights than for your innocent toil; while you continue your labors for the benefit of all the orders of the state, send your youth to be educated at this Institute. Here they will learn to scorn the dangers of the ocean, and they will search for your relief and your solace in faraway coasts. Here they will learn to multiply the objects of your labors, to improve the instruments and machines that assist you, and to perfect the useful arts that you continually employ. Here they will learn to pierce those tall rocks that surround you, and penetrate deep into the earth's bosom, taking from its intimate bowels the resources that Providence deposited in it for your relief; resources denied to sloth and indolent pride, and reserved for intelligence and diligent labor. Send them, instruct them, and you will multiply the regard that good and sensible souls already feel toward you.

And you, my dear *Gijoneses*, privileged by your proximity to this Institute, do not let your pride grow because of it. It is not for you alone that this monument to science has been built, but for all Asturians; and the closer you are to it, the greater your responsibility to honor and defend it. Make good use of this advantage, and build upon it your claim to the love and respect of your brothers. Let hospitality be your first virtue from now on. Wherever they come from, receive them with open arms, and an open heart; form with them a single people, united by the love of knowledge that beckons all. Let this be indeed a firm and long-lasting tie of fraternal love, one that extinguishes forever the vile parties that have divided you, gathering you together with one will, one design: that of working for the good of the country.

Spaniards, whoever you are, see here your vocation: follow it, and find happiness in the knowledge of nature. And if, awed by its arcane mysteries, you do not dare remove the veil that conceals its mysterious operations from mortal eyes, study at least its history in the profusion of things that lie before you. Contemplate the animal kingdom, in the midst of which man reigns, bright like the sun among the stars of the heavens; and see how its individuals, after filling the earth with activity and joy, docilely come to him to help him in his labors, or hide from his power and respect his empire. Watch how the earth is ennobled by the leafy pomp of the plant kingdom, and how from the humblest blade of grass to the tallest Cedar of Lebanon, an immensity of resources and succor is made available for man's desire after enhancing their majesty. See how nature weighs down the mineral kingdom, provider of so many goods and evils, with mountains, concealing it in her deepest caverns; and how, despite it all, it trusts man with the keys to it, acknowledging his will and his dominion. Admire the exuberance, the profusion, the variety of its productions, and work hurriedly to transform them for the common good.

Happy is he, one and a thousand times happy, whose studies have this delicious and sublime end! Yes: too much time and effort have been dedicated to study the forces of nature only to afflict and perturb them; the instruments of its ruin and desolation have been perfected for too long. You, beloved compatriots, are not called to profane the name and offices of wisdom. Devote it entirely to those innocent and peaceful arts that honor and console mankind. Dedicate it to the multiplication and perfection of their instruments and methods, and open with them the springs of abundance and of life that a frenzied ambition hopes to keep closed. Help the reign of reason and universal concord finally succeed these days of confusion and scandal that humanity looks upon with sadness and horror.

Above all, my children (and you must forgive me the use of this epithet, and blame it on the tenderness of my affection), above all, devote your learning to that art that is wisdom's most intimate friend and nature's perfection. Consecrate it to the first, the most necessary, the most beneficial: innocent agriculture. Watch the immense mass of inorganic matter that seems destined to deepen our misery; turn your attention to the earth, this universal mother whose youth is renewed with the annual cycle of the heavens, and study at all times that marvelous virtue of fomenting the seeds that are entrusted to her bosom, for in their reproduction lie the multiplication and solace of mankind. And if the precious and useful gifts that she has presented to you do not satisfy your desires, open up its bowels and discover new sources of wealth and prosperity. What goods are not kept within its dark abyss! Rocks, salts, metals, bitumen … ah! Do not be dazzled by greed before so much treasure. Choose the most useful and innocent, and stop above all in this admirable and abundant fossil that Providence has given us to increase our plenty.

There is an object worthy of your most diligent efforts. The country calls you to study nature and to know it. Do not turn your eyes away from it, even if it seems humble or grotesque to you. Soon it will help give shelter and warmth; it will succor industry; it will be a great aid to Spain's commerce and navigation. Your brothers in the eastern and southern provinces desire it and expect it from you. A day will come when the other nations will be your tributaries, running anxiously to our coasts for supplies; or purchasing it from the ships that carry this solace to the frozen inhabitants of one and the other pole. Then Asturias will know abundance and happiness. Then, with your agriculture improved, your arts encouraged, your commerce and navigation enhanced, you will multiply like the sand on your beaches, and peace and joy will live among you.

Oh happy days! Days of plenty; days of ease; days of glory for Asturias! Happy shall be those who live to see them, and renewing the memory of this solemn day, commemorate it in the years to come! Happy are those who hear the hymns of gratitude and praise that will be sung by our descendants for the glory of our good king who, fixing the place of science in this land, opened the doors that led to such rejoicing! Then, his blessings will also recall the tender and venerable name of the patriotic minister who prepared the path to knowledge, and it will be carried from generation to generation to the remotest posterity. And if the enthusiasm of acknowledgment awakens a tender memory of my small efforts, of this zeal for your well-being that today consumes me, then my ashes, which will not lie far from you, will have received the only award that my heart desires, and will beckon to you from the grave to study nature, to look for useful truths within her, and to devote your time and efforts, your knowledge and all of your zeal, to the good of your country and the solace of mankind.

ON THE NEED TO COMBINE
THE STUDY OF LITERATURE WITH
THE STUDY OF THE SCIENCES*

Gijón (Asturias) 1797

Gentlemen:

The first time that I had the honor of addressing you from this podium, on that memorable and glorious day on which, with the purest joy and hopes of promise, we opened the doors of this new Institute and welcomed you to it, you learned that my first care was to lift your eyes to the importance and usefulness of the sciences that you had come to study. And if there was any merit in my words, if the ardent zeal of procuring your good fortune lent them any strength, you will not have forgotten the tender solicitude with which I exhorted you to embrace the truth that I presented. And? After three years, when you have come to the glorious end of this cycle [of your studies], and as we prepare to present to the public the first fruits of your diligence and our conduct, must we continue to persuade and convince you of such a well-known truth?

Perhaps this is what public opinion demands from us, and we would acquiesce to it were we not certain of swaying it more strongly with deeds instead of words. Yes, gentlemen, despite the progress achieved through our constancy and yours, and in the midst of the justice with which it is honored by those good souls that, mindful of the importance of public education, yearn for its improvement, I know that malignant spirits hover around you, censuring your efforts. Enemies of useful instruction and of the public good, which depends upon it, they discredit the objects of your teaching and, under the false pretenses of friendship and compassion, they question its advantages and the benefits you will gain from it. It is the struggle of light against darkness that I foresaw and spoke to you about on that solemn day; and it is faced by all public establishments that wage war on ignorance and aspire to promote true instruction.

But what could I say to those men who murmur against what they do not understand and persecute that which they cannot reach, moved not by zeal but by a spirit of contradiction, not by their own convictions, but by envy and malice? No, do not expect me to respond with anything other than our silence and our conduct. Let them witness today

---

* Given to the Real Instituto Asturiano de Náutica y Mineralogía. "Oración sobre la necesidad de unir el estudio de la literatura al de las ciencias."

the fruit of your studies, and they will hold their tongues. That will be our best exposition, and what will most confound them, so do not heed their mutterings and carry on with your useful tasks, like worker bees happily laboring in their hives while the drones buzz and linger above.

A new object, no less censured by these cynical imitators of Zoilus and no less beneficial to you, beckons my attention and yours: in the course of the teaching of arts and letters [*buenas letras*] that we began this year, you have seen that it is our intention to unite the literary arts with the study of science. And this union, long desired but never established in our imperfect education system, will seem strange to some, and impossible to others, and perhaps even you will think it useless or ineffectual.

It is our intention to satisfy all of you today, because we are accountable to all of you. We are accountable to the government, which has charged us with perfecting this establishment; we are accountable to the public, for whose good it is consecrated; and since you have trusted us with your education, we are accountable primarily to you. Would I dare ask you for further sacrifices of your energy and waking hours if I did not see the promise of a great and certain benefit in this sacrifice? Therein is the subject of my speech. Have no fear, my children, that prodding you to the study of literature will in some way diminish your love of science. No, indeed: I shall always regard the sciences as the primary, the most worthwhile, object of your education. For only they can enlighten your spirit; they alone can enrich it; they alone can transmit the precious truths discovered in antiquity, and, at the same time, awaken in your souls the desire to discover new ones, so that this rich treasure grows more and more; only they can put an end to the useless disputes and absurd opinions that surround us; and, finally, only they can dissipate the obscure atmosphere of error that lingers above the earth, so that light and knowledge can enhance the innate nobility of the human species.

But the fact that science is the primary object of your education does not mean that it should be the only one; the literary arts will not be any less useful to you and, I dare say, any less necessary.

For what are the sciences without their aid? While science enlightens the spirit, literature enhances it; while science enriches it, literature polishes and refines it; while science rectifies our judgment and gives it exactitude and firmness, literature gives it discernment, taste, beauty and perfection. These offices are performed by literature because everything that is related to the expression of our ideas belongs to its jurisdiction. And see here the great line of demarcation that divides human knowledge. It shows us that science is employed in acquiring and treasuring ideas, and literature in enunciating them; through science we learn about all the beings that surround us, we discern their essence, we penetrate their properties and, uplifted, we reach for their highest source. But therein ends the ministry of science, and that of literature begins, for after following science in its rapid ascent, it takes all the riches, gives them a new form, polishes and makes them beautiful, and communicates and transmits them from one generation to the next.

To reach this sublime end, I do not propose long and painful studies: the span of our lives is so brief, and our youth vanishes so rapidly, that I would consider it fortunate if we could spare some moments of leisure. This, at least, has been my intention when I have reduced the study of the literary arts to that of rhetoric, and condensed therein all of the arts identified and named by the *metodistas*.

And why not use this moment to combat one of the greatest vices of our education, the vice that has most thwarted the progress of the sciences and of the human spirit? Undoubtedly, the subdivision of the sciences, as well as that of the arts, has contributed marvelously to their perfection. A man who dedicates his entire life to one branch of instruction can without a doubt learn and meditate upon it more; he can accumulate a greater number of observations and experiences; and he can treasure a greater sum of lights and knowledge. That is how the tree of science grew: that is how its branches multiplied and extended; and that is how, nourished and fortified, each of them gave more abundant and flavorful fruit.

But this subdivision, so positive for progress, became fatal for the study of science; for as its limits became fixed, the acquisition of scientific knowledge became more difficult; and when it was extended to elementary instruction, it made such learning take longer and become more tiring, if not impossible and interminable. How is it that this inconvenience had gone unnoticed until now? How have we missed that, with the tree of knowledge truncated, the root separated from the trunk, the trunk from its branches and its fruit scattered and dismembered, the intimate union that all human knowledge shares is destroyed? And with it, the ultimate end of all studies, for without comprehending it, without intuiting it, all knowledge is vain.

And how have we not prevented another greater evil that derives from the same principle? You shall observe how multiplying the degrees in the scientific scale, our precious youth—which is the hope of future generations—is paralyzed in them. You shall see how we burden their memories with irrelevant rules and precepts; we have them inquire into the methods for the acquisition of truth at the very moment in which they should be in the process of acquiring and possessing it. This is how the road to wisdom is unnecessarily prolonged, without ever reaching its goal; this is how, instead of love, we inspire tedium and aversion to study—since they feel themselves growing old without benefiting from their efforts—; this is also how society is plagued with vain and verbose men who call themselves learned, without having cultivated the understanding that enlightens the spirit, nor the sentiments that improve the heart. To escape this hurdle, just as we have condensed all of the elements of the exact sciences into the teaching of math, and all of the natural sciences into the teaching of physics, we will condense all of the elements of arts and letters into the teaching of how to express ourselves. Do grammar, rhetoric and poetics, and even dialectics and logic, have any end other than that of the proper expression of our ideas? Is their ministry not the exact communication of our thoughts through clear words, placed in the order and way that is most convenient to the object of our discourses?

Well, this is what our new teaching embraces. Do not fear that to impart it we will oppress your memory with that inopportune farrago of definitions and rules to which these studies are vulgarly reduced. Not in the least: the simple logic of language, reduced to a few luminous principles, derived from the purest origin of reason, enlightened by the observation of the greatest models in the art of expression, constitute the sum of this instruction. The work will be light, but if your dedication concurs with our desires and the tender labors of the professor who is in charge of your teaching, it will bear rich fruit.

But perhaps hearing me speak of the great models, some among you are wondering if I am going to call you to embark upon the long and arduous study of the dead languages, to transport you to the centuries and regions that produced them. No, gentlemen, I confess that I think it would be to your advantage to drink the sublime nectar of the genius produced by Greece and Rome from those pure fountains. But we must ask: would this advantage be worth the time and effort that it would cost you to reach it? How far will it go, this veneration, this blind idolatry, so to speak, that we profess toward antiquity? Why not shake off once and for all this stale preoccupation with which we have so foolishly enslaved our reason, and to which we sacrifice the prime of our lives?

I admit, in good faith, that it would be folly to deny the excellence of those great models. No, among us there has not been, nor have there been among any of the most learned nations, someone comparable to Homer or Pindar, Horace or the Mantuan; or equal to Xenophon or Titus Livius or Demosthenes or Cicero. But where does this shameful disparity come from? Why is it that there is less genius in the works of modern scholars, with greater learning, than in those of the ancients? The reason is evident, says a modern scholar: the ancients created, and we merely imitate; the ancient studied nature in nature, and we study it in them. Why, then, do we not follow their footsteps, and, in order to equal them, study as they did? That is how we should imitate them!

And that is how we wish to guide you through this new teaching. Its end is to plant in your souls the seed of a taste for all the arts of language. To help it grow, to help it germinate, we will place before you plenty of models: ancient ones in translation, modern ones in their original forms. Study the living languages, especially your own; cultivate them, but dedicate more time to observation and meditation than to fruitless readings; and, shaking off once and for all the chains of imitation, separate yourselves from the flock of *metodistas* and copyists, and dare to rise to the contemplation of nature. The celebrated men of antiquity learned from it, their talents were formed and enriched, those talents that we admire not only for their excellence but also for their amplitude and versatility. Judge them not for what they said and learned, but for what they did. And you will appreciate the worth of men who seemed born for all the professions and employments; like the soldiers of Cadmus, who burst forth from the earth armed and prepared to fight, they burst forth from the hands of their teachers to shine in all their undertakings and public offices. Look at Pericles, the support and delight of Athens for his profound politics and eloquence, whose wisdom made him the star of the lyceum, and whose sensibility and good taste made him a friend of Sophocles, Phidias and Aspasia. Look at Cicero, commanding armies, governing provinces, subduing factious rebels, saving the country, all the while applying the sublime precepts of public and private morality in the offices he held and in his teachings. Or Xenophon, directing the glorious retreat of 10,000 men, and later immortalizing it with his pen; or Caesar, who fought, spoke and wrote with the same splendor; or Pliny, a fount of wisdom, who amid discharging the offices of magistrate and military officer studied the mysteries of nature and described their most inimitable richness with his brush.

Study, like them, the natural and rational universe, and, like them, contemplate this great model, this sublime type of what is beautiful and perfect, majestic and grand in the physical and moral order, for this is how you will equal those illustrious luminaries. Do

you wish to become great poets? Then, like Homer, observe how men face the important trials of their public and private lives; or, like Euripides, study the human heart in
the tumult and fluctuations of passion; or contemplate the delights of rustic life like
Theocritus and Virgil. You want to become eloquent orators, lucid historians, illustrious
and profound politicians? Then, like Hortensius and Tullius, Sallust and Tacitus, study,
inquire into those secret relations, those large and sudden movements that link human
events with an invisible hand, conduct the destinies of men, and force and bring about
their political vicissitudes. Here are the steps that you must follow, the great model that
you must imitate. Born in a sweet and temperate climate, in a land where nature has
gathered the most sublime and august sceneries; blessed with a strong and penetrating
intelligence; and supported by a language of majesty and harmony, if you cultivate it, if
you learn to employ it wisely, you will sing like Pindar, narrate like Thucydides, persuade
like Socrates, argue like Plato and Aristotle and even devise proofs with as much preci-
sion as Euclid.

Happy is he who in aspiring to equal these celebrated men, struggles to reach those
precious talents! How much glory, how much pleasure will his efforts provide! But if false
modesty slackens the innocent desire for literary fame in some of you; if sloth makes others prefer humble and easy pleasures, do not think that the teaching that I propose to you
is any less necessary. For who would not benefit from it in their individual affairs? Believe
me: fidelity of judgment; a fine and delicate discernment; in a word, the good taste
inspired by this learning, is the most necessary talent for the enjoyment of life. It is necessary not only for speaking and writing, but also for listening and reading, and I dare say,
even for feeling and thinking. Because you must know that good taste is like our reason's
sense of touch, so that if by touching and feeling a form we determine its extension and
contours, its softness or hardness, its roughness or softness; similarly, it is by touching and
feeling with the criteria of taste that we discover beauty or imperfections in our words or
those of others, and can accurately judge their merit and worth.

This critical sense is also the source of all the pleasures that the mind produces in our
soul, both in literature and in the arts, and that delicious sensation is always proportion-
ate to the degree of exactitude with which we distinguish beauty from defect. This critical sense is what elevates us with the sublime raptures of Fray Luis de León, or torments
us with Silveira's metaphors, and it is this critical sense that captivates us with Murillo's
brushstrokes, or annoys us with El Greco's brusqueness; it is because of this sense that we
cry with Virgil and Racine, and we laugh with Moreto and Cervantes; and because of
this critical discernment we are unimpressed by the rambling wordiness of a charlatan.
Because of it we are also tied with golden shackles to the lips of the eloquent man. This
sense perfects our ideas, our feelings, and unveils beauty and grace in arts, and in nature;
it makes us love them, and savor them, and it leaves us without reason in the light of their
enchantment.

Perfect, my children, this precious sense, and it will be your guide in all your studies,
and exercise the primary influence in your opinions and your conduct. It will place in
your hands works marked with the seal of truth and genius, and make them drop those
fraught with ignorance and error. Perfect it, make it immune to extravagance and medi-
ocrity, and the day will come when the repulsive horde of embryos, mutants, monstrosities

and literary aberrations with which the bad taste of the past centuries has infested the republic of letters will be forever banished from your sight spread. Then, comparing the need we have of a good and beneficial doctrine, with the brevity of the time we have to attain it, we will finally condemn to the flames of eternal oblivion all those enigmas, sophisms and minutiae, fables and fabrications and trickeries, all those paradoxes, all that filth, nonsense and folly, that has accumulated in the enormous encyclopedia of barbarity and pedantry.

These great favors await public education once the combination of the study of literature and science is finally achieved. Once attained, regardless of your vocation or of your destiny, you will stand before the public like worthy members of the nation that instructs you; and which, after all, should be the ultimate purpose of your instruction. For what is the use of learning if it is not devoted to the common good? No, your homeland will not honor you for what you know, but for what you do. And what good will it do you to treasure many truths, if you do not know how to communicate them?

Nevertheless, to communicate truth it must be made persuasive, and to be persuasive, it must be spoken kindly. It is necessary to remove the dark, scientific apparatus, take its purest and clearest results, simplify it, accommodate it to the understanding of the general public and imbue it with that force, that grace, which, capturing the imagination, sways all who hear it.

And who do you think should claim this victory but the art of speaking well? Do not doubt it: the domain of science is exercised only upon reason. All of the sciences speak with reason, none with the heart. Because assent is for reason, and will is for choice. And sometimes the heart, jealously guarding its independence, rebels against the forces of reason and does not want to be subjected or conquered by anything but feelings. Therein is literature's highest calling: the power to sway and move hearts, to light them, to charm them and to subject them to its empire.

Such is the strength of its enchantment, and such will be the strength of the man whose solid instruction includes a way with words, perfected by literature. Committed to public service, with what splendor would he not fulfill the tasks that his country asks of him? While science enlightens the sphere of the action in which he must employ his talents; while it helps him see clearly the objects that he must promote for the public interest and the means with which to reach them, and the ends to which he must conduct them, literature will pave the way. Directing or exhorting, speaking or writing, his words will always be fortified by reason and sweetened by eloquence; and exciting the sentiments and will of the public, his acceptance will be secured along with universal gratitude.

Let us compare to this respectable man one of those speculating scholars who, disdaining this precious talent, owes his position in public office to the vague opinion of his theories. You will see that the only passion that his learning inspires in him is pride; the only sentiment, contempt; the only amusement is solitary retreat; and when he employs his talents, he is as in a foreign country, where he cannot discover the sphere of his action nor the extent of his forces, nor can he succeed in finding the proper means to rule or make himself obeyed. Abstract in his principles, inflexible in his maxims, inimical to society, insensible to the delicate subtleties of civility, if he is forced by duty to turn from his nocturnal lucubration to a social event, he will appear careless in his appearance,

embarrassed in his demeanor and taciturn or inopportunely mysterious in his conversation, destined to be society's scarecrow and a discredit to knowledge.

But literature, which is an enemy of control and a lover of sweet independence, is
much better suited to private life, in which it indulgently exerts and deploys its graces.
While scientific knowledge, in its elevated atmosphere, disdains condescending to partake
of familiar conversation and contact, or is disdained by them, you will see that erudition
polishes and tempers this contact, it enhances and perfects it, and thus it contributes to
the splendor of society, and to its advantage as well. Yes, gentlemen: also to its advantage. By Jove, is society anything other than a great company to which everybody must
contribute their strength and intelligence, devoting them to the good of all? Courteous,
amiable, expressive: nobody will compel or persuade better; loving, kind, compassionate
in his sentiments: nobody will be more capable of directing and reassuring; with a sweet
and friendly demeanor, and grace and urbanity in his words, who will better entertain,
gratify and appease his fellow men?

See there why the man adorned with this pleasant and conciliatory talent will always
be a friend and solace to others. Who would resist the empire of his eloquence? Full of
vigor and attraction, always enjoyable and interesting, his words always relevant to the
matter that he is presenting at that moment, they will attract the attention and applause
of his audience. And whether he narrates or expounds, whether he reflects or elaborates,
whether he laughs or feels, he will always be the soul of the conversation and the company's delight.

But alas! More than once he will be cast out by ignorance and ill breeding. Alas!
Tormented by the stupid silences, churlish jokes and the mordant and dastardly slander
that characterizes them, he will withdraw to his gratifying retreat. But follow him, and
you will see how charming his solitude is. There, reinstated in himself and given over
to the study and contemplation that delight him, he finds that innocent pleasure whose
ineffable sweetness is only experienced and enjoyed by those who love literature. There,
in sweet dealings with the Muses, he spends placid hours alone and at peace, surrounded
by the illustrious geniuses who have cultivated them throughout the ages. And above
all, he exercises his imagination, this powerful faculty of the human spirit that, flying
everywhere unfettered, fills his soul with great ideas and sentiments; deeply moving or
elevating it, until riding on the fiery wings of enthusiasm it is lifted above nature and into
a new universe filled with charm and wonder, where it rapturously enjoys the company
of the imaginary beings that she has created.

Some of you may tell me that this is an illusion, and you would be right: but it is an
innocent illusion, pleasant and beneficial. And which of the world's pleasures, which of
its joys, are not illusions? Is what we call happiness anything but an illusion? Is it more
real for an ambitious man with an all-consuming thirst for glory, power and wealth? Or
for an intemperate man who pays for brief instants of sensual pleasure with long installments of bitterness and disquiet? Is it more real in the sweat and exhaustion of hunting,
or in the anxiety and uncertainty of gambling? Is it more real in the continuous wan-
dering from street to street of indolent men who spend their days in idle walks, bored,
and overwhelmed by the weight of their own sloth? No, my children: if something on
this earth deserves to be called happiness, it is that intimate moral sentiment that results

from the employment of our mind in the quest for truth and the practice of virtue. And which studies can arouse this pure satisfaction and inspire these delicious sentiments if not those of literature? Even those scorned by presumptuous scholars for being vain or frivolous contribute to improve and enlighten the soul. Poetry, among its sweet fictions and wise joys, gives the soul sublime ideas and feelings at every step, moving and elevating it, tearing it from the claws of vulgar vices and compelling it to love and follow virtue. And while eloquence, colorfully adorning the mind's triumphant arguments, suggests the purest sentiments and most illustrious examples of virtue and honesty, history, with its august perspective, presents the truths and errors, the virtues and vices, and the inescapable vicissitudes with which eternal Providence elevated nations and empires across the centuries, and then destroyed them, sweeping them from the face of the earth. And although in this magnificent theater, the soul sees a great number of men guided by greed and ambition, it is consoled by the sight of the few who, models of virtue, shine here and there in the field of history like great oaks that stand in a forest devoured by flames, surviving out of their own willpower and eminence.

And, by Jove, does philosophy not belong to the study of literature? Yes, my children: it is its most noble province. Do not think that these studies are far or distant from each other, for everything is linked together in the plan of human knowledge. Could we examine the expression of our ideas, without analyzing how they were generated? And could we analyze that, without finding the source in ourselves? And could we contemplate the self, without rising up to the supreme origin that is the wellspring of all beings, as well as of all truths? Therein is the exalted end to which I want to conduct you through this new teaching. Run to it, my children: hurry especially toward that sublime region of philosophy that helps us know the Creator, and know ourselves, and that along with the knowledge of the supreme good, it reveals also all of the natural obligations and civil duties of man.

Study ethics: in it you will find that pure morality professed by all virtuous men across the centuries, which was later enlightened, perfected and sanctified by the Gospel, and is both the peak and the foundation of our august religion. It is guided by truth and its end is virtue. Oh! Why should this not be the sublime end of all studies and instruction? What fatality dooms our institutes of public education to be wary of making men wise and also virtuous? And why is the science of virtue not taught in public schools?

I would be so fortunate, my children, if someday I were to establish this study, and crown your teachings and my desires with it! The work of Plato and Epictetus, Cicero and Seneca, will enlighten your spirit and arouse your heart. Our sacrosanct religion will elevate your ideas; give you temperance in prosperity, strength in times of tribulation and the justice of principles and feelings that characterize true virtue. When you have reached this summit, you will prefer to live in virtue than to be powerful; you will sing sweet melodies when faced by horrendous torments, or die adoring the divine Providence, jubilant in the midst of misfortune.

INDEX

Lightning Source UK Ltd.
Milton Keynes UK
UKOW01n2215210217

294964UK00001B/13/P

9 781783 086290